Optimizing Linux® Pe

A Hands-On Guide to Linux®
Performance Tools

Phillip G. Ezolt

invent

www.hp.com/hpbooks

PRENTICE
HALL
PTR

Pearson Education

Upper Saddle River, NJ • Boston• Indianapolis • San Francisco

New York • Toronto • Montreal • London • Munich • Paris • Madrid

Capetown • Sydney • Tokyo • Singapore • Mexico City

The publisher offers excellent discounts on this book when ordered in quantity for bulk purchases or special sales, which may include electronic versions and/or custom covers and content particular to your business, training goals, marketing focus, and branding interests. For more information, please contact:

> U. S. Corporate and Government Sales
> (800) 382-3419
> corpsales@pearsontechgroup.com

For sales outside the U. S., please contact:

> International Sales
> international@pearsoned.com

Visit us on the Web: www.phptr.com

Library of Congress Number: 2004117118

ISBN 0-13-148682-9

Text printed in the United States on recycled paper at RR Donnelley & Sons Company in Crawfordsville, IN

First printing, March 2005

This book is dedicated to my wife Sarah, (the best in the world), who gave up so many weekends to make this book possible. Thank you, Thank you, Thank you!

Table of Contents

Why Is Performance Important?

If you have ever sat waiting for a computer to do something, (while pounding on your desk, cursing, and wondering, "What is *taking* so long?"), you know why it is important to have a fast and well-tuned computer system. Although not all performance problems can be easily solved, understanding *why* things are slow can mean the difference between fixing the problem in software, upgrading the slow hardware, or simply throwing the whole computer out the window. Fortunately, most operating systems, Linux in particular, provide the tools to figure out why the machine runs slowly. By using a few basic tools, you can determine where the system is slowing down and fix the parts that are running inefficiently.

Although a slow system is particularly annoying to end users, application developers have an even more important reason to performance tune their applications: An efficient application runs on more systems. If you write sluggish applications that need a zippy computer, you eliminate customers who have slower computers. After all, not everyone has the latest hardware. A well-tuned application is usable by more customers, resulting in a bigger potential user base. In addition, if potential customers must choose between two different applications with similar functionality, they often choose the one that runs faster or is more efficient. Finally, a long-lived application likely goes through several rounds of optimization to cope with different customer demands, so it is crucial to know how to track down performance problems.

If you are a system administrator, you have a responsibility to the users of the system to make sure that it runs at an adequate performance level. If the system runs slowly, users complain. If you can determine the problem and fix it quickly, they stop complaining. As a bonus, if you can solve their problem by tuning the application or operating system (and thus keep them from having to buy new hardware), you make company bean counters happy. Knowing how to effectively use performance tools can mean the difference between spending days or spending hours on a performance problem.

Linux: Strengths and Weakness

If you use Linux, maintain it, and develop on it, you are in a strange but good situation. You have unprecedented access to source code, developers, and mailing lists, which often document design decisions years after they are made. Linux is an excellent environment in which to find and fix performance problems. This contrasts a proprietary environment, where it can be difficult to get direct access to software developers, may be hard to find written discussions about most design decisions, and is nearly impossible to access source code. In addition to this productive environment, Linux also has powerful performance tools that enable you to find and fix performance problems. These tools rival their proprietary counterparts.

Even with these impressive benefits, the Linux ecosystem still has challenges to overcome. Linux performance tools are scattered everywhere. Different groups with different aims develop the tools, and as a result, the tools are not necessarily in a centralized location. Some tools are included in standard Linux distributions, such as Red Hat, SUSE, and Debian; others are scattered throughout the Internet. If you're trying to solve a performance problem, you first have to know that the tools you need exist, and then figure out where to find them. Because no single Linux performance tool solves every type of performance problem, you also must figure out how to use them jointly to determine what is broken. This can be a bit of an art, but becomes easier with experience. Although most of the general strategies can be documented, Linux does not have any guide that tells you how to aggregate performance tools to actually solve a problem. Most of the tools or subsystems have information about tuning the particular subsystem, but not how to use them with other tools. Many performance problems span several areas of the system, and unless you know how to use the tools collectively, you will not be able the fix the problem.

How Can This Book Help You?

You will learn many things from this book, including the following:

* What the various performance tools measure
* How to use each tool
* How to combine the tools to solve a performance problem
* How to start with a poorly performing system and pinpoint the problem
* How the methods are used to solve real-world problems (case studies)

Using the methods in this book, you can make a well-organized and diagnosed problem description that you can pass on to the original developers. If you're lucky, they will solve the problem for you.

Why Learn How to Use Performance Tools?

Why should anyone put effort into tuning a system or application?

* A well-tuned system can do more work with fewer resources.
* A well-tuned application can run on older hardware.
* A well-tuned desktop can save users time.
* A well-tuned server provides a higher service quality for more users.

If you know how to effectively diagnose performance problems, you can take a targeted approach to solving the problem instead of just taking a shot in the dark and hoping that it works. If you are an application developer, this means that you can quickly figure out what piece of code is causing the problem. If you are a system administrator, it means that you can figure out what part of the system needs to be tuned, or upgraded, without wasting time unsuccessfully trying different solutions. If you are an end user, you can figure out which applications are lagging and report the problem to the developers (or update your hardware, if necessary).

Linux has reached a crossroads. Most of the functionality for a highly productive system is already complete. The next evolutionary step is for Linux and its applications to be tuned to compete with and surpass the performance of other operating systems. Some of this performance optimization has already begun. For example, the SAMBA, Apache, and TUX Web server projects have, through significant time investments, tuned and optimized the system and code. Other performance optimizations—such as the Native POSIX Thread Library (NPTL), which dramatically improves threading performance; and object prelinking, which improves application startup time—are just starting to be integrated into Linux. Linux is ripe for performance improvements.

Can I Tune for Performance?

The best thing about performance optimization is that you do not need to know the details of the entire application or system to effectively fix performance problems. Performance optimization requires a complementary set of skills to those of a typical application developer.

You need to be observant and persistent. It takes more of a detective than a programmer to hunt down and eliminate performance problems. It is exhilarating to find and fix these. When you start, performance is terrible. However, you track down the cause, rip it out by the roots, and, if you're lucky, the system then runs twice as fast. *Voilà*!

To get to the *voilà*, you must understand the powerful but sometimes confusing world of Linux performance tools. This takes some work, but in the end, it is worth it. The tools can show you aspects of your application and system that you never expected to see.

Who Should Read This Book?

This book helps Linux software developers, system administrators, and end users to use the Linux performance tools to find the performance problems in a given system. Beginning performance investigators learn the basics of performance investigation and analysis. Medium to advanced performance investigators, especially those with performance experience on other proprietary operating systems, learn about the Linux equivalents of commands from other systems with which they may already be familiar.

Software developers learn how to pinpoint the exact line of source code that causes a performance problem. System administrators who are performance tuning a system learn about the tools that show why a system is slowing down, and they can then use that information to tune the system. Finally, although not the primary focus of the book, end users learn the basic skills necessary to figure out which applications are consuming all the system resources.

How Is This Book Organized?

This book teaches an audience of various levels of experience to find and fix performance problems. To accomplish this, the chapters are presented so that you can pick and choose to read different parts of the book without reading the entire book straight through.

Chapter 1 is devoted to the basic methods of performance problem hunting. It contains a series of non-Linux–specific tips and suggestions that prove useful for tracking down performance issues. These guidelines are general suggestions for performance problem hunting and can be applied to tracking down performance issues on any type of computer system.

Chapters 2 through 8 (the bulk of this book) cover the various tools available to measure different performance statistics on a Linux system. These chapters explain what various tools measure, how they are invoked, and provide an example of each tool being used. Each chapter demonstrates tools that measure aspects of different Linux subsystems, such as system CPU, user CPU, memory, network I/O, and disk I/O. If a tool measures aspects of more than one subsystem, it is presented in more than one chapter. Each chapter describes multiple tools, but only the appropriate tool options for a particular subsystem are presented in a given chapter. The descriptions follow this format:

1. *Introduction*—This section explains what the tool is meant to measure and how it operates.

2. *Performance tool options*—This section does not just rehash the tool's documentation. Instead, it explains which options are relevant to the current topic and what those options mean. For example, some performance tool man pages identify the events that a tool measures but do not explain what

the events mean. This section explains the meaning of the events and how they are relevant to the current subsystem.

3. *Example*—This section provides one or more examples of the tool being used to measure performance statistics. This section shows the tool being invoked and any output that it generates.

Chapter 9 is Linux specific and contains a series of steps to use when confronted with a slow-performing Linux system. It explains how to use the previously described Linux performance tools in concert to pinpoint the cause of the performance problem. This chapter is the most useful if you want to start with a misbehaving Linux system and just diagnose the problem without necessarily understanding the details of the tools. Chapters 10 through 12 present case studies in which the methodologies and tools previously described are used together to solve real-world problems. The case studies highlight Linux performance tools used to find and fix different types of performance problems: a CPU-bound application, a latency-sensitive application, and an I/O bound application.

Chapter 13 overviews the performance tools and the opportunities Linux has for improvement.

This book also has two appendixes. Appendix A contains a table of the performance tools discussed in this book and includes a URL to the latest version of each tool. Appendix A also identifies which Linux distributions support each particular tool. Finally, Appendix B contains information that explains how to install `oprofile`, which is a very powerful but hard-to-install tool on a few major Linux distributions.

Acknowledgments

First, I want to thank to the good people at Prentice Hall, including Jill Harry, Brenda Mulligan, Gina Kanouse, and Keith Cline.

Second, I want to thank all the people who reviewed the initial book proposal and added valuable technical reviews and suggestions, including Karel Baloun, Joe Brazeal, Bill Carr, Jonathan Corbet, Matthew Crosby, Robert Husted, Paul Lussier, Scott Mann, Bret Strong, and George Vish II. I also want to thank all the people who taught me what I know about performance and let me optimize Linux even though the value of Linux optimization was uncertain at the time, including John Henning, Greg Tarsa, Dave Stanley, Greg Gaertner, Bill Carr, and the whole BPE tools group (which supported and encouraged my work on Linux).

In addition, I want to thank the good folks of SPEC who took me in and taught me why benchmarks, when done well, help the entire industry. I especially want to thank Kaivalya Dixit, whose passion and integrity for benchmarking will be sorely missed.

Thanks also to all the people who helped me keep my sanity with many games of Carcassonne and Settlers of Catan, including Sarah Ezolt, Dave and Yoko Mitzel, Tim and Maureen Chorma, Ionel and Marina Vasilescu, Joe Doucette, and Jim Zawisza.

Finally, I want to thank my family, including Sasha and Mischief, who remind me that we always have time for a walk or to chase dental floss; Ron and Joni Elias, who cheer me on; Russell, Carol, and Tracy Ezolt, who gave their support and encouragement as I worked on this; and to my wife, Sarah, who is the most understanding and supportive person you can imagine.

About the Author

PHIL EZOLT discovered Linux more than nine years ago when pursuing an undergraduate electrical and computer engineering degree from Carnegie Mellon. For six years, Phil ported and designed Linux performance tools for Compaq's Alpha performance group and represented Compaq in the SPEC CPU subcommittee. During that time, he improved Linux performance on the industry standard SPEC Web and CPU benchmarks using the performance tools he ported and developed. Phil is currently part of a Hewlett-Packard team developing Sepia, a visualization technology that uses Linux XC clusters, OpenGL, and off-the-shelf graphics cards to parallelize real-time high-end visualizations. He is also currently pursing a master's degree in computer science from Harvard University and is a big fan of German-style board games.

1
Performance Hunting Tips

Solving performance problems without foresight and planning is painful. You waste time and are constantly frustrated as the cause of the problem repeatedly slips through your fingers. By following the right set of procedures, you can transform a frustrating performance hunt into an interesting detective story. Each piece of information leads you closer to the true culprit. People can not always be trusted. The evidence will be your only friend. As you investigate the problem, it will take unusual twists and turns, and the information that you discovered in the beginning of the hunt may turn out to be what helps you figure out the problem in the end. The best part is that you will have a thrill of adrenaline and sense of accomplishment when you finally nab the "bad guy" and fix the problem.

If you have never investigated a performance problem, the first steps can be overwhelming. However, by following a few obvious and nonobvious tips, you can save time and be well on your way to finding the cause of a performance problem. The goal of this chapter is to provide you with a series of tips and guidelines to help you hunt a performance problem. These tips show you how to avoid some of the common traps when investigating what is wrong with your system or application. Most of these tips were hard-learned lessons that resulted from wasted time and frustrating dead ends. These tips help you solve your performance problem quickly and efficiently.

After reading this chapter, you should be able to

* Avoid repeating the work of others.
* Avoid repeating your own work.

* Avoid false leads that result from gathering misleading information.
* Create a useful reference document about your investigation.

Although no performance investigation is flawless (you will almost always say, "If only I would have thought of that *first*"), these tips help you to avoid some of the common mistakes of a performance investigation.

1.1   General Tips

1.1.1   Take Copious Notes (Save Everything)

Probably the *most* important thing that you can do when investigating a performance problem is to record every output that you see, every command that you execute, and every piece of information that you research. A well-organized set of notes allows you to test a theory about the cause of a performance problem by simply looking at your notes rather than rerunning tests. This saves a huge amount of time. Write it down to create a permanent record.

When starting a performance investigation, I usually create a directory for the investigation, open a new "Notes" file in GNU emacs, and start to record information about the system. I then store performance results in this directory and store interesting and related pieces of information in the Notes file. I suggest that you add the following to your performance investigation file and directory:

* *Record the hardware/software configuration*—This involves recording information about the hardware configuration (amount of memory and type of CPU, network, and disk subsystem) as well as the software environment (the OS and software versions and the relevant configuration files). This information may seem easy to reproduce later, but when tracking down a problem, you may significantly change a system's configuration. Careful and meticulous notes can be used to figure out the system's configuration during a particular test.

  Example: Save the output of `cat /proc/pci`, `dmesg`, and `uname -a` for each test.

* *Save and organize performance results*—It can be valuable to review performance results a long time after you run them. Record the results of a test with the configuration of the system. This allows you to compare how different configurations affect the performance results. It would be possible just to rerun the test if needed, but usually testing a configuration is a time-consuming process. It is more efficient just to keep your notes well organized and avoid repeating work.

* *Write down the command-line invocations*—As you run performance tools, you will often create complicated and complex command lines that measure the exact areas of the system that interest you. If you want to rerun a test, or run the same test on a different application, reproducing these command lines can be annoying and hard to do right on the first try. It is better just to record exactly what you typed. You can then reproduce the exact command line for a future test, and when reviewing past results, you can also see exactly what you measured. The Linux command `script` (described in detail in Chapter 8, "Utility Tools: Performance Tool Helpers") or "cut and paste" from a terminal is a good way to do this.

* *Record research information and URLs*—As you investigate a performance problem, it is import to record relevant information you found on the Internet, through e-mail, or through personal interactions. If you find a Web site that seems relevant, cut and paste the text into your notes. (Web sites can disappear.) However, also save the URL, because you might need to review the page later or the page may point to information that becomes important later in an investigation.

As you collect and record all this information, you may wonder why it is worth the effort. Some information may seem useless or misleading now, but it might be useful in the future. (A good performance investigation is like a good detective show: Although the clues are confusing at first, everything becomes clear in the end.) Keep the following in mind as you investigate a problem:

> *The implications of results may be fuzzy*—It is not always clear what a performance tool is telling you. Sometimes, you need more information to understand the implications of a particular result. At a later point, you might

look back at seemingly useless test results in a new light. The old information may actually disprove or prove a particular theory about the nature of the performance problem.

All information is useful information (which is why you save it)—It might not be immediately clear why you save information about what tests you have run or the configuration of the system. It can prove immensely useful when you try to explain to a developer or manager why a system is performing poorly. By recording and organizing everything you have seen during your investigation, you have proof to support a particular theory and a large base of test results to prove or disprove other theories.

Periodically reviewing your notes can provide new insights—When you have a big pool of information about your performance problem, review it periodically. Taking a fresh look allows you to concentrate on the results, rather than the testing. When many test results are aggregated and reviewed at the same time, the cause of the problem may present itself. Looking back at the data you have collected allows you test theories without actually running any tests.

Although it is inevitable that you will have to redo some work as you investigate a problem, the less time that you spend redoing old work, the more efficient you will be. If you take copious notes and have a method to record the information as you discover it, you can rely on the work that you have already done and avoid rerunning tests and redoing research. To save yourself time and frustration, keep reliable and consistent notes.

For example, if you investigate a performance problem and eventually determine the cause to be a piece of hardware (slow memory, slow CPU, and so on), you will probably want to test this theory by upgrading that slow hardware and rerunning the test. It often takes a while to get new hardware, and a large amount of time might pass before you can rerun your test. When you are finally able, you want to be able to run an identical test on the new and old hardware. If you have saved your old test invocations and your test results, you will know immediately how to configure the test for the new hardware, and will be able to compare the new results with the old results that you have stored.

1.1.2 Automate Redundant Tasks

As you start to tweak the system to improve performance, it can become easy to make mistakes when typing complicated commands. Inadvertently using incorrect parameters or configurations can generate misleading performance information. It is a good idea to automate performance tool invocations and application tests:

> *Performance tool invocations*—Some Linux performance tools require a fairly complicated command line. Do yourself a favor and store them in a shell script, or put the complete commands in a reference file that you can use to cut and paste. This saves you frustration, and gives you some certainty that the command line you use to invoke the tools is the correct one.
>
> *Application tests*—Most applications have complicated configurations either through a command line or a configuration file. You will often rerun the application you are testing many times. You save frustration if you script the invocation. Although typing a 30-character command might seem easy at first, after you have done it 10 times you will appreciate the automation.

If you automate as much as you can, you will reduce mistakes. Automation with scripting can save time and help to avoid misleading information caused by improper tool and test invocations.

For example, if you are trying to monitor a system during a particular workload or length of time, you might not be present when the test finishes. It proves helpful to have a script that, after the test has completed, automatically collects, names, and saves all the generated performance data and places it automatically in a "Results" directory. After you have this piece of infrastructure in place, you can rerun your tests with different optimizations and tunings without worrying about whether the data will be saved. Instead, you can turn your full attention to figuring out the cause of the problem rather than managing test results.

1.1.3 Choose Low-Overhead Tools If Possible

In general, the act of observing a system modifies its behavior. (For you physics buffs, this is known as the Heisenberg uncertainty principle.)

Specifically, when using performance tools, they change the way that the system behaves. When you investigate a problem, you want to see how the application performs and must deal with the error introduced by performance tools. This is a necessary evil, but you must know that it exists and try to minimize it. Some performance tools provide a highly accurate view of the system, but use a high-overhead way of retrieving the information. Tools with a very high overhead change system behavior more than tools with lower overhead. If you only need a coarse view of the system, it is better to use the tools with lower overhead even though they are not as accurate.

For example, the tool ps can give you a pretty good, but coarse, overview of the quantity and type of memory that an application is using. More accurate but invasive tools, such as memprof or valgrind, also provide this information, but may change the behavior of the system by using more memory or CPU than the original application would alone.

1.1.4 Use Multiple Tools to Understand the Problem

Although it would be extraordinarily convenient if you needed only one tool to figure out the cause of a performance problem, this is rarely the case. Instead, each tool you use provides a hint of the problem's cause, and you must use several tools in concert to really understand what is happening. For example, one performance tool may tell you that the system has a high amount of disk I/O, and another tool may show that the system is using a large amount of swap. If you base your solution only on the results of the first tool, you may simply purchase a faster disk drive (and find that the performance problem has only improved slightly). Using the tools together, however, you determine that the high amount of disk I/O results from the high amount of swap that is being used. In this case, you might reduce the swapping by buying more memory (and thus cause the high disk I/O to disappear).

Using multiple performance tools together often gives you a much clearer picture of the performance problem than is possible with any single tool.

Parable of the Blind Men and the Elephant

Three blind men approach a mighty elephant to try to figure out what it is like. The first man pulls on the tail and says, "The elephant is like a rope." The second man touches the elephant's leg and says, "The elephant is like a tree." The third man touches the elephant's side and says, "The elephant is like a mighty wall."

Obviously, not one of them had the correct answer. If they had shared and combined their impressions, however, they might have discovered the truth about the elephant. Don't be like the blind men with the elephant. Use multiple performance tools together to verify the cause of a problem.

1.1.5 Trust Your Tools

One of the most exciting and frustrating times during a performance hunt is when a tool shows an "impossible" result. Something that "cannot" happen has clearly happened. The first instinct is to believe that the tools are broken. Do not be fooled. The tools are impartial. Although they can be incorrect, it is more likely that the application is doing what it should not be doing. Use the tools to investigate the problem.

For example, the Gnome calculator uses more than 2,000 system calls just to launch and then exit. Without the performance tools to prove this fact, it seems unlikely that this many system calls would be necessary to just start and stop an application. However, the performance tools can show where and why it is happening.

1.1.6 Use the Experience of Others (Cautiously)

When investigating any performance problem, you may find the task overwhelming. Do not go it alone. Ask the developers whether they have seen similar problems. Try to find someone else who has already solved the problem that you are experiencing. Search the Web for similar problems and, hopefully, solutions. Send e-mail to user lists and to developers.

This piece of advice comes with a word of warning: Even the developers who think that they know their applications are not always right. If the developer disagrees with the performance tool data, the developer might be wrong. Show developers your data and how you came to a particular conclusion. They will usually help you to reinterpret the data or fix the problem. Either way, you will be a little bit further along in your investigation. Do not be afraid to disagree with developers if your data shows something happening that should not be happening.

For example, you can often solve performance problems by following instructions you find from a Google search of similar problems. When investigating a Linux problem, many times, you will find that others have run into it before (even if it was years ago) and have reported a solution on a public mailing list. It is easy to use Google, and it can save you days of work.

1.2 Outline of a Performance Investigation

This section outlines a series of essential steps as you begin a performance investigation. Because the ultimate goal is to fix the problem, the best idea is to research the problem before you even touch a performance tool. Following a particular protocol is an efficient way to solve your problem without wasting valuable time.

1.2.1 Finding a Metric, Baseline, and Target

The first step in a performance investigation is to determine the current performance and figure out how much it needs to be improved. If your system is significantly under-performing, you may decide that it is worth the time to investigate. However, if the system is performing close to its peak values, it might not be worth an investigation. Figuring out the peak performance values helps you to set reasonable performance expectations and gives you a performance goal, so that you know when to stop optimizing. You can always tweak the system just a little more, and with no performance target, you can waste a lot of time squeezing out that extra percent of performance, even though you may not actually need it.

1.2.1.1 Establish a Metric

To figure out when you have finished, you must create or use an already established metric of your system's performance. A metric is an objective measurement that indicates how the system is performing. For example, if you are optimizing a Web server, you could choose "serviced Web requests per second." If you do not have an objective way to measure the performance, it can be nearly impossible to determine whether you are making any progress as you tune the system.

1.2.1.2 Establish a Baseline

After you figure out how you are going to measure the performance of a particular system or application, it is important to determine your current performance levels. Run the application and record its performance before any tuning or optimization; this is called the baseline value, and it is the starting point for the performance investigation.

1.2.1.3 Establish a Target

After you pick a metric and baseline for the performance, it is important to pick a target. This target guides you to the end of the performance hunt. You can indefinitely tweak a system, and you can always get it just a little better with more and more time. If you pick your target, you will know when have finished. To pick a reasonable goal, the following are good starting points:

* *Find others with a similar configuration and ask for their performance measurements*—This is an ideal situation. If you can find someone with a similar system that performs better, not only will you be able to pick a target for your system, you may also be able to work with that person to determine why your configuration is slower and how your configurations differ. Using another system as a reference can prove immensely useful when investigating a problem.

* *Find results of industry standard benchmarks*—Many Web sites compare benchmark results of various aspects of computing systems. Some of the benchmark results can be achieved only with a heroic effort, so they might not represent realistic use. However, many benchmark sites have the

configuration used for particular results. These configurations can provide clues to help you tune the system.

* *Use your hardware with a different OS or application*—It may be possible to run a different application on your system with a similar function. For example, if you have two different Web servers, and one performs slowly, try a different one to see whether it performs any better. Alternatively, try running the same application on a different operating system. If the system performs better in either of these cases, you know that your original application has room for improvement.

If you use existing performance information to guide your target goal, you have a much better chance of picking a target that is aggressive but not impossible to reach.

Grabbing the Low-Hanging Fruit

Another approach to the performance hunt is pick a certain amount of time for the hunt and, instead of picking a target, optimize as much as possible within that time period. If an application has never been optimized for a given workload, it often has a few problems with relatively easy fixes. These easy fixes are called the "low-hanging fruit."

Why "low-hanging fruit"? An analogy to a performance investigation is to imagine that you were hungry and standing at the base of an apple tree. You would likely grab for the apple closest to the ground and easiest for you to reach. These low-hanging apples will satisfy your hunger just as well as the harder-to-reach apples farther up the tree; however, picking them requires much less work. Similarly, if you are optimizing an application in a limited amount of time, you might just try to fix the easiest and obvious problems (low-hanging fruit) rather than making some of the more difficult and fundamental changes.

1.2.2 Track Down the Approximate Problem

Use the performance tools to take a first cut at determining the cause of the problem. By taking an initial rough cut at the problem, you get a high-level idea of the problem. The goal of the rough cut is to gather enough information to pass along to the other users and developers of this program, so that they can provide advice and tips. It is vitally important to have a well-written explanation of what you think the problem might be and what tests led you to that conclusion.

1.2.3 See Whether the Problem Has Already Been Solved

Your next goal should be to determine whether others have already solved the problem. A performance investigation can be a lengthy and time-consuming affair. If you can just reuse the work of others, you will be done before you start. Because your goal is simply to improve the performance of the system, the best way to solve a performance problem is to rely on what someone else has already done.

Although you must take specific advice regarding performance problems with a grain of salt, the advice can be enlightening, enabling you to see how others may have investigated a similar problem, how they tried to solve the problem, and whether they succeeded.

Here are a few different places to look for performance advice:

* *Search the Web for similar error messages/problems*—This is usually my first line of investigation. Web searches often reveal lots of information about the application or the particular error condition that you are seeing. They can also lead to information about another user's attempt to optimize the systems, and possibly tips about what worked and what did not. A successful search can yield pages of information that directly applies to your performance problem. Searching with Google or Google groups is a particularly helpful way to find people with similar performance problems.

* *Ask for help on the application mailing lists*—Most popular or publicly developed software has an e-mail list of people who use that software. This is a perfect place to find answers to performance questions. The readers and

contributors are usually experienced at running the software and making it perform well. Search the archive of the mailing list, because someone may have asked about a similar problem. Subsequent replies to the original message might describe a solution. If they do not, send an e-mail to the person who originally wrote about the problem and ask whether he or she figured out how to resolve it. If that fails, or no one else had a similar problem, send an e-mail describing your problem to the list; if you are lucky, someone may have already solved your problem.

* *Send an e-mail to the developer*—Most Linux software includes the e-mail address of the developer somewhere in the documentation. If an Internet search and the mailing list fails, you can try to send an e-mail to the developer directly. Developers are usually very busy, so they might not have time to answer. However, they know the application better than anyone else. If you can provide the developer with a coherent analysis of the performance problem, and are willing to work with the developer, he or she might be able to help you. Although his idea of the cause of the performance problem might not be correct, the developer might point you in a fruitful direction.

* *Talk to the in-house developers*—Finally, if this is a product being developed in-house, you can call or e-mail the in-house developers. This is pretty much the same as contacting the external developers, but the in-house people might be able to devote more time to your problem or point you to an internal knowledge base.

By relying on the work of others, you might be able to solve your problem before you even begin to investigate. At the very least, you will most likely be able to find some promising avenues to investigate, so it is always best to see what others have found.

1.2.4 The Case Begins (Start to Investigate)

Now that you have exhausted the possibility of someone else solving the problem, the performance investigation must begin. Later chapters describe the tools and methods in detail, but here are a few tips to make things work better:

* *Isolate the problem*—If at all possible, eliminate any extraneous programs or applications that are running on the system you are investigating. A heavily loaded system with many different running applications can skew the information gathered by the performance tools and ultimately lead you down false paths.

* *Use system difference to find causes*—If you can find a similar system that performs well, it can be a powerful aid in debugging your problem. One of the problems of using performance tools is that you do not necessarily have a good way of knowing whether the results from a performance tool indicate a problem. If you have a good system and a bad one, you can run the same performance tool on both systems and compare the results. If the results differ, you might be able to determine the cause of the problem by figuring out how the systems differ.

* *Change one thing at a time*—This very important. To really determine where the problem lies, you should only make one change at a time. This might be time-consuming and cause you to run many different tests, but it is really the only way to figure out whether you have solved the problem.

* *Always remeasure after optimizing*—If you are tweaking a system, it is important to remeasure everything after you change something. When you start modifying the system configuration, all the performance information that you previously generated might not be valid anymore. Usually, as you solve a performance problem, others jump in to take its place. The new problems may be very different from the old problems, so you really have to rerun your performance tools to make sure you are investigating the right problem.

Following these tips can help you avoid false leads and help to determine the cause of a performance problem.

1.2.5 Document, Document, Document

As mentioned previously, it is really important to document what you are doing so that you can go back at a later date and review it. If you have hunted down the performance problem, you will have a big file of notes and URLs fresh in your mind. They may be a jumbled disorganized mess, but as of now, you understand what they mean and how they are organized. After you solve the problem, take some time to rewrite what you have discovered and why you think that it is true. Include performance results that you've measured and experiments that you've done. Although it might seem like a lot of work, it can be very valuable. After a few months, it is easy to forget all the tests that you have done, and if you do not write down your results, you may end up redoing it. If you write a report when the tests are fresh in your mind, you will not have to do the work again, and can instead just rely on what you have written down.

1.3 Chapter Summary

Hunting a performance problem should be a satisfying and exciting process. If you have a good method in place to research and analyze, it will be repaid back many times as you hunt the problem. First, determine whether other people have had similar problems; if they have, try their solutions. Be skeptical of what they tell you, but look for others with experience of a similar problem. Create a reasonable metric and target for your performance hunt; the metric enables you to know when you have finished. Automate performance tests. Be sure to save test results and configuration information when you generate them so that you can review the results later. Keep your results organized and record any research and other information that you find that relates to your problem. Finally, periodically review your notes to find information that you might have missed the first time. If you follow these guidelines, you will have a clear goal and a clear procedure to investigate the problem.

This chapter provided a basic background for a performance investigation, and the following chapters cover the Linux-specific performance tools themselves. You learn how to use the tools, what type of information they can provide, and how to use them in combination to find performance problems on a particular system.

2

Performance Tools: System CPU

This chapter overviews the system-wide Linux performance tools. These tools are your first line of defense when tracking a performance problem. They can show you how the overall system is performing and which areas are misbehaving. This chapter discusses the statistics that these tools can measure and how to use the individual tools to gather those statistics. After reading this chapter, you should

- Understand the basic metrics of system-wide performance, including CPU usage
- Understand which tools can retrieve these system-wide performance metrics

2.1 CPU Performance Statistics

Each system-wide Linux performance tool provides different ways to extract similar statistics. Although no tool displays all the statistics, some of the tools display the same statistics. Rather than describe the meaning of the statistics multiple times (once for each tool), we review them once before all the tools are described.

2.1.1 Run Queue Statistics

In Linux, a process can be either runnable or blocked waiting for an event to complete. A blocked process may be waiting for data from an I/O device or the results of a system call. If a process is runnable, that means that it is competing for the CPU time with the other processes that are also runnable. A runnable process is not necessarily using the CPU, but when the Linux scheduler is deciding which process to run next, it picks from the list of runnable processes. When these processes are runnable, but waiting to use the processor, they form a line called the run queue. The longer the run queue, the more processes wait in line.

The performance tools commonly show the number of processes that are runnable and the number of processes that are blocked waiting for I/O. Another common system statistic is that of load average. The load on a system is the total amount of running and runnable process. For example, if two processes were running and three were available to run, the system's load would be five. The load average is the amount of load over a given amount of time. Typically, the load average is taken over 1 minute, 5 minutes, and 15 minutes. This enables you to see how the load changes over time.

2.1.2 Context Switches

Most modern processors can run only one process or thread at a time. Although some processors, such hyperthreaded processors, can actually run more than one process simultaneously, Linux treats them as multiple single-threaded processors. To create the illusion that a given single processor runs multiple tasks simultaneously, the Linux kernel constantly switches between different processes. The switch between different processes is called a context switch, because when it happens, the CPU saves all the context information from the old process and retrieves all the context information for the new process. The context contains a large amount of information that Linux tracks for each process, including, among others, which instruction the process is executing, which memory it has allocated, and which files the process has open. Switching these contexts can involve moving a large amount of information, and a context switch can be quite expensive. It is a good idea to minimize the number of context switches if possible.

To avoid context switches, it is important to know how they can happen. First, context switches can result from kernel scheduling. To guarantee that each process receives a fair share of processor time, the kernel periodically interrupts the running process and, if appropriate, the kernel scheduler decides to start another process rather than let the current process continue executing. It is possible that your system will context switch every time this periodic interrupt or timer occurs. The number of timer interrupts per second varies per architecture and kernel version. One easy way to check how often the interrupt fires is to use the /proc/interrupts file to determine the number of interrupts that have occurred over a known amount of time. This is demonstrated in Listing 2.1.

Listing 2.1

```
root@localhost asm-i386]# cat /proc/interrupts | grep timer
; sleep 10 ; cat /proc/interrupts | grep timer
  0:    24060043           XT-PIC  timer
  0:    24070093           XT-PIC  timer
```

In Listing 2.1, we ask the kernel to show us how many times the timer has fired, wait 10 seconds, and then ask again. That means that on this machine, the timer fires at a rate of (24,070,093 − 24,060,043) interrupts / (10 seconds) or ~1,000 interrupts/sec. If you have significantly more context switches than timer interrupts, the context switches are most likely caused by an I/O request or some other long-running system call (such as a sleep). When an application requests an operation that can not complete immediately, the kernel starts the operation, saves the requesting process, and tries to switch to another process if one is ready. This allows the processor to keep busy if possible.

2.1.3 Interrupts

In addition, periodically, the processor receives an interrupt by hardware devices. These interrupts are usually triggered by a device that has an event that needs to be handled by the kernel. For example, if a disk controller has just finished retrieving a block from the drive and is ready for the kernel to use it, the disk controller may trigger an interrupt. For each interrupt the kernel receives, an interrupt handler is run if it has been registered for that interrupt; otherwise, the interrupt is ignored. These interrupt handlers run at a very high priority in the system and typically execute very quickly. Sometimes, the interrupt handler has work that needs to be done, but does not require the high priority, so it launches a "bottom half," which is also known as a soft-interrupt handler. If there are a high number of interrupts, the kernel can spend a large amount of time servicing these interrupts. The file `/proc/interrupts` can be examined to show which interrupts are firing on which CPUs.

2.1.4 CPU Utilization

CPU utilization is a straightforward concept. At any given time, the CPU can be doing one of seven things. First, it can be idle, which means that the processor is not actually doing any work and is waiting for something to do. Second, the CPU can be running user code, which is specified as "user" time. Third, the CPU can be executing code in the Linux kernel on behalf of the application code. This is "system" time. Fourth, the CPU can be executing user code that has been "nice"ed or set to run at a lower priority than normal processes. Fifth, the CPU can be in `iowait`, which mean the system is spending its time waiting for I/O (such as disk or network) to complete. Sixth, the CPU can be in `irq` state, which means it is in high-priority kernel code handling a hardware interrupt. Finally, the CPU can be in `softirq` mode, which means it is executing kernel code that was also triggered by an interrupt, but it is running at a lower priority (the bottom-half code). This can happen when a device interrupt occurs, but the kernel needs to do some work with it before it is ready to hand it over to user space (for example, with a network packet).

Most performance tools specify these values as a percentage of the total CPU time. These times can range from 0 percent to 100 percent, but all three total 100 percent. A system with a high "system" percentage is spending most of its time in the kernel. Tools such as `oprofile` can help determine where this time is being spent. A system that has a high "user" time spends most of its time running applications. The next chapter shows how to use performance tools to track down problems in these cases. If a system is spending most of its time `iowait` when it should be doing work, it is most likely waiting for I/O from a device. It may be a disk, network card, or something else causing the slowdown.

2.2 Linux Performance Tools: CPU

Here begins our discussion of performance tools that enable you to extract information previously described.

2.2.1 vmstat (Virtual Memory Statistics)

vmstat stands for virtual memory statistics, which indicates that it will give you information about the virtual memory system performance of your system. Fortunately, it actually does much more than that. vmstat is a great command to get a rough idea of how your system performs as a whole. It tells you

- How many processes are running
- How the CPU is being used
- How many interrupts the CPU receives
- How many context switches the scheduler performs

It is an excellent tool to use to get a rough idea of how the system performs.

2.2.1.1 CPU Performance-Related Options

vmstat can be invoked with the following command line:

```
vmstat [-n] [-s] [delay [count]]
```

vmstat can be run in two modes: sample mode and average mode. If no parameters are specified, vmstat stat runs in average mode, where vmstat displays the average value for all the statistics since system boot. However, if a delay is specified, the first sample will be the average since system boot, but after that vmstat samples the system every delay seconds and prints out the statistics. Table 2-1 describes the options that vmstat accepts.

Table 2-1 *vmstat* Command-Line Options

Option	Explanation
-n	By default, vmstat periodically prints out the column headers for each performance statistic. This option disables that feature so that after the initial header, only performance data displays. This proves helpful if you want to import the output of vmstat into a spreadsheet.

continues

Table 2-1 *vmstat* Command-Line Options (Continued)

Option	Explanation
-s	This displays a one-shot details output of system statistics that vmstat gathers. The statistics are the totals since the system booted.
delay	This is the amount of time between vmstat samples.

vmstat provides a variety of different output statistics that enable you to track different aspects of the system performance. Table 2-2 describes those related to CPU performance. The next chapter covers those related to memory performance.

Table 2-2 CPU-Specific *vmstat* Output

Column	Explanation
r	This is the number of currently runnable processes. These processes are not waiting on I/O and are ready to run. Ideally, the number of runnable processes would match the number of CPUs available.
b	This is the number of processes blocked and waiting for I/O to complete.
forks	The is the number of times a new process has been created.
in	This is the number of interrupts occurring on the system.
cs	This is the number of context switches happening on the system.
us	The is the total CPU time as a percentage spent on user processes (including "nice" time).
sy	The is the total CPU time as a percentage spent in system code. This includes time spent in the system, irq, and softirq state.
wa	The is the total CPU time as a percentage spent waiting for I/O.
id	The is the total CPU time as a percentage that the system is idle.

vmstat provides a good low-overhead view of system performance. Because all the performance statistics are in text form and are printed to standard output, it is easy to capture the data generated during a test and process or graph it later. Because vmstat is such a low-overhead tool, it is practical to keep it running on a console or in a window even on a very heavily loaded server when you need to monitor the health of the system at a glance.

2.2.1.2 Example Usage

As shown in Listing 2.2, if vmstat is run with no command-line parameters, it displays the average values for the statistics that it records since the system booted. This example shows that the system was nearly idle since boot, as indicated by the CPU usage columns, under us, sys, wa, and id. The CPU spent 5 percent of the time since boot on user application code, 1 percent on system code, and the rest, 94 percent sitting idle.

Listing 2.2

```
[ezolt@scrffy tmp]$ vmstat
procs ------------memory---------- ---swap-- -----io---- --system--
----cpu----
 r  b   swpd   free   buff   cache   si   so    bi    bo   in    cs us sy id
wa
 1  0 181024  26284  35292 503048    0    0     3     2    6     1  5  1 94 0
```

Although vmstat's statistics since system boot can be useful to determine how heavily loaded the machine has been, vmstat is most useful when it runs in sampling mode, as shown in Listing 2.3. In sampling mode, vmstat prints the systems statistics after the number of seconds passed with the delay parameter. It does this sampling count a number of times. The first line of statistics in Listing 2.3 contains the system averages since boot, as before, but then the periodic sample continues after that. This example shows that there is very little activity on the system. We can see that no processes were blocked during the run by looking at the 0 in the b. We can also see, by looking in the r column, that fewer than 1 processes were running when vmstat sampled its data.

Listing 2.3

```
[ezolt@scrffy tmp]$ vmstat 2 5
procs ----------memory---------- ---swap-- -----io---- --system-- ----cpu----
 r  b   swpd   free   buff  cache   si   so    bi    bo   in    cs us sy id wa
 1  0 181024  26276  35316 502960    0    0     3     2    6     1  5  1 94  0
 1  0 181024  26084  35316 502960    0    0     0     0 1318   772  1  0 98  0
 0  0 181024  26148  35316 502960    0    0     0    24 1314   734  1  0 98  0
 0  0 181024  26020  35316 502960    0    0     0     0 1315   764  2  0 98  0
 0  0 181024  25956  35316 502960    0    0     0     0 1310   764  2  0 98  0
```

vmstat is an excellent way to record how a system behaves under a load or during a test condition. You can use vmstat to display how the system is behaving and, at the same time, save the result to a file by using the Linux tee command. (Chapter 8, "Utility Tools: Performance Tool Helpers," describes the tee command in more detail.) If you only pass in the delay parameter, vmstat will sample indefinitely. Just start it before the test, and interrupt it after the test has completed. The output file can be imported into a spreadsheet, and used to see how the system reacts to the load or various system events. Listing 2.4 shows the output of this technique. In this example, we can look at the interrupt and context switches that the system is generating. We can see the total number of interrupts and context switches in the in and cs columns respectively.

The number of context switches looks good compared to the number of interrupts. The scheduler is switching processes less than the number of timer interrupts that are firing. This is most likely because the system is nearly idle, and most of the time when the timer interrupt fires, the scheduler does not have any work to do, so it does not switch from the idle process.

(Note: There is a bug in the version of vmstat that generated the following output. It causes the system average line of output to display incorrect values. This bug has been reported to the maintainer of vmstat and will be fixed soon, hopefully.)

Listing 2.4

```
[ezolt@scrffy ~/edid]$ vmstat 1 | tee /tmp/output
procs ----------memory---------- ---swap-- -----io---- --system-- ----cpu----
 r  b   swpd   free   buff  cache   si   so    bi    bo   in    cs us sy id wa
 0  1 201060  35832  26532 324112    0    0     3     2    6     2  5  1 94  0
 0  0 201060  35888  26532 324112    0    0    16     0 1138   358  0  0 99  0
```

```
0   0 201060  35888  26540 324104     0     0     0    88 1163  371  0  0 100  0
0   0 201060  35888  26540 324104     0     0     0     0 1133  345  0  0 100  0
0   0 201060  35888  26540 324104     0     0     0    60 1174  351  0  0 100  0
0   0 201060  35920  26540 324104     0     0     0     0 1150  408  0  0 100  0
[Ctrl-C]
```

More recent versions of vmstat can even extract more detailed information about a grab bag of different system statistics, as shown in Listing 2.5.

The next chapter discusses the memory statistics, but we look at the CPU statistics now. The first group of statistics, or "CPU ticks," shows how the CPU has spent its time since system boot, where a "tick" is a unit of time. Although the condensed vmstat output only showed four CPU states—us, sy, id, and wa—this shows how all the CPU ticks are distributed. In addition, we can see the total number of interrupts and context switches. One new addition is that of forks, which is basically the number of new processes that have been created since system boot.

Listing 2.5

```
[ezolt@scrffy ~/edid]$ vmstat -s
    1034320  total memory
     998712  used memory
     698076  active memory
     176260  inactive memory
      35608  free memory
      26592  buffer memory
     324312  swap cache
    2040244  total swap
     201060  used swap
    1839184  free swap
    5279633  non-nice user cpu ticks
   28207739  nice user cpu ticks
    2355391  system cpu ticks
  628297350  idle cpu ticks
     862755  IO-wait cpu ticks
         34  IRQ cpu ticks
    1707439  softirq cpu ticks
```
continues

Listing 2.5   (Continued)

```
 21194571 pages paged in
 12677400 pages paged out
    93406 pages swapped in
   181587 pages swapped out
1931462143 interrupts
 785963213 CPU context switches
1096643656 boot time
   578451 forks
```

vmstat provides a broad range of information about the performance of a Linux system. It is one of the core tools to use when investigating a problem with a system.

2.2.2 top (v. 2.0.x)

top is the Swiss army knife of Linux system-monitoring tools. It does a good job of putting a very large amount of system-wide performance information in a single screen. What you display can also be changed interactively; so if a particular problem creeps up as your system runs, you can modify what top is showing you.

By default, top presents a list, in decreasing order, of the top CPU-consuming processes. This enables you to quickly pinpoint which program is hogging the CPU. Periodically, top updates the list based on a delay that you can specify. (It is initially 3 seconds.)

2.2.2.1 CPU Performance-Related Options

top is invoked with the following command line:

```
top [d delay] [C] [H] [i] [n iter] [b]
```

top actually takes options in two modes: command-line options and runtime options. The command-line options determine how top displays its information. Table 2-3 shows the command-line options that influence the type and frequency of the performance statistics that top displays.

Table 2-3   *top* Command-Line Options

Option	Explanation
d delay	Delay between statistic updates.
n iterations	Number of iterations before exiting. top updates the statistics iterations times.
i	Don't display processes that aren't using any of the CPU.
H	Show all the individual threads of an application rather than just display a total for each application.
c	In a hyperthreaded or SMP system, display the summed CPU statistics rather than the statistics for each CPU.

As you run top, you might want to fine-tune what you are observing to investigate a particular problem. The output of top is highly customizable. Table 2-4 describes options that change statistics shown during top's runtime.

Table 2-4

Option	Explanation
f or F	This displays a configuration screen that enables you to select which process statistics display on the screen.
o or O	This displays a configuration screen that enables you to change the order of the displayed statistics.

The options described in Table 2-5 turn on or off the display of various system-wide information. It can be helpful to turn off unneeded statistics to fit more processes on the screen.

Table 2-5   *top* Runtime Output Toggles

Option	Explanation
l	This toggles whether the load average and uptime information will be updated and displayed.

continues

Table 2-5   *top* Runtime Output Toggles (Continued)

Option	Explanation
t	This toggles the display of how each CPU spends its time. It also toggles information about how many processes are currently running. Shows all the individual threads of an application instead of just displaying a total for each application.
m	This toggles whether information about the system memory usage will be shown on the screen. By default, the highest CPU consumers are displayed first. However, it might be more useful to sort by other characteristics.

Table 2-6 describes the different sorting modes that top supports. Sorting by memory consumption is particular useful to figure out which process consumes the most amount of memory.

Table 2-6   *top* Output Sorting/Display Options

Option	Explanation
P	Sorts the tasks by their CPU usage. The highest CPU user displays first.
T	Sorts the tasks by the amount of CPU time they have used so far. The highest amount displays first.
N	Sorts the tasks by their PID. The lowest PID displays first.
A	Sorts the tasks by their age. The newest PID is shown first. This is usually the opposite of "sort by PID."
i	Hides tasks that are idle and are not consuming CPU.

top provides system-wide information in addition to information about specific processes. Table 2-7 covers these statistics.

Table 2-7 *top* Performance Statistics

Option	Explanation
us	CPU time spent in user applications.
sy	CPU time spent in the kernel.
ni	CPU time spent in "nice"ed processes.
id	CPU time spent idle.
wa	CPU time spent waiting for I/O.
hi	CPU time spent in the irq handlers.
si	CPU time spent in the softirq handlers.
load average	The 1-minute, 5-minute, and 15-minute load average.
%CPU	The percentage of CPU that a particular process is consuming.
PRI	The priority value of the process, where a higher value indicates a higher priority. RT indicates that the task has real-time priority, a priority higher than the standard range.
NI	The nice value of the process. The higher the nice value, the less the system has to execute the process. Processes with high nice values tend to have very low priorities.
WCHAN	If a process is waiting on an I/O, this shows which kernel function it is waiting in.
STAT	This is the current status of a process, where the process is either sleeping (S), running (R), zombied (killed but not yet dead) (Z), in an uninterruptable sleep (D), or being traced (T).
TIME	The total amount CPU time (user and system) that this process has used since it started executing.
COMMAND	That command that this process is executing.
LC	The number of the last CPU that this process was executing on.
FLAGS	This toggles whether the load average and uptime information will be updated and displayed.

top provides a large amount of information about the different running processes and is a great way to figure out which process is a resource hog.

2.2.2.2 Example Usage

Listing 2.6 is an example run of top. Once it starts, it periodically updates the screen until you exit it. This demonstrates some of the system-wide statistics that top can generate. First, we see the load average of the system over the past 1, 5, and 15 minutes. As we can see, the system has started to get busy recently (because doom-3.x86). One CPU is busy with user code 90 percent of the time. The other is only spending ~13 percent of its time in user code. Finally, we can see that 73 of the processes are sleeping, and only 3 of them are currently running.

Listing 2.6

```
catan> top
 08:09:16  up 2 days, 18:44,  4 users,  load average: 0.95, 0.44, 0.17
76 processes: 73 sleeping, 3 running, 0 zombie, 0 stopped
CPU states:  cpu    user    nice   system    irq  softirq  iowait    idle
            total   51.5%   0.0%    3.9%    0.0%    0.0%    0.0%    44.6%
            cpu00   90.0%   0.0%    1.2%    0.0%    0.0%    0.0%     8.8%
            cpu01   13.0%   0.0%    6.6%    0.0%    0.0%    0.0%    80.4%
Mem:   2037140k av, 1132120k used,  905020k free,       0k shrd,   86220k buff
        689784k active,             151528k inactive
Swap: 2040244k av,      0k used, 2040244k free                  322648k cached
```

PID	USER	PRI	NI	SIZE	RSS	SHARE	STAT	%CPU	%MEM	TIME	CPU	COMMAND
7642	root	25	0	647M	379M	7664	R	49.9	19.0	2:58	0	doom.x86
7661	ezolt	15	0	1372	1372	1052	R	0.1	0.0	0:00	1	top
1	root	15	0	528	528	452	S	0.0	0.0	0:05	1	init
2	root	RT	0	0	0	0	SW	0.0	0.0	0:00	0	migration/0
3	root	RT	0	0	0	0	SW	0.0	0.0	0:00	1	migration/1
4	root	15	0	0	0	0	SW	0.0	0.0	0:00	0	keventd
5	root	34	19	0	0	0	SWN	0.0	0.0	0:00	0	ksoftirqd/0
6	root	34	19	0	0	0	SWN	0.0	0.0	0:00	1	ksoftirqd/1
9	root	25	0	0	0	0	SW	0.0	0.0	0:00	0	bdflush
7	root	15	0	0	0	0	SW	0.0	0.0	0:00	0	kswapd
8	root	15	0	0	0	0	SW	0.0	0.0	0:00	1	kscand
10	root	15	0	0	0	0	SW	0.0	0.0	0:00	1	kupdated
11	root	25	0	0	0	0	SW	0.0	0.0	0:00	0	mdrecoveryd

Now pressing F while top is running brings the configuration screen shown in Listing 2.7. When you press the keys indicated (A for PID, B for PPID, etc.), top toggles whether these statistics display in the previous screen. When all the desired statistics are selected, press Enter to return to top's initial screen, which now shows the current values of selected statistics. When configuring the statistics, all currently activated fields are capitalized in the Current Field Order line and have an asterisk (*) next to their name.

Listing 2.7

```
[ezolt@wintermute doc]$ top
(press 'F' while running)
   Current Field Order: AbcDgHIjklMnoTP|qrsuzyV{EFW[X
Toggle fields with a-z, any other key to return:
* A: PID        = Process Id
  B: PPID       = Parent Process Id
  C: UID        = User Id
* D: USER       = User Name
* E: %CPU       = CPU Usage
* F: %MEM       = Memory Usage
  G: TTY        = Controlling tty
* H: PRI        = Priority
* I: NI         = Nice Value
  J: PAGEIN     = Page Fault Count
  K: TSIZE      = Code Size (kb)
  L: DSIZE      = Data+Stack Size (kb)
* M: SIZE       = Virtual Image Size (kb)
  N: TRS        = Resident Text Size (kb)
  O: SWAP       = Swapped kb
* P: SHARE      = Shared Pages (kb)
  Q: A          = Accessed Page count
  R: WP         = Write Protected Pages
  S: D          = Dirty Pages
* T: RSS        = Resident Set Size (kb)
  U: WCHAN      = Sleeping in Function
* V: STAT       = Process Status
* W: TIME       = CPU Time
* X: COMMAND    = Command
```

continues

Listing 2.7   (Continued)

```
Y: LC          = Last used CPU (expect this to change regularly)
Z: FLAGS       = Task Flags (see linux/sched.h)
```

To show you how customizable top is, Listing 2.8 shows a highly configured output screen, which shows only the top options relevant to CPU usage.

Listing 2.8

```
08:16:23  up 2 days, 18:52,  4 users,  load average: 1.07, 0.92, 0.49
76 processes: 73 sleeping, 3 running, 0 zombie, 0 stopped
CPU states:  cpu    user    nice  system    irq  softirq  iowait    idle
            total   48.2%   0.0%    1.5%   0.0%    0.0%    0.0%    50.1%
            cpu00    0.3%   0.0%    0.1%   0.0%    0.0%    0.0%    99.5%
            cpu01   96.2%   0.0%    2.9%   0.0%    0.0%    0.0%     0.7%
Mem:  2037140k av, 1133548k used,  903592k free,      0k shrd,   86232k buff
690812k active,              151536k inactive
Swap: 2040244k av,      0k used, 2040244k free               322656k cached

  PID USER     PRI  NI WCHAN        FLAGS LC STAT %CPU   TIME CPU COMMAND
 7642 root      25   0             100100  1 R    49.6 10:30   1 doom.x86
    1 root      15   0             400100  0 S     0.0  0:05   0 init
    2 root      RT   0                140  0 SW    0.0  0:00   0 migration/0
    3 root      RT   0                140  1 SW    0.0  0:00   1 migration/1
    4 root      15   0                 40  0 SW    0.0  0:00   0 keventd
    5 root      34  19                 40  0 SWN   0.0  0:00   0 ksoftirqd/0
    6 root      34  19                 40  1 SWN   0.0  0:00   1 ksoftirqd/1
    9 root      25   0                 40  0 SW    0.0  0:00   0 bdflush
    7 root      15   0                840  0 SW    0.0  0:00   0 kswapd
    8 root      15   0                 40  0 SW    0.0  0:00   0 kscand
   10 root      15   0                 40  0 SW    0.0  0:00   0 kupdated
   11 root      25   0                 40  0 SW    0.0  0:00   0 mdrecoveryd
   20 root      15   0             400040  0 SW    0.0  0:00   0 katad-1
```

top provides an overview of system resource usage with a focus on providing information about how various processes are consuming those resources. It is best used when interacting with the system directly because of the user-friendly and tool-unfriendly format of its output.

2.2.3 top (v. 3.x.x)

Recently, the version of top provided by the most recent distributions has been completely overhauled, and as a result, many of the command-line and interaction options have changed. Although the basic ideas are similar, it has been streamlined, and a few different display modes have been added.

Again, top presents a list, in decreasing order, of the top CPU-consuming processes.

2.2.3.1 CPU Performance-Related Options

top is invoked with the following command line:

```
top  [-d delay] [-n iter] [-i]  [-b]
```

top actually takes options in two modes: command-line options and runtime options. The command-line options determine how top displays its information. Table 2-8 shows the command-line options that influence the type and frequency of the performance statistics that top will display.

Table 2-8   *top* Command-Line Options

Option	Explanation
-d delay	Delay between statistic updates.
-n iterations	Number of iterations before exiting. top updates the statistics' iterations times.
-i	This option changes whether or not idle processes display.
-b	Run in batch mode. Typically, top shows only a single screenful of information, and processes that don't fit on the screen never display. This option shows all the processes and can be very useful if you are saving top's output to a file or piping the output to another command for processing.

As you run top, you may want to fine-tune what you are observing to investigate a particular problem. Like the 2.x version of top, the output of top is highly customizable. Table 2-9 describes options that change statistics shown during top's runtime.

Table 2-9   *top* Runtime Options

Option	Explanation
A	This displays an "alternate" display of process information that shows top consumers of various system resources.
I	This toggles whether top will divide the CPU usage by the number of CPUs on the system.
	For example, if a process was consuming all of both CPUs on a two-CPU system, this toggles whether top displays a CPU usage of 100% or 200%.
f	This displays a configuration screen that enables you to select which process statistics display on the screen.
o	This displays a configuration screen that enables you to change the order of the displayed statistics.

The options described in Table 2-10 turn on or off the display of various system-wide information. It can be helpful to turn off unneeded statistics to fit more processes on the screen.

Table 2-10   *top* Runtime Output Toggles

Option	Explanation
1 (numeral 1)	This toggles whether the CPU usage will be broken down to the individual usage or shown as a total.
l	This toggles whether the load average and uptime information will be updated and displayed.

top v3.x provides system-wide information in addition to information about specific processes similar to those of top v2.x. These statistics are covered in Table 2-11.

Table 2-11   *top* Performance Statistics

Option	Explanation
us	CPU time spent in user applications.
sy	CPU time spent in the kernel.
ni	CPU time spent in "nice"ed processes.
id	CPU time spent idle.
wa	CPU time spent waiting for I/O.
hi	CPU time spent in the irq handlers.
si	CPU time spent in the softirq handlers.
load average	The 1-minute, 5-minute, and 15-minute load average.
%CPU	The percentage of CPU that a particular process is consuming.
PRI	The priority value of the process, where a higher value indicates a higher priority. RT indicates that the task has real-time priority, a priority higher than the standard range.
NI	The nice value of the process. The higher the nice value, the less the system has to execute the process. Processes with high nice values tend to have very low priorities.
WCHAN	If a process is waiting on an I/O, this shows which kernel function it is waiting in.
TIME	The total amount CPU time (user and system) that this process has used since it started executing.
COMMAND	That command that this process is executing.
S	This is the current status of a process, where the process is either sleeping (S), running (R), zombied (killed but not yet dead) (Z), in an uninterruptable sleep (D), or being traced (T).

top provides a large amount of information about the different running processes and is a great way to figure out which process is a resource hog. The v.3 version of top has trimmed-down top and added some alternative views of similar data.

2.2.3.2 Example Usage

Listing 2.9 is an example run of top v3.0. Again, it will periodically update the screen until you exit it. The statistics are similar to those of top v2.x, but are named slightly differently.

Listing 2.9

```
catan> top
top - 08:52:21 up 19 days, 21:38, 17 users,  load average: 1.06, 1.13, 1.15
Tasks: 149 total,  1 running, 146 sleeping,  1 stopped,  1 zombie
Cpu(s):  0.8% us,  0.4% sy,  4.2% ni, 94.2% id,  0.1% wa,  0.0% hi,  0.3% si
Mem:    1034320k total, 1023188k used,    11132k free,    39920k buffers
Swap:   2040244k total,  214496k used,  1825748k free,   335488k cached

  PID USER      PR  NI  VIRT  RES  SHR S %CPU %MEM    TIME+  COMMAND
26364 root      16   0  400m  68m 321m S  3.8  6.8 379:32.04 X
26737 ezolt     15   0 71288  45m  21m S  1.9  4.5   6:32.04 gnome-terminal
29114 ezolt     15   0 34000  22m  18m S  1.9  2.2  27:57.62 gnome-system-mo
 9581 ezolt     15   0  2808 1028 1784 R  1.9  0.1   0:00.03 top
    1 root      16   0  2396  448 1316 S  0.0  0.0   0:01.68 init
    2 root      RT   0     0    0    0 S  0.0  0.0   0:00.68 migration/0
    3 root      34  19     0    0    0 S  0.0  0.0   0:00.01 ksoftirqd/0
    4 root      RT   0     0    0    0 S  0.0  0.0   0:00.27 migration/1
    5 root      34  19     0    0    0 S  0.0  0.0   0:00.01 ksoftirqd/1
    6 root      RT   0     0    0    0 S  0.0  0.0   0:22.49 migration/2
    7 root      34  19     0    0    0 S  0.0  0.0   0:00.01 ksoftirqd/2
    8 root      RT   0     0    0    0 S  0.0  0.0   0:37.53 migration/3
    9 root      34  19     0    0    0 S  0.0  0.0   0:00.01 ksoftirqd/3
   10 root       5 -10     0    0    0 S  0.0  0.0   0:01.74 events/0
   11 root       5 -10     0    0    0 S  0.0  0.0   0:02.77 events/1
   12 root       5 -10     0    0    0 S  0.0  0.0   0:01.79 events/2
```

Now pressing f while top is running brings the configuration screen shown in Listing 2.10. When you press the keys indicated (A for PID, B for PPID, etc.), top toggles whether these statistics display in the previous screen. When all the desired statistics are selected, press Enter to return to top's initial screen, which now shows the current values of selected statistics. When you are configuring the statistics, all currently activated fields are capitalized in the Current Field Order line and have and asterisk (*) next to their name. Notice that most of statistics are similar, but the names have slightly changed.

Listing 2.10

```
(press 'f' while running)
Current Fields: _AEHIOQTWKNMbcdfgjplrsuvyzX  for window 1:Def
Toggle fields via field letter, type any other key to return


  * A: PID        = Process Id            u: nFLT      = Page Fault count
  * E: USER       = User Name             v: nDRT      = Dirty Pages count
  * H: PR         = Priority              y: WCHAN     = Sleeping in Function
  * I: NI         = Nice value            z: Flags     = Task Flags <sched.h>
  * O: VIRT       = Virtual Image (kb)  * X: COMMAND   = Command name/line
  * Q: RES        = Resident size (kb)
  * T: SHR        = Shared Mem size (kb)  Flags field:
  * W: S          = Process Status
  * K: %CPU       = CPU usage             0x00000001  PF_ALIGNWARN
  * N: %MEM       = Memory usage (RES)    0x00000002  PF_STARTING
  * M: TIME+      = CPU Time, hundredths  0x00000004  PF_EXITING
    b: PPID       = Parent Process Pid    0x00000040  PF_FORKNOEXEC
    c: RUSER      = Real user name        0x00000100  PF_SUPERPRIV
    d: UID        = User Id               0x00000200  PF_DUMPCORE
    f: GROUP      = Group Name            0x00000400  PF_SIGNALED
    g: TTY        = Controlling Tty       0x00000800  PF_MEMALLOC
    j: #C         = Last used cpu (SMP)   0x00002000  PF_FREE_PAGES (2.5)
    p: SWAP       = Swapped size (kb)     0x00008000  debug flag (2.5)
    l: TIME       = CPU Time              0x00024000  special threads (2.5)
    r: CODE       = Code size (kb)        0x001D0000  special states (2.5)
    s: DATA       = Data+Stack size (kb)  0x00100000  PF_USEDFPU (thru 2.4)
```

Listing 2.11 shows the new output mode of top, where many different statistics are sorted and displayed on the same screen.

Listing 2.11

```
(press 'F' while running)
1:Def - 09:00:48 up 19 days, 21:46, 17 users,  load average: 1.01, 1.06, 1.10
Tasks: 144 total,  1 running, 141 sleeping,  1 stopped,  1 zombie
Cpu(s):  1.2% us,  0.9% sy,  0.0% ni, 97.9% id,  0.0% wa,  0.0% hi,  0.0% si
Mem:   1034320k total, 1024020k used,    10300k free,    39408k buffers
Swap: 2040244k total,  214496k used, 1825748k free,   335764k cached


 1  PID USER       PR  NI  VIRT   RES   SHR S %CPU %MEM    TIME+   COMMAND
  29114 ezolt      16   0 34112   22m   18m S  3.6  2.2  28:15.06 gnome-system-mo
  26364 root       15   0  400m   68m  321m S  2.6  6.8 380:01.09 X
   9689 ezolt      16   0  3104  1092  1784 R  1.0  0.1   0:00.09 top
 2  PID PPID    TIME+  %CPU %MEM  PR  NI S  VIRT SWAP  RES  UID COMMAND
  30403 24989  0:00.03  0.0  0.1  15   0 S  5808 4356 1452 9336 bash
  29510 29505  7:19.59  0.0  5.9  16   0 S  125m  65m  59m 9336 firefox-bin
  29505 29488  0:00.00  0.0  0.1  16   0 S  5652 4576 1076 9336 run-mozilla.sh
 3  PID %MEM  VIRT SWAP  RES CODE DATA  SHR nFLT nDRT S  PR  NI %CPU COMMAND
   8414 25.0  374m 121m 252m  496 373m  98m 1547    0 S  16   0  0.0 soffice.bin
  26364  6.8  400m 331m  68m 1696 398m 321m 2399    0 S  15   0  2.6 X
  29510  5.9  125m  65m  59m   64 125m  31m  253    0 S  16   0  0.0 firefox-bin
  26429  4.7 59760  10m  47m  404  57m  12m 1247    0 S  15   0  0.0 metacity
 4  PID PPID  UID USER       RUSER    TTY         TIME+  %CPU %MEM S COMMAND
   1371    1   43 xfs        xfs      ?         0:00.10  0.0  0.1 S xfs
   1313    1   51 smmsp      smmsp    ?         0:00.08  0.0  0.2 S sendmail
    982    1   29 rpcuser    rpcuser  ?         0:00.07  0.0  0.1 S rpc.statd
    963    1   32 rpc        rpc      ?         0:06.23  0.0  0.1 S portmap
```

top v3.x provides a slightly cleaner interface to top. It simplifies some aspects of it and provides a nice "summary" information screen that displays many of the resource consumers in the system.

2.2.4 procinfo (Display Info from the /proc File System)

Much like vmstat, procinfo provides a view of the system-wide performance character-istics. Although some of the information that it provides is similar to that of vmstat, it also provides information about the number of interrupts that the CPU received for each device. Its output format is a little more readable than vmstat, but it takes up much more screen space.

2.2.4.1 CPU Performance-Related Options

procinfo is invoked with the following command:

procinfo [-f] [-d] [-D] [-n sec] [-f file]

Table 2-12 describes the different options that change the output and the frequency of the samples that procinfo displays.

Table 2-12   *procinfo* Command-Line Options

Option	Explanation
-f	Runs procinfo in full-screen mode
-d	Displays statistics change between samples rather than totals
-D	Displays statistic totals rather than rate of change
-n sec	Number of seconds to pause between each sample
-Ffile	Sends the output of procinfo to a file

Table 2-13 shows the CPU statistics that procinfo gathers.

Table 2-13   *procinfo* CPU Statistics

Option	Explanation
user	This is the amount of user time that the CPU has spent in days, hours, and minutes.
nice	This is the amount of nice time that the CPU has spent in days, hours, and minutes.
system	This is the amount of system time that the CPU has spent in days, hours, and minutes.
idle	This is the amount of idle time that the CPU has spent in days, hours, and minutes.
irq 0- N	This displays the number of the irq, the amount that has fired, and which kernel driver is responsible for it.

Much like vmstat or top, procinfo is a low-overhead command that is good to leave running in a console or window on the screen. It gives a good indication of a system's health and performance.

2.2.4.2 Example Usage

Calling procinfo without any command options yields output similar to Listing 2.12. Without any options, procinfo displays only one screenful of status and then exits. procinfo is more useful when it is periodically updated using the -n second options. This enables you to see how the system's performance is changing in real time.

Listing 2.12

```
[ezolt@scrffy ~/mail]$ procinfo
Linux 2.4.18-3bigmem (bhcompile@daffy) (gcc 2.96 20000731 ) #1 4CPU [scrffy]

Memory:      Total       Used       Free     Shared    Buffers     Cached
Mem:       1030784     987776      43008          0      35996     517504
Swap:      2040244      17480    2022764
```

```
Bootup: Thu Jun  3 09:20:22 2004   Load average: 0.47 0.32 0.26 1/118 10378


user  :      3:18:53.99   2.7%  page in :  1994292  disk 1:       20r       0w
nice  :      0:00:22.91   0.0%  page out:  2437543  disk 2:   247231r  131696w
system:      3:45:41.20   3.1%  swap in :      996
idle  :  4d 15:56:17.10  94.0%  swap out:     4374
uptime:  1d  5:45:18.80         context : 64608366


irq  0:  10711880 timer            irq 12:   1319185 PS/2 Mouse
irq  1:     94931 keyboard         irq 14:   7144432 ide0
irq  2:         0 cascade [4]       irq 16:        16 aic7xxx
irq  3:         1                  irq 18:   4152504 nvidia
irq  4:         1                  irq 19:         0 usb-uhci
irq  6:         2                  irq 20:   4772275 es1371
irq  7:         1                  irq 22:    384919 aic7xxx
irq  8:         1 rtc              irq 23:   3797246 usb-uhci, eth0
```

As you can see from Listing 2.12, procinfo provides a reasonable overview of the system. We can see that, once again for the user, nice, system, and idle time, the system is not very busy. One interesting thing to notice is that procinfo claims that the system has spent more idle time than the system has been running (as indicated by the uptime). This is because the system actually has four CPUs, so for every day of wall time, four days of CPU time passes. The load average confirms that the system has been relatively work-free for the recent past. For the past minute, on the average, the system had less than one process ready to run; a load average of .47 indicates that a single process was ready to run only 47 percent of the time. On a four-CPU system, this large amount of CPU power is going to waste.

procinfo also gives us a good view of what devices on the system are causing interrupts. We can see that the Nvidia card (nvidia), IDE controller (ide0), Ethernet device (eth0), and sound card (es1371) have a relatively high number of interrupts. This is as one would expect for a desktop workstation.

procinfo has the advantage of putting many of the system-wide performance statistics within a single screen, enabling you to see how the system is performing as a whole. It lacks details about network and disk performance, but it provide a good system-wide detail of the CPU and memory performance. One limitation that can be significant is the fact that procinfo does not report when the CPU is in the iowait, irq, or softirq mode.

2.2.5 gnome-system-monitor

gnome-system-monitor is, in many ways, a graphical counterpart of top. It enables you to graphically monitor individual processes and observe the load on the system based on the graphs that it displays.

2.2.5.1 CPU Performance-Related Options

gnome-system-monitor can be invoked from the Gnome menu. (Under Red Hat 9 and greater, this is under System Tools > System Monitor.) However, it can also be invoked using the following command:

```
gnome-system-monitor
```

gnome-system-monitor has no relevant command-line options that affect the CPU performance measurements. However, some of the statistics shown can be modified by selecting gnome-system-monitor's Edit > Preferences menu entry.

2.2.5.2 Example Usage

When you launch gnome-system-monitor, it creates a window similar to Figure 2-1. This window shows information about the amount of CPU and memory that a particular process is using. It also shows information about the parent/child relationships between each process.

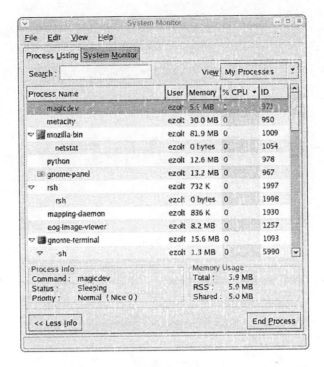

Figure 2-1

Figure 2-2 shows a graphical view of system load and memory usage. This is really what distinguishes gnome-system-monitor from top. You can easily see the current state of the system and how it compares to the previous state.

The graphical view of data provided by gnome-system-monitor can make it easier and faster to determine the state of the system, and how its behavior changes over time. It also makes it easier to navigate the system-wide process information.

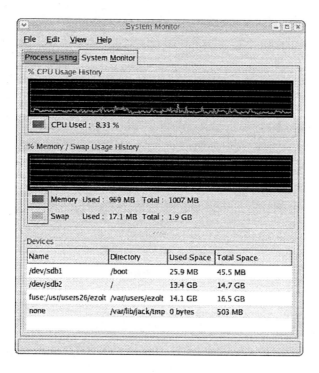

Figure 2-2

2.2.6 mpstat (Multiprocessor Stat)

mpstat is a fairly simple command that shows you how your processors are behaving based on time. The biggest benefit of mpstat is that it shows the time next to the statistics, so you can look for a correlation between CPU usage and time of day.

If you have multiple CPUs or hyperthreading-enabled CPUs, mpstat can also break down CPU usage based on the processor, so you can see whether a particular processor is doing more work than the others. You can select which individual processor you want to monitor or you can ask mpstat to monitor all of them.

2.2.6.1 CPU Performance-Related Options

mpstat can be invoked using the following command line:

```
mpstat [ -P { cpu | ALL } ]  [ delay [ count ] ]
```

Once again, delay specifies how often the samples will be taken, and count determines how many times it will be run. Table 2-14 describes the command-line options of mpstat.

Table 2-14 *mpstat* Command-Line Options

Option	Explanation
-P { cpu | ALL }	This option tells mpstat which CPUs to monitor. cpu is the number between 0 and the total CPUs minus 1.
delay	This specifies how long mpstat waits between samples.

mpstat provides similar information to the other CPU performance tools, but it allows the information to be attributed to each of the processors in a particular system. Table 2-15 describes the options that it supports.

Table 2-15 *mpstat* CPU Statistics

Option	Explanation
user	This is the percentage of user time that the CPU has spent during the previous sample.
nice	This is the percentage of time that the CPU has spent during the previous sample running low-priority (or nice) processes.
system	This is the percentage of system time that the CPU has spent during the previous sample.
iowait	This is the percentage of time that the CPU has spent during the previous sample waiting on I/O.
irq	This is the percentage of time that the CPU has spent during the previous sample handling interrupts.
softirq	This is the percentage of time that the CPU has spent during the previous sample handling work that needed to be done by the kernel after an interrupt has been handled.
idle	This is the percentage of time that the CPU has spent idle during the previous sample.

mpstat is a good tool for providing a breakdown of how each of the processors is performing. Because mpstat provides a per-CPU breakdown, you can identify whether one of the processors is becoming overloaded.

2.2.6.2 Example Usage

First, we ask mpstat to show us the CPU statistics for processor number 0. This is shown in Listing 2.13.

Listing 2.13

```
[ezolt@scrffy sysstat-5.1.1]$ ./mpstat -P 0 1 10
Linux 2.6.8-1.521smp (scrffy)    10/20/2004

07:12:02 PM  CPU  %user  %nice  %sys %iowait  %irq  %soft  %idle  intr/s
07:12:03 PM    0   9.80   0.00   1.96    0.98  0.00   0.00  87.25  1217.65
07:12:04 PM    0   1.01   0.00   0.00    0.00  0.00   0.00  98.99  1112.12
07:12:05 PM    0   0.99   0.00   0.00    0.00  0.00   0.00  99.01  1055.45
07:12:06 PM    0   0.00   0.00   0.00    0.00  0.00   0.00 100.00  1072.00
07:12:07 PM    0   0.00   0.00   0.00    0.00  0.00   0.00 100.00  1075.76
07:12:08 PM    0   1.00   0.00   0.00    0.00  0.00   0.00  99.00  1067.00
07:12:09 PM    0   4.90   0.00   3.92    0.00  0.00   0.98  90.20  1045.10
07:12:10 PM    0   0.00   0.00   0.00    0.00  0.00   0.00 100.00  1069.70
07:12:11 PM    0   0.99   0.00   0.99    0.00  0.00   0.00  98.02  1070.30
07:12:12 PM    0   3.00   0.00   4.00    0.00  0.00   0.00  93.00  1067.00
Average:       0   2.19   0.00   1.10    0.10  0.00   0.10  96.51  1085.34
```

Listing 2.14 shows a similar command on very unloaded CPUs that both have hyperthreading. You can see how the stats for all the CPUs are shown. One interesting observation in this output is the fact that one CPU seems to handle all the interrupts. If the system was heavy loaded with I/O, and all the interrupts were being handed by a single processor, this could be the cause of a bottleneck, because one CPU is overwhelmed, and the rest are waiting for work to do. You would be able to see this with mpstat, if the processor handling all the interrupts had no idle time, whereas the other processors did.

Listing 2.14

```
[ezolt@scrffy sysstat-5.1.1]$ ./mpstat -P ALL 1 2
Linux 2.6.8-1.521smp (scrffy)   10/20/2004
```

07:13:21 PM	CPU	%user	%nice	%sys	%iowait	%irq	%soft	%idle	intr/s
07:13:22 PM	all	3.98	0.00	1.00	0.25	0.00	0.00	94.78	1322.00
07:13:22 PM	0	2.00	0.00	0.00	1.00	0.00	0.00	97.00	1137.00
07:13:22 PM	1	6.00	0.00	2.00	0.00	0.00	0.00	93.00	185.00
07:13:22 PM	2	1.00	0.00	0.00	0.00	0.00	0.00	99.00	0.00
07:13:22 PM	3	8.00	0.00	1.00	0.00	0.00	0.00	91.00	0.00
07:13:22 PM	CPU	%user	%nice	%sys	%iowait	%irq	%soft	%idle	intr/s
07:13:23 PM	all	2.00	0.00	0.50	0.00	0.00	0.00	97.50	1352.53
07:13:23 PM	0	0.00	0.00	0.00	0.00	0.00	0.00	100.00	1135.35
07:13:23 PM	1	6.06	0.00	2.02	0.00	0.00	0.00	92.93	193.94
07:13:23 PM	2	0.00	0.00	0.00	0.00	0.00	0.00	101.01	16.16
07:13:23 PM	3	1.01	0.00	1.01	0.00	0.00	0.00	100.00	7.07
Average:	CPU	%user	%nice	%sys	%iowait	%irq	%soft	%idle	intr/s
Average:	all	2.99	0.00	0.75	0.12	0.00	0.00	96.13	1337.19
Average:	0	1.01	0.00	0.00	0.50	0.00	0.00	98.49	1136.18
Average:	1	6.03	0.00	2.01	0.00	0.00	0.00	92.96	189.45
Average:	2	0.50	0.00	0.00	0.00	0.00	0.00	100.00	8.04
Average:	3	4.52	0.00	1.01	0.00	0.00	0.00	95.48	3.52

mpstat can be used to determine whether the CPUs are fully utilized and relatively balanced. By observing the number of interrupts each CPU is handling, it is possible to find an imbalance. Details on how to control where interrupts are routing are provided in the kernel source under Documentation/IRQ-affinity.txt.

2.2.7 sar (System Activity Reporter)

sar has yet another approach to collecting system data. sar can efficiently record system performance data collected into binary files that can be replayed at a later date. sar is a low-overhead way to record information about how the system is performing.

The sar command can be used to record performance information, replay previous recorded information, and display real-time information about the current system. The output of the sar command can be formatted to make it easy to pipe to relational databases or to other Linux commands for processing.

2.2.7.1 CPU Performance-Related Options

sar can be invoked with the following command line:

sar [options] [delay [count]]

Although sar reports about many different areas of Linux, the statistics are of two different forms. One set of statistics is the instantaneous value at the time of the sample. The other is a rate since the last sample. Table 2-16 describes the command-line options of sar.

Table 2-16   *sar* Command-Line Options

Option	Explanation
-c	This reports information about how many processes are being created per second.
-I {irq | SUM | ALL | XALL}	This reports the rates that interrupts have been occurring in the system.
-P {cpu | ALL}	This option specifies which CPU the statistics should be gathered from. If this isn't specified, the system totals are reported.
-q	This reports information about the run queues and load averages of the machine.
-u	This reports information about CPU utilization of the system. (This is the default output.)
-w	This reports the number of context switches that occurred in the system.
-o filename	This specifies the name of the binary output file that will store the performance statistics.

Option	Explanation
-f filename	This specifies the filename of the performance statistics.
delay	The amount of time to wait between samples.
count	The total number of samples to record.

sar offers a similar set (with different names) of the system-wide CPU performance statistics that we have seen in the proceeding tools. The list is shown in Table 2-17.

Table 2-17 *sar* CPU Statistics

Option	Explanation
user	This is the percentage of user time that the CPU has spent during the previous sample.
nice	This is the percentage of time that the CPU has spent during the previous sample running low-priority (or nice) processes.
system	This is the percentage of system time that the CPU has spent during the previous sample.
iowait	This is the percentage of time that the CPU has spent during the previous sample waiting on I/O.
idle	This is the percentage of time that the CPU was idle during the previous sample.
runq-sz	This is the size of the run queue when the sample was taken.
plist-sz	This is the number of processes present (running, sleeping, or waiting for I/O) when the sample was taken.
ldavg-1	This was the load average for the last minute.
ldavg-5	This was the load average for the past 5 minutes.
ldavg-15	This was the load average for the past 15 minutes.
proc/s	This is the number of new processes created per second. (This is the same as the forks statistic from vmstat.)
cswch	This is the number of context switches per second.
intr/s	The number of interrupts fired per second.

One of the significant benefits of sar is that it enables you to save many different types of time-stamped system data to log files for later retrieval and review. This can prove very handy when trying to figure out why a particular machine is failing at a particular time.

2.2.7.2 Example Usage

This first command shown in Listing 2.15 takes three samples of the CPU every second, and stores the results in the binary file /tmp/apache_test. This command does not have any visual output and just returns when it has completed.

Listing 2.15

```
[ezolt@wintermute sysstat-5.0.2]$ sar -o /tmp/apache_test 1 3
```

After the information has been stored in the /tmp/apache_test file, we can display it in various formats. The default is human readable. This is shown in Listing 2.16. This shows similar information to the other system monitoring commands, where we can see how the processor was spending time at a particular time.

Listing 2.16

```
[ezolt@wintermute sysstat-5.0.2]$ sar -f /tmp/apache_test
Linux 2.4.22-1.2149.nptl (wintermute.phil.org)   03/20/04
```

17:18:34	CPU	%user	%nice	%system	%iowait	%idle
17:18:35	all	90.00	0.00	10.00	0.00	0.00
17:18:36	all	95.00	0.00	5.00	0.00	0.00
17:18:37	all	92.00	0.00	6.00	0.00	2.00
Average:	all	92.33	0.00	7.00	0.00	0.67

However, sar can also output the statistics in a format that can be easily imported into a relational database, as shown in Listing 2.17. This can be useful for storing a large amount of performance data. Once it has been imported into a relational database, the performance data can be analyzed with all of the tools of a relational database.

Listing 2.17

```
[ezolt@wintermute sysstat-5.0.2]$ sar -f /tmp/apache_test  -H
wintermute.phil.org;1;2004-03-20 22:18:35 UTC;-1;90.00;0.00;10.00;0.00;0.00
wintermute.phil.org;1;2004-03-20 22:18:36 UTC;-1;95.00;0.00;5.00;0.00;0.00
wintermute.phil.org;1;2004-03-20 22:18:37 UTC;-1;92.00;0.00;6.00;0.00;2.00
```

Finally, sar can also output the statistics in a format that can be easily parsed by standard Linux tools such as awk, perl, python, or grep. This output, which is shown in Listing 2.18, can be fed into a script that will pull out interesting events, and possibly even analyze different trends in the data.

Listing 2.18

```
[ezolt@wintermute sysstat-5.0.2]$ sar -f /tmp/apache_test   -h
wintermute.phil.org     1     1079821115     all     %user   90.00
wintermute.phil.org     1     1079821115     all     %nice   0.00
wintermute.phil.org     1     1079821115     all     %system 10.00
wintermute.phil.org     1     1079821115     all     %iowait 0.00
wintermute.phil.org     1     1079821115     all     %idle   0.00
wintermute.phil.org     1     1079821116     all     %user   95.00
wintermute.phil.org     1     1079821116     all     %nice   0.00
wintermute.phil.org     1     1079821116     all     %system 5.00
wintermute.phil.org     1     1079821116     all     %iowait 0.00
wintermute.phil.org     1     1079821116     all     %idle   0.00
wintermute.phil.org     1     1079821117     all     %user   92.00
wintermute.phil.org     1     1079821117     all     %nice   0.00
wintermute.phil.org     1     1079821117     all     %system 6.00
wintermute.phil.org     1     1079821117     all     %iowait 0.00
wintermute.phil.org     1     1079821117     all     %idle   2.00
```

In addition to recording information in a file, sar can also be used to observe a system in real time. In the example shown in Listing 2.19, the CPU state is sampled three times with one second between them.

Listing 2.19

```
[ezolt@wintermute sysstat-5.0.2]$ sar 1 3
Linux 2.4.22-1.2149.nptl (wintermute.phil.org)   03/20/04

17:27:10      CPU     %user    %nice    %system   %iowait    %idle
17:27:11      all     96.00    0.00     4.00      0.00       0.00
17:27:12      all     98.00    0.00     2.00      0.00       0.00
17:27:13      all     92.00    0.00     8.00      0.00       0.00
Average:      all     95.33    0.00     4.67      0.00       0.00
```

The default display's purpose is to show information about the CPU, but other information can also be displayed. For example, sar can show the number of context switches per second, and the number of memory pages that have been swapped in or out. In Listing 2.20, sar samples the information two times, with one second between them. In this case, we ask sar to show us the total number of context switches and process creations that occur every second. We also ask sar for information about the load average. We can see in this example that this machine has 163 process that are in memory but not running. For the past minute, on average 1.12 processes have been ready to run.

Listing 2.20

```
[ezolt@scrffy manuscript]$ sar -w -c -q 1 2
Linux 2.6.8-1.521smp (scrffy)   10/20/2004


08:23:29 PM    proc/s
08:23:30 PM     0.00


08:23:29 PM    cswch/s
08:23:30 PM    594.00


08:23:29 PM    runq-sz  plist-sz  ldavg-1  ldavg-5  ldavg-15
08:23:30 PM         0       163     1.12     1.17     1.17


08:23:30 PM    proc/s
```

```
08:23:31 PM        0.00


08:23:30 PM    cswch/s
08:23:31 PM    812.87


08:23:30 PM    runq-sz  plist-sz   ldavg-1   ldavg-5   ldavg-15
08:23:31 PM          0       163      1.12      1.17       1.17


Average:       proc/s
Average:         0.00


Average:       cswch/s
Average:        703.98


Average:       runq-sz  plist-sz   ldavg-1   ldavg-5   ldavg-15
Average:             0       163      1.12      1.17       1.17
```

As you can see, sar is a powerful tool that can record many different performance statistics. It provides a Linux-friendly interface that enables you to easily extract and analyze the performance data.

2.2.8 oprofile

oprofile is a performance suite that uses the performance counter hardware available in nearly all modern processors to track where CPU time is being spent on an entire system, and individual processes. In addition to measuring where CPU cycles are spent, oprofile can measure very low-level information about how the CPU is performing. Depending on the events supported by the underlying processor, it can measure such things as cache misses, branch mispredictions and memory references, and floating-point operations.

oprofile does not record every event that occurs; instead, it works with the processor's performance hardware to sample every count events, where count is a value that users specify when they start oprofile. The lower the value of count, the more accurate the results are, but the higher the overhead of oprofile. By keeping count to a reasonable value, oprofile can run with a very low overhead but still give an amazingly accurate account of the performance of the system.

Sampling is very powerful, but be careful for some nonobvious gotchas when using it. First, sampling may say that you are spending 90 percent of your time in a particular routine, but it does not say why. There can be two possible causes for a high number of cycles attributed to a particular routine. First, it is possible that this routine is the bottleneck and is taking a long amount of time to execute. However, it may also be that the function is taking a reasonable amount of time to execute, but is called a large number of times. You can usually figure out which is the case by looking at the samples around, the particularly hot line, or by instrumenting the code to count the number of calls that are made to it.

The second problem of sampling is that you are never quite sure where a function is being called from. Even if you figure out that the function is being called many times and you track down all of the functions that call it, it is not necessarily clear which function is doing the majority of the calling.

2.2.8.1 CPU Performance-Related Options

oprofile is actually a suite of pieces that work together to collect CPU performance statistics. There are three main pieces of oprofile:

* The oprofile kernel module manipulates the processor and turns on and off sampling.
* The oprofile daemon collects the samples and saves them to disk.
* The oprofile reporting tools take the collected samples and show the user how they relate to the applications running on the system.

The oprofile suite hides the driver and daemon manipulation in the opcontrol command. The opcontrol command is used to select which events the processor will sample and start the sampling.

When controlling the daemon, you can invoke opcontrol using the following command line:

```
opcontrol [--start] [--stop] [--dump]
```

This option's control, the profiling daemon, enables you to start and stop sampling and to dump the samples from the daemon's memory to disk. When sampling, the opro-file daemon stores a large amount of samples in internal buffers. However, it is only possibly to analyze the samples that have been written (or dumped) to disk. Writing to disk can be an expensive operation, so oprofile only does it periodically. As a result, after running a test and profiling with oprofile, the results may not be available imme-diately, and you will have to wait until the daemon flushes the buffers to disk. This can be very annoying when you want to begin analysis immediately, so the opcontrol com-mand enables you to force the dump of samples from the oprofile daemon's internal buffers to disk. This enables you to begin a performance investigation immediately after a test has completed.

Table 2-18 describes the command-line options for the opcontrol program that enable you to control the operation of the daemon.

Table 2-18   *opcontrol* Daemon Control

Option	Explanation
-s/--start	Starts profiling unless this uses a default event for the current processor
-d/--dump	Dumps the sampling information that is currently in the kernel sample buffers to the disk.
--stop	This will stop the profiling.

By default, oprofile picks an event with a given frequency that is reasonable for the processor and kernel that you are running it on. However, it has many more events that can be monitored than the default. When you are listing and selecting an event, opcon-trol is invoked using the following command line:

```
opcontrol [--list-events] [-event=:name:count:unitmask:kernel:user:]
```

The event specifier enables you to select which event is going to be sampled; how fre-quently it will be sampled; and whether that sampling will take place in kernel space, user space, or both. Table 2-19 describes the command-line option of opcontrol that enables you to select different events to sample.

Table 2-19 *opcontrol* Event Handling

Option	Explanation
`-l/--list-events`	Lists the different events that the processor can sample.
`-event=:name:count:` `unitmask:kernel:user:`	Used to specify what events will be sampled. The event name must be one of the events that the processor supports. A valid event can be retrieved from the `--list-events` option. The `count` parameter specifies that the processor will be sampled every `count` times that event happens. The `unitmask` modifies what the event is going to sample. For example, if you are sampling "reads from memory," the unit mask may allow you to select only those reads that didn't hit in the cache. The `kernel` parameter specifies whether `oprofile` should sample when the processor is running in kernel space. The `user` parameter specifies whether `oprofile` should sample when the processor is running in user space.
`--vmlinux = kernel`	Specifies which uncompressed kernel image `oprofile` will use to attribute samples to various kernel functions.

After the samples have been collected and saved to disk, `oprofile` provides a different tool, `opreport`, which enables you to view the samples that have been collected. `opreport` is invoked using the following command line:

```
opreport [-r] [-t]
```

Typically, `opreport` displays all the samples collected by the system and which executables (including the kernel) are responsible for them. The executables with the highest number of samples are shown first, and are followed by all the executables with samples. In a typical system, most of the samples are in a handful of executables at the top of the list, with a very large number of executables contributing a very small number of samples. To deal with this, `opreport` enables you to set a threshold, and only executables with that percentage of the total samples or greater will be shown. Alternatively, `opreport` can reverse the order of the executables that are shown, so those with a high contribution are shown last. This way, the most important data is printed last, and it will not scroll off the screen.

Table 2-20 describes these command-line options of opreport that enable you to format the output of the sampling.

Table 2-20 *opreport* Report Format

Option	Explanation
--reverse-sort / -r	Reverses the order of the sort. Typically, the images that caused the most events display first.
--threshold / -t [percentage]	Causes opreport to only show images that have contributed percentage or more amount of samples. This can be useful when there are many images with a very small number of samples and you are only interested in the most significant.

Again, oprofile is a complicated tool, and these options show only the basics of what oprofile can do. You learn more about the capabilities of oprofile in later chapters.

2.2.8.2 Example Usage

oprofile is a very powerful tool, but it can also be difficult to install. Appendix B, "Installing oprofile," contains instructions on how to get oprofile installed and running on a few of the major Linux distributions.

We begin the use of oprofile by setting it up for profiling. This first command, shown in Listing 2.21, uses the opcontrol command to tell the oprofile suite where an uncompressed image of the kernel is located. oprofile needs to know the location of this file so that it can attribute samples to exact functions within the kernel.

Listing 2.21

```
[root@wintermute root]# opcontrol --vmlinux=/boot/vmlinux-\
2.4.22-1.2174.nptlsmp
```

After we set up the path to the current kernel, we can begin profiling. The command in Listing 2.22 tells oprofile to start sampling using the default event. This event varies depending on the processor, but the default event for this processor is CPU_CLK_ UNHALTED. This event samples all of the CPU cycles where the processor is not halted. The 233869 means that the processor will sample the instruction the processor is executing every 233,869 events.

Listing 2.22

```
[root@wintermute root]# opcontrol -s
Using default event: CPU_CLK_UNHALTED:233869:0:1:1
Using log file /var/lib/oprofile/oprofiled.log
Daemon started.
Profiler running.
```

Now that we have started sampling, we want to begin to analyze the sampling results. In Listing 2.23, we start to use the reporting tools to figure out what is happening in the system. opreport reports what has been profiled so far.

Listing 2.23

```
[root@wintermute root]# opreport
opreport op_fatal_error:
No sample file found: try running opcontrol --dump
or specify a session containing sample files
```

Uh oh! Even though the profiling has been happening for a little while, we are stopped when opreport specifies that it cannot find any samples. This is because the opreport command is looking for the samples on disk, but the oprofile daemon stores the samples in memory and only periodically dumps them to disk. When we ask opreport for a list of the samples, it does not find any on disk and reports that it cannot find any samples. To alleviate this problem, we can force the daemon to flush the samples immediately by issuing a dump option to opcontrol, as shown in Listing 2.24. This command enables us to view the samples that have been collected.

Listing 2.24

```
[root@wintermute root]# opcontrol --dump
```

After we dump the samples to disk, we try again, and ask `oprofile` for the report, as shown in Listing 2.25. This time, we have results. The report contains information about the processor that it was collected on and the types of events that were monitored. The report then lists in descending order the number of events that occurred and which executable they occurred in. We can see that the Linux kernel is taking up 50 percent of the total cycles, emacs is taking 14 percent, and libc is taking 12 percent. It is possible to dig deeper into executable and determine which function is taking up all the time, but that is covered in Chapter 4, "Performance Tools: Process-Specific CPU."

Listing 2.25

```
[root@wintermute root]# opreport
CPU: PIII, speed 467.739 MHz (estimated)
Counted CPU_CLK_UNHALTED events (clocks processor is not halted)
with a unit mask of 0x00 (No unit mask) count 233869
     3190 50.4507 vmlinux-2.4.22-1.2174.nptlsmp
      905 14.3128 emacs
      749 11.8456 libc-2.3.2.so
      261  4.1278 ld-2.3.2.so
      244  3.8589 mpg321
      233  3.6850 insmod
      171  2.7044 libperl.so
      128  2.0244 bash
      113  1.7871 ext3.o
   ....
```

When we started the `oprofile`, we just used the default event that `opcontrol` chose for us. Each processor has a very rich set of events that can be monitored. In Listing 2.26, we ask `opcontrol` to list all the events that are available for this particular CPU. This list is quite long, but in this case, we can see that in addition to `CPU_CLK_UNHALTED`, we can also monitor DATA_MEM_REFS and DCU_LINES_IN. These are memory events caused by the memory subsystem, and we investigate them in later chapters.

Listing 2.26

```
[root@wintermute root]# opcontrol -l
oprofile: available events for CPU type "PIII"

See Intel Architecture Developer's Manual Volume 3, Appendix A and
Intel Architecture Optimization Reference Manual (730795-001)

CPU_CLK_UNHALTED: (counter: 0, 1)
        clocks processor is not halted (min count: 6000)
DATA_MEM_REFS: (counter: 0, 1)
        all memory references, cachable and non (min count: 500)
DCU_LINES_IN: (counter: 0, 1)
        total lines allocated in the DCU (min count: 500)
....
```

The command needed to specify which events we will monitor can be cumbersome, so fortunately, we can also use oprofile's graphical oprof_start command to graphically start and stop sampling. This enables us to select the events that we want graphically without the need to figure out the exact way to specify on the command line the events that we want to monitor.

In the example of op_control shown in Figure 2-3, we tell oprofile that we want to monitor DATA_MEM_REFS and L2_LD events at the same time. The DATA_MEM_REFS event can tell us which applications use the memory subsystem a lot and which use the level 2 cache. In this particular processor, the processor's hardware has only two counters that can be used for sampling, so only two events can be used simultaneously.

Now that we have gathered the samples using the graphical interface to operofile, we can now analyze the data that it has collected. In Listing 2.27, we ask opreport to display the profile of samples that it has collected in a similar way to how we did when we were monitoring cycles. In this case, we can see that the libmad library has 31 percent of the data memory references of the whole system and appears to be the heaviest user of the memory subsystem.

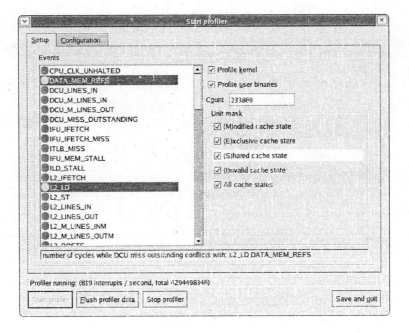

Figure 2-3

Listing 2.27

```
[root@wintermute root]# opreport
CPU: PIII, speed 467.739 MHz (estimated)
Counted DATA_MEM_REFS events (all memory references, cachable and non)
with a unit mask of 0x00 (No unit mask) count 30000
Counted L2_LD events (number of L2 data loads) with a unit mask of 0x0f
(All cache states) count 233869
    87462 31.7907        17  3.8636 libmad.so.0.1.0
    24259  8.8177        10  2.2727 mpg321
    23735  8.6272        40  9.0909 libz.so.1.2.0.7
    17513  6.3656        56 12.7273 libgklayout.so
    17128  6.2257        90 20.4545 vmlinux-2.4.22-1.2174.nptlsmp
    13471  4.8964         4  0.9091 libpng12.so.0.1.2.2
    12868  4.6773        20  4.5455 libc-2.3.2.so
....
```

The output provided by opreport displays all the system libraries and executables that contain any of the events that we were sampling. Note that not all the events have been recorded; because we are sampling, only a subset of events are actually recorded. This is usually not a problem, because if a particular library or executable is a performance problem, it will likely cause high-cost events to happen many times. If the sampling is random, these high-cost events will eventually be caught by the sampling code.

2.3 Chapter Summary

This chapter focused on the system-wide performance metric of CPU usage. These metrics mainly demonstrate how the operating system and machine are behaving, rather than a particular application.

This chapter demonstrated how performance tools, such as sar and vmstat, can be used to extract this system-wide performance information from a running system. These tools are the first line of defense when diagnosing a system problem. They help to determine how the system is behaving and which subsystem or application may be particularly stressed. The next chapter focuses on the system-wide performance tools that enable you to analyze the memory usage of the entire system.

3

Performance Tools: System Memory

This chapter overviews the system-wide Linux memory performance tools. This chapter discusses the memory statistics that these tools can measure and how to use the individual tools to gather those statistics. After reading this chapter, you should

- Understand the basic metrics of system-wide performance, including memory usage
- Understand which tools can retrieve system-wide memory performance metrics

3.1 Memory Performance Statistics

Each system-wide Linux performance tool provides different ways to extract similar statistics. Although no tool displays all the statistics, some of the tools display the same statistics. The beginning of this chapter reviews the details of these statistics, and those descriptions are then referenced as the tools are described.

3.1.1 Memory Subsystem and Performance

In modern processors, saving information to and retrieving information from the memory subsystem usually takes longer than the CPU executing code and manipulating that information. The CPU usually spends a significant amount of time idle, waiting for instructions and data to be retrieved from memory before it can execute them or operate based on them. Processors have various levels of cache that compensate for the slow memory performance. Tools such as `oprofile` can show where various processor cache misses can occur.

3.1.2 Memory Subsystem (Virtual Memory)

Any given Linux system has a certain amount of RAM or physical memory. When addressing this physical memory, Linux breaks it up into chunks or "pages" of memory. When allocating or moving around memory, Linux operates on page-sized pieces rather than individual bytes. When reporting some memory statistics, the Linux kernel reports the number of pages per second, and this value can vary depending on the architecture it is running on. Listing 3.1 creates a small application that displays the number of bytes per page for the current architecture.

Listing 3.1

```
#include <unistd.h>
int main(int argc, char *argv[])
{
    printf("System page size: %d\n",getpagesize());
}
```

On the IA32 architecture, the page size is 4KB. In rare cases, these page-sized chunks of memory can cause too much overhead to track, so the kernel manipulates memory in much bigger chunks, known as HugePages. These are on the order of 2048KB rather than 4KB and greatly reduce the overhead for managing very large amounts of memory. Certain applications, such as Oracle, use these huge pages to load an enormous amount of data in memory while minimizing the overhead that the Linux kernel needs to manage it. If HugePages are not completely filled with data, these can waste a significant amount of memory. A half-filled normal page wastes 2KB of memory, whereas a half-filled HugePage can waste 1,024KB of memory.

The Linux kernel can take a scattered collection of these physical pages and present to applications a well laid-out virtual memory space.

3.1.2.1 Swap (Not Enough Physical Memory)

All systems have a fixed amount of physical memory in the form of RAM chips. The Linux kernel allows applications to run even if they require more memory than available with the physical memory. The Linux kernel uses the hard drive as a temporary memory. This hard drive space is called swap space.

Although swap is an excellent way to allow processes to run, it is terribly slow. It can be up to 1,000 times slower for an application to use swap rather than physical memory. If a system is performing poorly, it usually proves helpful to determine how much swap the system is using.

3.1.2.2 Buffers and Cache (Too Much Physical Memory)

Alternatively, if your system has much more physical memory than required by your applications, Linux will cache recently used files in physical memory so that subsequent accesses to that file do not require an access to the hard drive. This can greatly speed up applications that access the hard drive frequently, which, obviously, can prove especially useful for frequently launched applications. The first time the application is launched, it needs to be read from the disk; if the application remains in the cache, however, it needs to be read from the much quicker physical memory. This disk cache differs from the processor cache mentioned in the previous chapter. Other than oprofile, valgrind, and kcachegrind, most tools that report statistics about "cache" are actually referring to disk cache.

In addition to cache, Linux also uses extra memory as buffers. To further optimize applications, Linux sets aside memory to use for data that needs to be written to disk. These set-asides are called buffers. If an application has to write something to the disk, which would usually take a long time, Linux lets the application continue immediately but saves the file data into a memory buffer. At some point in the future, the buffer is flushed to disk, but the application can continue immediately.

It can be discouraging to see very little free memory in a system because of the cache and buffer usage, but this is not necessarily a bad thing. By default, Linux tries to use as much of your memory as possible. This is good. If Linux detects any free memory, it caches applications and data in the free memory to speed up future accesses. Because it is usually a few orders of magnitude faster to access things from memory rather than disk, this can dramatically improve overall performance. When the system needs the cache memory for more important things, the cache memory is erased and given to the system. Subsequent access to the object that was previously cached has to go out to disk to be filled.

3.1.2.3 Active Versus Inactive Memory

Active memory is currently being used by a process. Inactive memory is memory that is allocated but has not been used for a while. Nothing is essentially different between the two types of memory. When required, the Linux kernel takes a process's least recently used memory pages and moves them from the active to the inactive list. When choosing which memory will be swapped to disk, the kernel chooses from the inactive memory list.

3.1.2.4 High Versus Low Memory

For 32-bit processors (for example, IA32) with 1GB or more of physical of memory, Linux must manage the physical memory as high and low memory. The high memory is not directly accessible by the Linux kernel and must be mapped into the low-memory range before it can be used. This is not a problem with 64-bit processors (such as AMD64/ EM6T, Alpha, or Itanium) because they can directly address additional memory that is available in current systems.

3.1.2.5 Kernel Usage of Memory (Slabs)

In addition to the memory that applications allocate, the Linux kernel consumes a certain amount for bookkeeping purposes. This bookkeeping includes, for example, keeping track of data arriving from network and disk I/O devices, as well as keeping track of which processes are running and which are sleeping. To manage this bookkeeping, the kernel has a series of caches that contains one or more slabs of memory. Each slab consists of a set of one or more objects. The amount of slab memory consumed by the kernel depends on which parts of the Linux kernel are being used, and can change as the type of load on the machine changes.

3.2 Linux Performance Tools: CPU and Memory

Here begins our discussion of performance tools that enable you to extract the memory performance information described previously.

3.2.1 vmstat (Virtual Memory Statistics) II

As you have seen before, vmstat can provide information about many different performance aspects of a system—although its primary purpose, as shown next, is to provide information about virtual memory system performance. In addition to the CPU performance statistics described in the previous chapter, it can also tell you the following:

- How much swap is being used
- How the physical memory is being used
- How much memory is free

As you can see, vmstat provides (via the statistics it displays) a wealth of information about the health and performance of the system in a single line of text.

3.2.1.1 System-Wide Memory-Related Options

In addition to the CPU statistics vmstat can provide, you can invoke vmstat with the following command-line options when investigating memory statistics:

```
vmstat [-a] [-s] [-m]
```

As before, you can run vmstat in two modes: sample mode and average mode. The added command-line options enable you to get the performance statistics about how the Linux kernel is using memory. Table 3-1 describes the options that vmstat accepts.

Table 3-1   *vmstat* Command-Line Options

Option	Explanation
-a	This changes the default output of memory statistics to indicate the active/inactive amount of memory rather than information about buffer and cache usage.
-s (procps 3.2 or greater)	This prints out the vm table. This is a grab bag of differentstatistics about the system since it has booted. It cannot be run in sample mode. It contains both memory and CPU statistics.
-m (procps 3.2 or greater)	This prints out the kernel's slab info. This is the same information that can be retrieved by typing cat /proc/slabinfo. This describes in detail how the kernel's memory is allocated and can be helpful to determine what area of the kernel is consuming the most memory.

Table 3-2 provides a list of the memory statistics that vmstat can provide. As with the CPU statistics, when run in normal mode, the first line that vmstat provides is the average values for all the rate statistics (so and si) and the instantaneous value for all the numeric statistics (swpd, free, buff, cache, active, and inactive).

Table 3-2   Memory-Specific *vmstat* Output Statistics

Column	Explanation
swpd	The total amount of memory currently swapped to disk.
free	The amount of physical memory not being used by the operating system or applications.
buff	The size (in KB) of the system buffers, or memory used to store data waiting to be saved to disk. This memory allows an application to continue execution immediately after it has issued a write call to the Linux kernel (instead of waiting until the data has been committed to disk).

Column	Explanation
cache	The size (in KB) of the system cache or memory used to store data previously read from disk. If an application needs this data again, it allows the kernel to fetch it from memory rather than disk, thus increasing performance.
active	The amount of memory actively being used. The active/inactive statistics are orthogonal to the buffer/cache; buffer and cache memory can be active and inactive.
inactive	The amount of inactive memory (in KB), or memory that has not been used for a while and is eligible to be swapped to disk.
si	The rate of memory (in KB/s) that has been swapped in from disk during the last sample.
so	The rate of memory (in KB/s) that has been swapped out to disk during the last sample.
pages paged in	The amount of memory (in pages) read from the disk(s) into the system buffers. (On most IA32 systems, a page is 4KB.)
pages paged out	The amount of memory (in pages) written to the disk(s) from the system cache. (On most IA32 systems, a page is 4KB.)
pages swapped in	The amount of memory (in pages) read from swap into system memory.
pages swapped in/out	The amount of memory (in pages) written from system memory to the swap.
used swap	The amount of swap currently being used by the Linux kernel.
free swap	The amount of swap currently available for use.
total swap	The total amount of swap that the system has; this is also the sum of used swap plus free swap.

vmstat provides a good overview of the current state of the virtual memory system for a given machine. Although it does not provide a complete and detailed list of every

Linux memory performance statistic available, it does provide a compact output that can indicate how the system memory is being used overall.

3.2.1.2 Example Usage

In Listing 3.2, as you saw in the previous chapter, if vmstat is invoked without any command-line options, it displays average values for performance statistics since system boot (si and so), and it shows the instantaneous values for the rest of them (swpd, free, buff, and cache). In this case, we can see that the system has about 500MB of memory that has been swapped to disk. ~14MB of the system memory is free. ~4MB is used for buffers that contain data that has yet to be flushed to disk. ~627MB is used for the disk cache that contains data that has been read off the disk in the past.

Listing 3.2

```
bash-2.05b$ vmstat
procs ----------memory---------- ---swap-- -----io---- --system-- ----cpu----
 r  b   swpd   free   buff  cache   si   so   bi   bo   in    cs us sy id wa
 0  0 511012  14840   4412 642072   33   31  204  247 1110  1548  8  5 73 14
```

In Listing 3.3, we ask vmstat to display information about the number of active and inactive pages. The amount of inactive pages indicates how much of the memory could be swapped to disk and how much is currently being used. In this case, we can see that 1310MB of memory is active, and only 78MB is considered inactive. This machine has a large amount of memory, and much of it is being actively used.

Listing 3.3

```
bash-2.05b$ vmstat -a
procs ----------memory---------- ---swap-- -----io---- --system-- ----cpu----
 r  b   swpd   free inact active   si   so   bi   bo   in    cs us sy id wa
 2  1 514004   5640 79816 1341208   33   31  204  247 1111  1548  8  5 73 14
```

Next, in Listing 3.4, we look at a different system, one that is actively swapping data in and out of memory. The si column indicates that swap data has been read in at a rate of 480KB, 832KB, 764KB, 344KB, and 512KB during each of those sample periods. The so column indicates that memory data has been written to swap at a rate of 9KB, 0KB, 916KB, 0KB, 1068KB, 444KB, 792KB, during each of the samples. These results could indicate that the system does not have enough memory to handle all the running processes. A simultaneously high swap-in and swap-out rate can occur when a process's memory is being saved to make way for an application that had been previously swapped to disk. This can be disastrous if two running programs both need more memory than the system can provide. For example, if two processes are using a large amount of memory, and both are trying to run simultaneously, each can cause the other's memory to be written to swap. When one of the programs needs a piece of memory, it kicks out one that the other applications needs. When the other application starts to run, it kicks out a piece of memory that the original program was using, and waits until its memory is loaded from the swap. This can cause both applications to grind to a halt while they wait for their memory to be retrieved from swap before they can continue execution. As soon as one makes a little bit of progress, it swaps out memory that the other process was using and causes the other program to slow down. This is called thrashing. When this happens, the system spends most of its time reading memory to and from the swap, and system performance dramatically slows down.

In this particular case, the swapping eventually stopped, so most likely the memory that was swapped to disk was not immediately needed by the original process. This means the swap usage was effective, the contents of the memory that was not being used was written to disk, and the memory was then given to the process that needed it.

Listing 3.4

```
[ezolt@localhost book]$ vmstat  1 100
procs ----------memory---------- ---swap-- -----io---- --system-- ----cpu----
 r  b   swpd   free   buff  cache   si   so    bi    bo    in    cs us sy id wa
 2  1 131560   2320   8640  53036    1    9   107    69  1137   426 10  7 74  9
 0  1 131560   2244   8640  53076  480    0   716     0  1048   207  6  1  0 93
 1  2 132476   3424   8592  53272  832  916  1356   916  1259   692 11  4  0 85
 1  0 132476   2400   8600  53280  764    0  1040    40  1288   762 14  5  0 81
 0  1 133544   2656   8624  53392  344 1068  1096  1068  1217   436  8  3  5 84
```

continues

Listing 3.4   (Continued)

0	1	133988	2300	8620	54288	512	444	1796	444	1090	230	5	1	2	92
0	0	134780	3148	8612	53688	0	792	0	792	1040	166	5	1	92	2
0	0	134780	3148	8612	53688	0	0	0	0	1050	158	4	1	95	0
0	0	134780	3148	8612	53688	0	0	0	0	1148	451	7	2	91	0
0	0	134780	3148	8620	53680	0	0	0	12	1196	477	8	2	78	12

. . . .

As shown in Listing 3.5, as you saw in the previous chapter, vmstat can show a vast array of different system statistics. Now as we look at it, we can see some of the same statistics that were present in some of the other output modes, such as active, inactive, buffer, cache, and used swap. However, it also has a few new statistics, such as total memory, which indicates that this system has a total of 1516MB of memory, and total swap, which indicates that this system has a total of 2048MB of swap. It can be helpful to know the system totals when trying to figure out what percentage of the swap and memory is currently being used. Another interesting statistic is the pages paged in, which indicates the total number of pages that were read from the disk. This statistic includes the pages that are read starting an application and those that the application itself may be using.

Listing 3.5

```
bash-2.05b$ vmstat -s
      1552528  total memory
      1546692  used memory
      1410448  active memory
        11100  inactive memory
         5836  free memory
         2676  buffer memory
       645864  swap cache
      2097096  total swap
       526280  used swap
      1570816  free swap
     20293225 non-nice user cpu ticks
     18284715 nice user cpu ticks
     17687435 system cpu ticks
    357314699 idle cpu ticks
```

```
 67673539 IO-wait cpu ticks
   352225 IRQ cpu ticks
  4872449 softirq cpu ticks
495248623 pages paged in
600129070 pages paged out
 19877382 pages swapped in
 18874460 pages swapped out
2702803833 interrupts
3763550322 CPU context switches
1094067854 boot time
 20158151 forks
```

Finally, in Listing 3.6, we see that vmstat can provide information about how the Linux kernel allocates its memory. As previously described, the Linux kernel has a series of "slabs" to hold its dynamic data structures. vmstat displays each of the slabs (Cache), shows how many of the elements are being used (Num), shows how many are allocated (Total), shows the size of each element (Size), and shows the amount of memory in pages (Pages) that the total slab is using. This can be helpful when tracking down exactly how the kernel is using its memory.

Listing 3.6

```
bash-2.05b$ vmstat -m
Cache                   Num   Total   Size   Pages
udf_inode_cache           0       0    416       9
fib6_nodes                7     113     32     113
ip6_dst_cache             9      17    224      17
ndisc_cache               1      24    160      24
raw6_sock                 0       0    672       6
udp6_sock                 0       0    640       6
tcp6_sock               404     441   1120       7
ip_fib_hash              39     202     16     202
ext3_inode_cache       1714    3632    512       8
...
```

vmstat provides an easy way to extract large amounts of information about the Linux memory subsystem. When combined with the other information provided on the default output screen, it provides a fair picture of the health and resource usage of the system.

3.2.2 top (2.x and 3.x)

As discussed in the previous chapter, top presents both system-wide and process-specific performance statistics. By default, top presents a list, in decreasing order, of the top CPU-consuming processes, but it can also be adjusted to sort by the total memory usage, enabling you to track down which process is using the most memory.

3.2.2.1 Memory Performance-Related Options

top does not have any special command-line options that manipulate its display of memory statistics. It is invoked with the following command line:

top

However, once running, top enables you to select whether system-wide memory information displays, and whether processes are sorted by memory usage. Sorting by memory consumption proves particularly useful to determine which process is consuming the most memory. Table 3-3 describes the different memory-related output toggles.

Table 3-3 *top* Runtime Toggles

Option	Explanation
m	This toggles whether information about the system memory usage will be shown on the screen.
M	Sorts the tasks by the amount of memory they are using. Because processes may have allocated more memory than they are using, this sorts by resident set size. Resident set size is the amount the processes are actually using rather than what they have simply asked for.

Table 3-4 describes the memory performance statistics that top can provide for both the entire system and individual processes. top has two different versions, 2.x and 3.x, which have slightly different names for output statistics. Table 3-4 describes the names for both versions.

Table 3-4   *top* Memory Performance Statistics

Option	Explanation
%MEM	This is the percentage of the system's physical memory that this process is using.
SIZE (v 2.x) VIRT (v 3.x)	This is the total size of the process's virtual memory usage. This includes all the memory that the application has allocated but is not using.
SWAP	This is the amount of swap (in KB) that the process is using.
RSS (v 2.x) RES (v 3.x)	This is the amount of physical memory that the application is actually using.
TRS (v 2.x) CODE (v 3.x)	The total amount of physical memory (in KB) that the process's executable code is using.
DSIZE (v 2.x) DATA (v 3.x)	The total amount of memory (in KB) dedicated to a process's data and stack.
SHARE (v 2.x) SHR (v 3.x)	The total amount of memory (in KB) that can be shared with other processors.
D (v 2.x) nDRT (v 3.x)	The number of pages that are dirty and need to be flushed to disk.
Mem: total, used, free	Of the physical memory, this indicates the total amount, the used amount, and the free amount.
swap: total, used, free	Of the swap, this indicates the total amount, the used amount, and the free amount.
active (v 2.x)	The amount of physical memory currently active.
inactive (v 2.x)	The amount of physical memory that is inactive and hasn't been used in a while.
buffers	The total amount of physical memory (in KB) used to buffer values to be written to disk.

top provides a large amount of memory information about the different running processes. As discussed in later chapters, you can use this information to determine exactly how an application allocates and uses memory.

3.2.2.2 Example Usage

Listing 3.7 is similar to the example run of top shown in the previous chapter. However, in this example, notice that in the buffers, we have a total amount of 1,024MB of physical memory, of which ~84MB is free.

Listing 3.7

```
[ezolt@wintermute doc]$ top
top - 15:47:03 up 24 days,  4:32, 15 users,  load average: 1.17, 1.19, 1.17
Tasks: 151 total,   1 running, 138 sleeping,  11 stopped,   1 zombie
Cpu(s):  1.2% us,  0.7% sy,  0.0% ni, 93.0% id,  4.9% wa,  0.0% hi,  0.1% si
Mem:   1034320k total,   948336k used,    85984k free,    32840k buffers
Swap:  2040244k total,   276796k used,  1763448k free,   460864k cached

  PID USER      PR  NI  VIRT  RES  SHR S %CPU %MEM    TIME+  COMMAND
26364 root      16   0  405m  71m 321m S  4.0  7.1 462:25.50 X
17345 ezolt     16   0  176m  73m  98m S  2.6  7.3  1:17.48 soffice.bin
18316 ezolt     16   0  2756 1096 1784 R  0.7  0.1  0:05.54 top
26429 ezolt     16   0 65588  52m  12m S  0.3  5.2 16:16.77 metacity
26510 ezolt     16   0 19728 5660  16m S  0.3  0.5 27:57.87 clock-applet
26737 ezolt     16   0 70224  35m  20m S  0.3  3.5  8:32.28 gnome-terminal
    1 root      16   0  2396  448 1316 S  0.0  0.0  0:01.72 init
    2 root      RT   0     0    0    0 S  0.0  0.0  0:00.88 migration/0
    3 root      34  19     0    0    0 S  0.0  0.0  0:00.01 ksoftirqd/0
    4 root      RT   0     0    0    0 S  0.0  0.0  0:00.35 migration/1
    5 root      34  19     0    0    0 S  0.0  0.0  0:00.01 ksoftirqd/1
    6 root      RT   0     0    0    0 S  0.0  0.0  0:34.20 migration/2
    7 root      34  19     0    0    0 S  0.0  0.0  0:00.01 ksoftirqd/2
```

Again, top can be customized to display only what you are interested in observing. Listing 3.8 shows a highly configured output screen that shows only memory performance statistics.

Listing 3.8

```
Mem:   1034320k total,    948336k used,     85984k free,      33024k buffers
Swap:  2040244k total,    276796k used,   1763448k free,     460680k cached

VIRT   RES   SHR  %MEM SWAP CODE DATA nFLT nDRT COMMAND
405m   71m  321m   7.1 333m 1696 403m 4328    0 X
70224  35m   20m   3.5  33m  280  68m 3898    0 gnome-terminal
2756  1104  1784   0.1 1652   52 2704    0    0 top
19728 5660   16m   0.5  13m   44  19m   17    0 clock-applet
2396   448  1316   0.0 1948   36 2360   16    0 init
   0     0     0   0.0    0    0    0    0    0 migration/0
   0     0     0   0.0    0    0    0    0    0 ksoftirqd/0
   0     0     0   0.0    0    0    0    0    0 migration/1
   0     0     0   0.0    0    0    0    0    0 ksoftirqd/1
   0     0     0   0.0    0    0    0    0    0 migration/2
   0     0     0   0.0    0    0    0    0    0 ksoftirqd/2
   0     0     0   0.0    0    0    0    0    0 migration/3
```

top provides a real-time update of memory statistics and a display of which processes are using which types of memory. This information becomes useful as we investigate application memory usage.

3.2.3 procinfo II

As we've seen before, procinfo provides a view of the system-wide performance characteristics. In addition to the statistics described in the previous chapter, procinfo provides a few memory statistics, similar to vmstat and top, that indicate how the current memory is being used.

3.2.3.1 Memory Performance-Related Options

`procinfo` does not have any options that change the output of the memory statistics displayed and, as a result, is invoked with the following command:

```
procinfo
```

`procinfo` displays the basic memory system memory statistics, similar to `top` and `vmstat`. These are shown in Table 3-5.

Table 3-5 *procinfo* CPU Statistics

Option	Explanation
Total	This is the total amount of physical memory.
Used	This is the amount of physical memory in use.
Free	This is the amount of unused physical memory.
Shared	This is an obsolete value and should be ignored.
Buffers	This is the amount of physical memory used as buffers for disk writes.
Page in	The number of blocks (usually 1KB) read from disk. (This is broken on 2.6.x kernels.)
Page out	The number of blocks (usually 1KB) written to disk. (This is broken on 2.6.x kernels.)
Swap in	The number of memory pages read in from swap. (This statistic is broken on 2.6.x kernels.)
Swap out	The number of memory pages written to swap. (This statistic is broken on 2.6.x kernels.)

Much like `vmstat` or `top`, `procinfo` is a low-overhead command that is good to leave running in a console or window on the screen. It gives a good indication of a system's health and performance.

3.2.3.2 Example Usage

Listing 3.9 is a typical output for procinfo. As you can see, it reports summary information about how the system is using virtual memory. In this case, the system has a total of 312MB of memory; 301MB is in use by the kernel and applications, 11MB is used by system buffers, and 11MB is not used at all.

Listing 3.9

```
[ezolt@localhost procinfo-18]$ ./procinfo
Linux 2.6.6-1.435.2.3smp (bhcompile@tweety.build.redhat.com) (gcc 3.3.3 20040412 )
#1
1CPU [localhost]


Memory:      Total       Used        Free      Shared     Buffers
Mem:        320468      308776       11692         0       11604
Swap:       655192      220696      434496


Bootup: Sun Oct 24 10:03:43 2004     Load average: 0.44 0.53 0.51 3/110 32243


user  :     0:57:58.92    9.0%  page in :        0
nice  :     0:02:51.09    0.4%  page out:        0
system:     0:20:18.43    3.2%  swap in :        0
idle  :     8:47:31.54   81.9%  swap out:        0
uptime:    10:44:01.94          context : 13368094


irq  0: 38645994 timer          irq  7:        2
irq  1:    90516 i8042          irq  8:        1 rtc
irq  2:        0 cascade [4]    irq  9:        2
irq  3:   742857 prism2_cs      irq 10:        2
irq  4:        6               irq 11:   562551 uhci_hcd, yenta, yen
irq  5:        2               irq 12:  1000803 i8042
irq  6:        8               irq 14:   207681 ide0
```

procinfo provides information about system performance in a single screen of information. Although it provides a few of the important statistics for memory, vmstat or top is much better suited for investigating system-wide memory usage.

3.2.4 gnome-system-monitor (II)

gnome-system-monitor is in many ways a graphical counterpart of top. It enables you to monitor individual process and observe the load on the system based on the graphs that it displays. It also provides rudimentary graphs of CPU and memory usage.

3.2.4.1 Memory Performance-Related Options

gnome-system-monitor can be invoked from the Gnome menu. (Under Red Hat 9 and higher, this is in System Tools > System Monitor.) However, it can also be invoked using the following command:

gnome-system-monitor

gnome-system-monitor has no relevant command-line options that affect the memory performance measurements.

3.2.4.2 Example Usage

When you launch gnome-system-monitor and select the System Monitor tab, you see a window similar to Figure 3-1. This window enables you to glance at the graph and see how much physical memory and swap is currently being used, and how its usage has changed over time. In this case, we see that 969MB of a total of 1,007MB is currently being used. The memory usage has been relatively flat for a while.

The graphical view of data provided by gnome-system-monitor can make it easier and faster; however, most of the details, such as how the memory is being used, are missing.

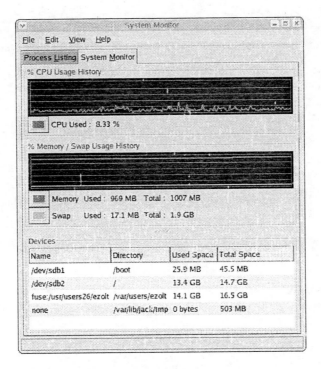

Figure 3-1

3.2.5 free

free provides an overall view of how your system is using your memory, including the amount of free memory. Although the free command may show that a particular system does not have much free memory, this is not necessarily bad. Instead of letting memory sit unused, the Linux kernel puts it to work as a cache for disk reads and as a buffer for disk writes. This can dramatically increase system performance. Because these cache and buffers can always be discarded and the memory can be used if needed by applications, free shows you the amount of free memory plus or minus these buffers.

3.2.5.1 Memory Performance-Related Options

free can be invoked using the following command line:

free [-l] [-t] [-s delay] [-c count]

Table 3-6 describes the parameters that modify the types of statistics that free displays. Much like vmstat, free can periodically display updated memory statistics.

Table 3-6   *free* Command-Line Options

Option	Explanation
-s delay	This option causes free to print out new memory statistics every delay seconds.
-c count	This option causes free to print out new statistics for count times.
-l	This option shows you how much high memory and how much low memory are being used.

free actually displays some of the most complete memory statistics of any of the memory statistic tools. The statistics that it displays are shown in Table 3-7.

Table 3-7   *free* Memory Statistics

Statistic	Explanation
Total	This is the total amount of physical memory and swap.
Used	This is the amount of physical memory and swap in use.
Free	This is the amount of unused physical memory and swap.
Shared	This is an obsolete value and should be ignored.
Buffers	This is the amount of physical memory used as buffers for disk writes.
Cached	This is the amount of physical memory used as cache for disk reads.
-/+ buffers/cache	In the Used column, this shows the amount of memory that would be used if buffers/cache were not counted as used memory. In the Free column, this shows the amount of memory that would be free if buffers/cache were counted as free memory.
Low	The total amount of low memory or memory directly accessible by the kernel.

Statistic	Explanation
High	The total amount of high memory or memory not directly accessible by the kernel.
Totals	This shows the combination of physical memory and swap for the Total, Used, and Free columns.

free provides information about the system-wide memory usage of Linux. It is a fairly complete range of memory statistics.

3.2.5.2 Example Usage

Calling free without any command options gives you an overall view of the memory subsystem.

As mentioned previously, Linux tries to use all the available memory if possible to cache data and applications. In Listing 3.10, free tells us that we are currently using 234,720 bytes of memory; however, if you ignore the buffers and cache, we are only using 122,772 bytes of memory. The opposite is true of the free column. We currently have 150,428 bytes of memory free; if you also count the buffers and cached memory (which you can, because Linux throws away those buffers if the memory is needed), however, we have 262,376 bytes of memory free.

Listing 3.10

```
[ezolt@wintermute procps-3.2.0]$ free
              total       used       free     shared    buffers     cached
Mem:         385148     234720     150428          0       8016     103932
-/+ buffers/cache:      122772     262376
Swap:        394080      81756     312324
```

Although you could just total the columns yourself, the -t flag shown in Listing 3.11 tells you the totals when adding both swap and real memory. In this case, the system had 376MB of physical memory and 384MB of swap. The total amount of memory available on the system is 376MB plus 384MB, or ~760MB. The total amount of free memory was 134MB of physical memory plus 259MB of swap, yielding a total of 393MB of free memory.

Listing 3.11

```
[ezolt@wintermute procps-3.2.0]$ free -t
                total      used      free    shared   buffers    cached
Mem:           385148    247088    138060         0      9052    115024
-/+ buffers/cache:       123012    262136
Swap:          394080     81756    312324
Total:         779228    328844    450384
```

Finally, free tells you the amount of high and low memory that the system is using. This is mainly useful on 32-bit machines (such as IA32) with 1GB or more of physical memory. (32-bit machines are the only machines that will have high memory.) Listing 3.12 shows a system with a very small amount of free memory, 6MB in total. It shows a system with 876MB of low memory and 640MB of high memory. This system also has much more cached memory than buffer memory, suggesting that it may be aggressively writing data to disk rather than leaving it in the buffer cache a long time.

Listing 3.12

```
fas% free -l
                total      used      free    shared   buffers    cached
Mem:          1552528   1546472      6056         0      7544    701408
Low:           897192    892800      4392
High:          655336    653672      1664
-/+ buffers/cache:       837520    715008
Swap:         2097096    566316   1530780
```

free gives a good idea of how the system memory is being used. It may take a little while to get used to output format, but it contains all the important memory statistics.

3.2.6 slabtop

slabtop is similar to top, but instead of displaying information about the CPU and memory usage of the processes in the system, slabtop shows in real-time how the kernel is allocating its various caches and how full they are. Internally, the kernel has a series of caches that are made up of one or more slabs. Each slab consists of a set of one or more objects. These objects can be active (or used) or inactive (unused). slabtop shows you the status of the different slabs. It shows you how full they are and how much memory they are using.

3.2.6.1 Memory Performance-Related Options

slabtop is invoked using the following command line:

```
slabtop [--delay n -sort={a | b | c | l | v | n | o | p | s | u}
```

The command-line options for slabtop are described in Table 3-8.

Table 3-8 *slabtop* Command-Line Options

Option	Explanation
--delay	This specifies how long slabtop waits between updates.
--sort {order}	This specifies the order of the output. order can be one of the following:
a	This sorts by the number of active objects in each slab.
b	This sorts by the total number of objects (active and inactive) in each slab for a particular cache.
c	This sorts by the total amount of memory each cache is using.
l	This sorts by the number of slabs used by each cache.
v	This sorts by the number of active slabs used by each cache.
n	This sorts by the name of the cache.
o	This sorts by the number of objects in the particular cache.
P	This sorts by the number of pages used per slab.
s	This sorts by the size of the objects in the cache.

slabtop provides a glimpse into the data structures of the Linux kernel. Each of these slab types is tied closed to the Linux kernel, and a description of each of these slabs is beyond the scope of this book. If a particular slab is using a large amount of kernel memory, reading the Linux kernel source code and searching the Web are two great ways to figure out what these slabs are used for.

3.2.6.2 Example Usage

As shown in Listing 3.13, by default, `slabtop` fills the entire console and continually updates the statistics every three seconds. In this example, you can see that the size-64 slab has the most objects, only half of which are active.

Listing 3.13

```
[ezolt@wintermute proc]$ slabtop
Active / Total Objects (% used)    : 185642 / 242415 (76.6%)
Active / Total Slabs (% used)      : 12586 / 12597 (99.9%)
Active / Total Caches (% used)     : 88 / 134 (65.7%)
Active / Total Size (% used)       : 42826.23K / 50334.67K (85.1%)
Minimum / Average / Maximum Object : 0.01K / 0.21K / 128.00K


  OBJS ACTIVE  USE OBJ SIZE  SLABS OBJ/SLAB CACHE SIZE NAME
 66124  34395  52%   0.06K   1084      61      4336K size-64
 38700  35699  92%   0.05K    516      75      2064K buffer_head
 30992  30046  96%   0.15K   1192      26      4768K dentry_cache
 21910  21867  99%   0.27K   1565      14      6260K radix_tree_node
 20648  20626  99%   0.50K   2581       8     10324K ext3_inode_cache
 11781   7430  63%   0.03K     99     119       396K size-32
  9675   8356  86%   0.09K    215      45       860K vm_area_struct
  6024   2064  34%   0.62K   1004       6      4016K ntfs_big_inode_cache
  4520   3633  80%   0.02K     20     226        80K anon_vma
  4515   3891  86%   0.25K    301      15      1204K filp
  4464   1648  36%   0.12K    144      31       576K size-128
  3010   3010 100%   0.38K    301      10      1204K proc_inode_cache
  2344    587  25%   0.50K    293       8      1172K size-512
  2250   2204  97%   0.38K    225      10       900K inode_cache
  2100    699  33%   0.25K    140      15       560K size-256
  1692   1687  99%   0.62K    282       6      1128K nfs_inode_cache
  1141   1141 100%   4.00K   1141       1      4564K size-4096
```

Because the information provided by slabtop is updated periodically, it is a great way to see how the Linux kernel's memory usage changes in response to different workloads.

3.2.7 sar (II)

All the advantages of using sar as a CPU performance tool, such as the easy recording of samples, extraction to multiple output formats, and time stamping of each sample, are still present when monitoring memory statistics. sar provides similar information to the other memory statistics tools, such as the current values for the amount of free memory, buffers, cached, and swap amount. However, it also provides the rate at which these value change and provides information about the percentage of physical memory and swap that is currently being consumed.

3.2.7.1 Memory Performance-Related Options

sar can be invoked with the following command line:

sar [-B] [-r] [-R]

By default, sar displays only CPU performance statistics; so to retrieve any of the memory subsystem statistics, you must use the options described in Table 3-9.

Table 3-9 sar Command-Line Options

Option	Explanation
-B	This reports information about the number of blocks that the kernel swapped to and from disk. In addition, for kernel versions after v2.5, it reports information about the number of page faults.
-W	This reports the number of pages of swap that are brought in and out of the system.
-r	This reports information about the memory being used in the system. It includes information about the total free memory, swap, cache, and buffers being used.

sar provides a fairly complete view of the Linux memory subsystem. One advantage that sar provides over other tools is that it shows the rate of change for many of the important values in addition to the absolute values. You can use these values to see exactly how memory usage is changing over time without having to figure out the differences between values at each sample. Table 3-10 shows the memory statistics that sar provides.

Table 3-10   *sar* Memory Statistics

Statistic	Explanation
pgpgin/s	The amount of memory (in KB) that the kernel paged in from disk.
pgpgout/s	The amount of memory (in KB) that the kernel paged out to disk.
fault/s	The total number of faults that that the memory subsystem needed to fill. These may or may not have required a disk access.
majflt/s	The total number of faults that the memory subsystem needed to fill and required a disk access.
pswpin/s	The amount of swap (in pages) that the system brought into memory.
pswpout/s	The amount of memory (in pages) that the system wrote to swap.
kbmemfree	This is the total physical memory (in KB) that is currently free or not being used.
kbmemused	This is the total amount of physical memory (in KB) currently being used.
%memused	This is the percentage of the total physical memory being used.
kbbuffers	This is the amount of physical memory used as buffers for disk writes.
kbcached	This is the amount of physical memory used as cache for disk reads.
kbswpfree	This is the amount of swap (in KB) currently free.
kbswpused	This is the amount of swap (in KB) currently used.
%swpused	This is the percentage of the swap being used.

Statistic	Explanation
kbswpcad	This is memory that is both swapped to disk and present in memory. If the memory is needed, it can be immediately reused because the data is already present in the swap area.
frmpg/s	The rate that the system is freeing memory pages. A negative number means the system is allocating them.
bufpg/s	The rate that the system is using new memory pages as buffers. A negative number means that number of buffers is shrinking, and the system is using less of them.

Although sar misses the high and low memory statistics, it provides nearly every other memory statistic. The fact that it can also record network CPU and disk I/O statistics makes it very powerful.

3.2.7.2 Example Usage

Listing 3.14 shows sar providing information about the current state of the memory subsystem. From the results, we can see that the amount of memory that the system used varies from 98.87 percent to 99.25 percent of the total memory. Over the course of the observation, the amount of free memory drops from 11MB to 7MB. The percentage of swap that is used hovers around ~11 percent. The system has ~266MB of data cache and about 12MB in buffers that can be written to disk.

Listing 3.14

```
[ezolt@scrffy manuscript]$ sar -r 1 5
Linux 2.6.8-1.521smp (scrffy)    10/25/2004
```

09:45:30 AM	kbmemfree	kbmemused	%memused	kbbuffers	kbcached	kbswpfree	kbswpused	%swpused	kbswpcad
09:45:31 AM	11732	1022588	98.87	12636	272284	1816140	224104	10.98	66080
09:45:32 AM	10068	1024252	99.03	12660	273300	1816140	224104	10.98	66080
09:45:33 AM	5348	1028972	99.48	12748	275292	1816140	224104	10.98	66080
09:45:35 AM	4932	1029388	99.52	12732	273748	1816140	224104	10.98	66080
09:45:36 AM	6968	1027352	99.33	12724	271876	1815560	224684	11.01	66660
Average:	7810	1026510	99.25	12700	273300	1816024	224220	10.99	66196

Listing 3.15 shows that the system is consuming the free memory at a rate of ~82 pages per second during the first sample. Later, it frees ~16 pages, and then consumes ~20 pages. The number pages of buffers grew only once during the observation, at a rate of 2.02 pages per second. Finally, the pages of cache shrunk by 2.02, but in the end, they expanded by 64.36 pages/second.

Listing 3.15

```
[ezolt@scrffy manuscript]$ sar -R 1 5
Linux 2.6.8-1.521smp (scrffy)    10/25/2004


09:57:22 AM    frmpg/s    bufpg/s    campg/s
09:57:23 AM     -81.19       0.00       0.00
09:57:24 AM       8.00       0.00       0.00
09:57:25 AM       0.00       2.02      -2.02
09:57:26 AM      15.84       0.00       0.00
09:57:27 AM     -19.80       0.00      64.36
Average:        -15.54       0.40      12.55
```

Listing 3.16 shows that the system wrote ~53 pages of memory to disk during the third sample. The system has a relatively high fault count, which means that memory pages are being allocated and used. Fortunately, none of these are major faults, meaning that the system does not have to go to disk to fulfill the fault.

Listing 3.16

```
[ezolt@scrffy dvi]$ sar -B 1 5
Linux 2.6.8-1.521smp (scrffy)    10/25/2004


09:58:34 AM   pgpgin/s pgpgout/s    fault/s   majflt/s
09:58:35 AM      0.00      0.00    1328.28       0.00
09:58:36 AM      0.00      0.00     782.18       0.00
09:58:37 AM      0.00     53.06     678.57       0.00
09:58:38 AM      0.00      0.00     709.80       0.00
09:58:39 AM      0.00      0.00     717.17       0.00
Average:         0.00     10.42     842.48       0.00
```

As you can see, sar is a powerful tool that enhances the functionality of the other system memory performance tools by adding the ability to archive, time stamp, and simultaneously collect many different types of statistics.

3.2.8 /proc/meminfo

The Linux kernel provides a user-readable text file called /proc/meminfo that displays current system-wide memory performance statistics. It provides a superset of the system-wide memory statistics that can be acquired with vmstat, top, free, and procinfo; but it is a little more difficult to use. If you want periodic updates, you must write a script or some code for such. If you want to store the memory performance information or coordinate it with CPU statistics, you must create a new tool or write a script. However, /proc/meminfo provides the most complete view of system memory usage.

3.2.8.1 Memory Performance-Related Options

The information in /proc/meminfo can be retrieved with the following command line:

```
cat /proc/meminfo
```

This command displays the array of statistics described in Table 3-11.

Table 3-11   /proc/meminfo Memory Statistics (All in KB)

Statistic	Explanation
MemTotal	The total amount of system physical memory.
MemFree	The total amount of free physical memory.
Buffers	The amount of memory used for pending disk writes.
Cached	The amount of memory used to cache disk reads.
SwapCached	The amount of memory that exists in both the swap and the physical memory.
Active	The amount of memory currently active in the system.
Inactive	The amount of memory currently inactive and a candidate for swap.

continues

Table 3-11   /proc/meminfo Memory Statistics (All in KB) (Continued)

Statistic	Explanation
HighTotal	The amount of high memory (in KB).
HighFree	The amount of free high memory (in KB).
LowTotal	The amount of low memory (in KB).
LowFree	The amount of free low memory (in KB).
SwapTotal	The amount of swap memory (in KB).
SwapFree	The amount of free swap memory (in KB).
Dirty	Memory waiting to be written to disk.
Writeback	Memory currently being written to disk.
Mapped	The total amount of memory brought into a process's virtual address space using mmap.
Slab	The total amount of kernel slab memory (in KB).
Committed_AS	The amount of memory required to almost never run out of memory with the current workload. Normally, the kernel hands out more memory than it actually has with the hope that applications overallocate. If all the applications were to use what they allocate, this is the amount of physical memory you would need.
PageTables	The amount of memory reserved for kernel page tables.
VmallocTotal	The amount of kernel memory usable for vmalloc.
VmallocUsed	The amount of kernel memory used for vmalloc.
VmallocChunk	The largest contiguous chunk of vmalloc'able memory.
HugePages_Total	The total size of all HugePages.
HugePages_Free	The total amount of free HugePages.

/proc/meminfo provides a wealth of information about the current state of the Linux memory subsystem.

3.8.2.2 Example Usage

Listing 3.17 shows an example output of /proc/meminfo. It shows some memory statistics that are similar to those we have seen with other tools. However, some statistics show new information. One, Dirty, shows that the system currently has 24KB of data waiting to be written to disk. Another, Commited_AS, shows that we need a little more memory (needed: 1068MB versus total: 1024MB) to avoid a potential out-of-memory situation.

Listing 3.17

```
[ezolt@scrffy /tmp]$ cat /proc/meminfo
MemTotal:        1034320 kB
MemFree:           10788 kB
Buffers:           29692 kB
Cached:           359496 kB
SwapCached:       113912 kB
Active:           704928 kB
Inactive:         222764 kB
HighTotal:             0 kB
HighFree:              0 kB
LowTotal:        1034320 kB
LowFree:           10788 kB
SwapTotal:       2040244 kB
SwapFree:        1756832 kB
Dirty:                24 kB
Writeback:             0 kB
Mapped:           604248 kB
Slab:              51352 kB
Committed_AS:    1093856 kB
PageTables:         9560 kB
VmallocTotal:    3088376 kB
VmallocUsed:       26600 kB
VmallocChunk:    3058872 kB
HugePages_Total:       0
HugePages_Free:        0
Hugepagesize:       2048 kB
```

/proc/meminfo is the most complete place to gather system-wide Linux memory statistics. Because you can treat it as a text file, any custom script or program can easily extract the statistics.

3.3 Chapter Summary

This chapter focused on system-wide memory performance metrics. These metrics mainly demonstrate how the operating system is using memory rather than a particular application.

This chapter demonstrated how performance tools such as sar and vmstat can be used to extract this system-wide memory performance information from a running system. The output of these tools indicates how the system as a whole is using available memory. The next chapter describes the tools available to investigate a single process's CPU usage.

4
Performance Tools: Process-Specific CPU

After using the system-wide performance tools to figure out which process is slowing down the system, you must apply the process-specific performance tools to figure out how the process is behaving. Linux provides a rich set of tools to track the important statistics of a process and application's performance.

After reading this chapter, you should be able to

* Determine whether an application's runtime is spent in the kernel or application.

* Determine what library and system calls an application is making and how long they are taking.

* Profile an application to figure out what source lines and functions are taking the longest time to complete.

4.1 Process Performance Statistics

The tools to analyze the performance of applications are varied and have existed in one form or another since the early days of UNIX. It is critical to understand how an application is interacting with the operating system, CPU, and memory system to understand its performance. Most applications are not self-contained and make many calls to the Linux kernel and different libraries. These calls to the Linux kernel (or system calls) may be as simple as "what's my PID?" or as complex as "read 12 blocks of data from the disk." Different systems calls will have different performance implications. Correspondingly, the library calls may be as simple as memory allocation or as complex as graphics window creation. These library calls may also have different performance characteristics.

4.1.1 Kernel Time Versus User Time

The most basic split of where an application may spend its time is between kernel and user time. Kernel time is the time spent in the Linux kernel, and user time is the amount of time spent in application or library code. Linux has tools such `time` and `ps` that can indicate (appropriately enough) whether an application is spending its time in application or kernel code. It also has commands such as `oprofile` and `strace` that enable you to trace which kernel calls are made on the behalf of the process, as well as how long each of those calls took to complete.

4.1.2 Library Time Versus Application Time

Any application with even a minor amount of complexity relies on system libraries to perform complex actions. These libraries may cause performance problems, so it is important to be able to see how much time an application spends in a particular library. Although it might not always be practical to modify the source code of the libraries directly to fix a problem, it may be possible to change the application code to call different or fewer library functions. The `ltrace` command and `oprofile` suite provide a way to analyze the performance of libraries when they are used by applications. Tools built in to the Linux loader, `ld`, helps you determine whether the use of many libraries slows down an application's start time.

4.1.3 Subdividing Application Time

When the application is known to be the bottleneck, Linux provides tools that enable you to profile an application to figure out where time is spent within an application. Tools such as `gprof` and `oprofile` can generate profiles of an application that pin down exactly which source line is causing large amounts of time to be spent.

4.2 The Tools

Linux has a variety of tools to help you determine which pieces of an application are the primary users of the CPU. This section describes these tools.

4.2.1 time

The time command performs a basic function when testing a command's performance, yet it is often the first place to turn. The time command acts as a stopwatch and times how long a command takes to execute. It measures three types of time. First, it measures the real or elapsed time, which is the amount of time between when the program started and finished execution. Next, it measures the user time, which is the amount of time that the CPU spent executing application code on behalf of the program. Finally, time measures system time, which is the amount of time the CPU spent executing system or kernel code on behalf of the application.

4.2.1.1 CPU Performance-Related Options

The time command (see Table 4-1) is invoked in the following manner:

```
time [-v] application
```

The application is timed, and information about its CPU usage is displayed on standard output after it has completed.

Table 4-1 *time* Command-Line Options

Option	Explanation
-v	This option presents a verbose display of the program's time and statistics. Some statistics are zeroed out, but more statistics are valid with Linux kernel v2.6 than with Linux kernel v2.4.
	Most of the valid statistics are present in both the standard and verbose mode, but the verbose mode provides a better description for each statistic.

Table 4-2 describes the valid output statistic that the `time` command provides. The rest are not measured and always display zero.

Table 4-2   CPU-Specific *time* Output

Column	Explanation
User time (seconds)	This is the number of seconds of CPU spent by the application.
System time (seconds)	This is the number of seconds spent in the Linux kernel on behalf of the application.
Elapsed (wall-clock) time (h:mm:ss or m:ss)	This is the amount of time elapsed (in wall-clock time) between when the application was launched and when it completed.
Percent of CPU this job got	This is the percentage of the CPU that the process consumed as it was running.
Major (requiring I/O) page faults	The number of major page faults or those that required a page of memory to be read from disk.
Minor (reclaiming a frame) page faults	The number of minor page faults or those that could be filled without going to disk.
Swaps	This is the number of times the process was swapped to disk.
Voluntary context switches	The number of times the process yielded the CPU (for example, by going to sleep).
Involuntary context switches:	The number of times the CPU was taken from the process.
Page size (bytes)	The page size of the system.
Exit status	The exit status of the application.

This command is a good way to start an investigation. It displays how long the application is taking to execute and how much of that time is spent in the Linux kernel versus your application.

4.2.1.2 Example Usage

The time command included on Linux is a part of the cross-platform GNU tools. The default command output prints a host of statistics about the commands run, even if Linux does not support them. If the statistics are not available, time just prints a zero. The following command is a simple invocation of the time command. You can see in Listing 4.1 that the elapsed time (~3 seconds) is much greater than the sum of the user (0.9 seconds) and system (0.13 seconds) time, because the application spends most of its time waiting for input and little time using the processor.

Listing 4.1

```
[ezolt@wintermute manuscript]$ /usr/bin/time gcalctool
0.91user 0.13system 0:03.37elapsed 30%CPU (0avgtext+0avgdata 0maxresident)k
0inputs+0outputs (2085major+369minor)pagefaults 0swaps
```

Listing 4.2 is an example of time displaying verbose output. As you can see, this output shows much more than the typical output of time. Unfortunately, most of the statistics are zeros, because they are not supported on Linux. For the most part, the information provided in verbose mode is identical to the output provided in standard mode, but the statistics' labels are much more descriptive. In this case, we can see that this process used 15 percent of the CPU when it was running, and spent 1.15 seconds running user code with .12 seconds running kernel code. It accrued 2,087 major page faults, or memory faults that did not require a trip to disk; it accrued 371 page faults that did require a trip to disk. A high number of major faults would indicate that the operating system was constantly going to disk when the application tried to use memory, which most likely means that the kernel was swapping a significant amount.

Listing 4.2

```
[ezolt@wintermute manuscript]$ /usr/bin/time --verbose gcalctool
        Command being timed: "gcalctool"
        User time (seconds): 1.15
        System time (seconds): 0.12
        Percent of CPU this job got: 15%
```

continues

Listing 4.2   (Continued)

```
Elapsed (wall clock) time (h:mm:ss or m:ss): 0:08.02
Average shared text size (kbytes): 0
Average unshared data size (kbytes): 0
Average stack size (kbytes): 0
Average total size (kbytes): 0
Maximum resident set size (kbytes): 0
Average resident set size (kbytes): 0
Major (requiring I/O) page faults: 2087
Minor (reclaiming a frame) page faults: 371
Voluntary context switches: 0
Involuntary context switches: 0
Swaps: 0
File system inputs: 0
File system outputs: 0
Socket messages sent: 0
Socket messages received: 0
Signals delivered: 0
Page size (bytes): 4096
Exit status: 0
```

Note that the bash shell has a built-in time command, so if you are running bash and execute time without specifying the path to the executable, you get the following output:

```
[ezolt@wintermute manuscript]$ time gcalctool

real    0m3.409s
user    0m0.960s
sys     0m0.090s
```

The bash built-in time command can be useful, but it provides a subset of the process execution information.

4.2.2 strace

strace is a tool that traces the system calls that a program makes while executing. System calls are function calls made into the Linux kernel by or on behalf of an application. strace can show the exact system calls that were made and proves incredibly useful to determine how an application is using the Linux kernel. Tracing down the frequency and length of system calls can be especially valuable when analyzing a large program or one you do not understand completely. By looking at the strace output, you can get a feel for how the application is using the kernel and what type of functions it depends on.

strace can also be useful when you completely understand an application, but if that application makes calls to system libraries (such as libc or GTK.) In this case, even though you know where the application makes every system call, the libraries might be making more system calls on behalf of your application. strace can quickly show you what calls these libraries are making.

Although strace is mainly intended to trace the interaction of processes with the kernel by showing the arguments and results for every system call an application makes, strace can also provide summary information that is a little less daunting. After the run of an application, strace can provide a table showing the frequency of each system call and the total time spent in calls of that type. This table can be a crucial first piece of information in understanding how your program is interacting with the Linux kernel.

4.2.2.1 CPU Performance-Related Options

The following invocation of strace is most useful for performance testing:

```
strace [-c] [-p pid] [-o file] [--help] [ command [ arg ...  ]]
```

If strace is run without any options, it displays all the system calls made by the given command on standard error. This can be helpful when trying to figure out why an application is spending a large amount of time in the kernel. Table 4-3 describes a few strace options that are also helpful when tracing a performance problem.

Table 4-3   *strace* Command-Line Options

Option	Explanation
-c	This causes strace to print out a summary of statistics rather than an individual list of all the system calls that are made.
-p pid	This attaches to the process with the given PID and starts tracing.
-o file	The output of strace will be saved in file.
--help	Lists a complete summary of the strace options

Table 4-4 explains the statistics present in output of the strace summary option. Each line of output describes a set of statistics for a particular system call.

Table 4-4   CPU-Specific *strace* Output

Column	Explanation
% time	Of the total time spent making system calls, this is the percentage of time spent on this one.
seconds	This the total number of seconds spent in this system call.
usecs/call	This is the number of microseconds spent per system call of this type.
calls	This is the total number of calls of this type.
errors	This is the number of times that this system call returned an error.

Although the options just described are most relevant to a performance investigation, strace can also filter the types of system calls that it traces. The options to select the system calls to trace are described in detail with the --help option and in the strace man page. For general performance tuning, it is usually not necessary to use them; if needed, however, they exist.

4.2.2.2 Example Usage

Listing 4.3 is an example of using strace to gather statistics about which system calls an application is making. As you can see, strace provides a nice profile of the system's calls made on behalf of an application, which, in this case, is oowriter. In this example, we look at how oowriter is using the read system call. We can see that read is taking the 20 percent of the time by consuming a total of 0.44 seconds. It is called 2,427 times and, on average, each call takes 184 microseconds. Of those calls, 26 return an error.

Listing 4.3

```
[ezolt@wintermute tmp]$ strace -c oowriter
execve("/usr/bin/oowriter", ["oowriter"], [/* 35 vars */]) = 0
Starting OpenOffice.org ...
```

% time	seconds	usecs/call	calls	errors	syscall
20.57	0.445636	184	2427	26	read
18.25	0.395386	229	1727		write
11.69	0.253217	338	750	514	access
10.81	0.234119	16723	14	6	waitpid
9.53	0.206461	1043	198		select
4.73	0.102520	201	511	55	stat64
4.58	0.099290	154	646		gettimeofday
4.41	0.095495	58	1656	15	lstat64
2.51	0.054279	277	196		munmap
2.32	0.050333	123	408		close
2.07	0.044863	66	681	297	open
1.98	0.042879	997	43		writev
1.18	0.025614	12	2107		lseek
0.95	0.020563	1210	17		unlink
0.67	0.014550	231	63		getdents64
0.58	0.012656	44	286		mmap2
0.53	0.011399	68	167	2	ioctl
0.50	0.010776	203	53		readv
0.44	0.009500	2375	4	3	mkdir

continues

Listing 4.3   (Continued)

0.33	0.007233	603	12	clone
0.29	0.006255	28	224	old_mmap
0.24	0.005240	2620	2	vfork
0.24	0.005173	50	104	rt_sigprocmask
0.11	0.002311	8	295	fstat64

strace does a good job of tracking a process, but it does introduce some overhead when it is running on an application. As a result, the number of calls that strace reports is probably more reliable than the amount of time that it reports for each call. Use the times provided by strace as a starting point for investigation rather than a highly accurate measurement of how much time was spent in each call.

4.2.3 ltrace

ltrace is similar in concept to strace, but it traces the calls that an application makes to libraries rather than to the kernel. Although it is primarily used to provide an exact trace of the arguments and return values of library calls, you can also use ltrace to summarize how much time was spent in each call. This enables you to figure out both what library calls the application is making and how long each is taking.

Be careful when using ltrace because it can generate misleading results. The time spent may be counted twice if one library function calls another. For example, if library function foo() calls function bar(), the time reported for function foo() will be all the time spent running the code in function foo() plus all the time spent in function bar().

With this caveat in mind, it still is a useful tool to figure out how an application is behaving.

4.2.3.1 CPU Performance-Related Options

ltrace provides similar functionality to strace and is invoked in a similar way:

```
ltrace [-c] [-p pid] [-o filename] [-S] [--help] command
```

In the preceding invocation, command is the command that you want ltrace to trace. Without any options to ltrace, it displays all the library calls to standard error. Table 4-5 describes the ltrace options that are most relevant to a performance investigation.

Table 4-5 *ltrace* Command-Line Options

Option	Explanation
-c	This option causes ltrace to print a summary of all the calls after the command has completed.
-S	ltrace traces system calls in addition to library calls, which is identical to the functionality strace provides.
-p pid	This traces the process with the given PID.
-o file	The output of strace is saved in file.
--help	Displays help information about ltrace.

Again, the summary mode provides performance statistics about the library calls made during an application's execution. Table 4-6 describes the meanings of these statistics.

Table 4-6 CPU-Specific *ltrace* Output

Column	Explanation
% time	Of the total time spent making library calls, this is the percentage of time spent on this one.
seconds	This is the total number of seconds spent in this library call.
usecs/call	This is the number of microseconds spent per library call of this type.
calls	This is the total number of calls of this type.
function	This is the name of the library call.

Much like strace, ltrace has a large number of options that can modify the functions that it traces. These options are described by the ltrace --help command and in detail in the ltrace man page.

4.2.3.2 Example Usage

Listing 4.4 is a simple example of ltrace running on the xeyes command. xeyes is an X Window application that pops up a pair of eyes that follow your mouse pointer around the screen.

Listing 4.4

```
[ezolt@localhost manuscript]$ ltrace -c /usr/X11R6/bin/xeyes
% time     seconds  usecs/call     calls      function
------ ----------- ----------- --------- --------------------
 18.65    0.065967       65967         1 XSetWMProtocols
 17.19    0.060803          86       702 hypot
 12.06    0.042654         367       116 XQueryPointer
  9.51    0.033632       33632         1 XtAppInitialize
  8.39    0.029684          84       353 XFillArc
  7.13    0.025204         107       234 cos
  6.24    0.022091          94       234 atan2
  5.56    0.019656          84       234 sin
  4.62    0.016337         139       117 XtAppAddTimeOut
  3.19    0.011297          95       118 XtWidgetToApplicationContext
  3.06    0.010827          91       118 XtWindowOfObject
  1.39    0.004934        4934         1 XtRealizeWidget
  1.39    0.004908        2454         2 XCreateBitmapFromData
  0.65    0.002291        2291         1 XtCreateManagedWidget
  0.12    0.000429         429         1 XShapeQueryExtension
  0.09    0.000332         332         1 XInternAtom
  0.09    0.000327          81         4 XtDisplay
  0.09    0.000320         106         3 XtGetGC
  0.05    0.000168          84         2 XSetForeground
  0.05    0.000166          83         2 XtScreen
```

```
0.04      0.000153       153      1 XtParseTranslationTable
0.04      0.000138       138      1 XtSetValues
0.04      0.000129       129      1 XmuCvtStringToBackingStore
0.03      0.000120       120      1 XtDestroyApplicationContext
0.03      0.000116       116      1 XtAppAddActions
0.03      0.000109       109      1 XCreatePixmap
0.03      0.000108       108      1 XtSetLanguageProc
0.03      0.000104       104      1 XtOverrideTranslations
0.03      0.000102       102      1 XtWindow
0.03      0.000096        96      1 XtAddConverter
0.03      0.000093        93      1 XtCreateWindow
0.03      0.000093        93      1 XFillRectangle
0.03      0.000089        89      1 XCreateGC
0.03      0.000089        89      1 XShapeCombineMask
0.02      0.000087        87      1 XclearWindow
0.02      0.000086        86      1 XFreePixmap
------   -----------    -------  --  --------------------
100.00    0.353739               2261 total
```

In Listing 4.4, the library functions XSetWMProtocols, hypot, and XQueryPointer take 18.65 percent, 17.19 percent, and 12.06 percent of the total time spent in libraries. The call to the second most time-consuming function, hypot, is made 702 times, and the call to most time-consuming function, XSetWMProtocols, is made only once. Unless our application can completely remove the call to XSetWMProtocols, we are likely stuck with whatever time it takes. It is best to turn our attention to hypot. Each call to this function is relatively lightweight; so if we can reduce the number of times that it is called, we may be able to speed up the application. hypot would probably be the first function to be investigated if the xeyes application was a performance problem. Initially, we would determine what hypot does, but it is unclear where it may be documented. Possibly, we could figure out which library hypot belongs to and read the documentation for that library. In this case, we do not have to find the library first, because a man page exists for the hypot function. Running man hypot tells us that the hypot function will calculate the distance (hypotenuse) between two points and is part of the math library, libm. However, functions in libraries may have no man pages, so we would need to be able to determine what library a function is part of without them. Unfortunately, `ltrace` does not make it at obvious which library a function is from. To figure it out, we have to use the Linux tools `ldd` and `objdump`. First, `ldd` is used to display which libraries are used by a dynamically linked application. Then, `objdump` is used to search each of those libraries for the given function. In Listing 4.5, we use `ldd` to see which libraries are used by the xeyes application.

Listing 4.5

```
[ezolt@localhost manuscript]$ ldd /usr/X11R6/bin/xeyes
        linux-gate.so.1 =>  (0x00ed3000)
        libXmu.so.6 => /usr/X11R6/lib/libXmu.so.6 (0x00cd4000)
        libXt.so.6 => /usr/X11R6/lib/libXt.so.6 (0x00a17000)
        libSM.so.6 => /usr/X11R6/lib/libSM.so.6 (0x00368000)
        libICE.so.6 => /usr/X11R6/lib/libICE.so.6 (0x0034f000)
        libXext.so.6 => /usr/X11R6/lib/libXext.so.6 (0x0032c000)
        libX11.so.6 => /usr/X11R6/lib/libX11.so.6 (0x00262000)
        libm.so.6 => /lib/tls/libm.so.6 (0x00237000)
        libc.so.6 => /lib/tls/libc.so.6 (0x0011a000)
        libdl.so.2 => /lib/libdl.so.2 (0x0025c000)
        /lib/ld-linux.so.2 => /lib/ld-linux.so.2 (0x00101000)
```

Now that the `ldd` command has shown the libraries that xeyes uses, we can use the `objdump` command to figure out which library the function is in. In Listing 4.6, we look for the `hypot` symbol in each of the libraries that xeyes is linked to. The `-T` option of `objdump` lists all the symbols (mostly functions) that the library relies on or provides. By using `fgrep` to look at output lines that have `.text` in it, we can see which libraries export the hypot function. In this case, we can see that the `libm` library is the only library that contains the `hypot` function.

Listing 4.6

```
[/tmp]$ objdump -T /usr/X11R6/lib/libXmu.so.6 | fgrep ".text" | grep "hypot"
[/tmp]$ objdump -T /usr/X11R6/lib/libXt.so.6  | fgrep ".text" | grep "hypot"
[/tmp]$ objdump -T /usr/X11R6/lib/libSM.so.6  | fgrep ".text" | grep "hypot"
```

```
[/tmp]$ objdump -T /usr/X11R6/lib/libICE.so.6  | fgrep ".text" | grep "hypot"
[/tmp]$ objdump -T /usr/X11R6/lib/libXext.so.6 | fgrep ".text" | grep "hypot"
[/tmp]$ objdump -T /usr/X11R6/lib/libX11.so.6  | fgrep ".text" | grep "hypot"
[/tmp]$ objdump -T /lib/tls/libm.so.6          | fgrep ".text" | grep "hypot"
00247520  w   DF .text  000000a9  GLIBC_2.0   hypotf
0024e810  w   DF .text  00000097  GLIBC_2.0   hypotl
002407c0  w   DF .text  00000097  GLIBC_2.0   hypot
[/tmp]$ objdump -T /lib/tls/libc.so.6          | fgrep ".text" | grep "hypot"
[/tmp]$ objdump -T /lib/libdl.so.2             | fgrep ".text" | grep "hypot"
[/tmp]$ objdump -T /lib/ld-linux.so.2          | fgrep ".text" | grep "hypot"
```

The next step might be to look through the source of xeyes to figure out where hypot is called and, if possible, reduce the number of calls made to it. An alternative solution is to look at the source of hypot and try to optimize the source code of the library.

By enabling you to investigate which library calls are taking a long time to complete, ltrace enables you to determine the cost of each library call that an application makes.

4.2.4 ps (Process Status)

ps is an excellent command to track a process's behavior as it runs.

It provides detailed static and dynamic statistics about currently running processes. ps provides static information, such as command name and PID, as well as dynamic information, such as current use of memory and CPU.

4.2.4.1 CPU Performance-Related Options

ps has many different options and can retrieve many different statistics about the state of a running application. The following invocations are those options most related to CPU performance and will show information about the given PID:

```
ps [-o etime,time,pcpu,command] [-u user] [-U user] [PID]
```

The command ps is probably one of the oldest and feature-rich commands to extract performance information, which can make its use overwhelming. By only looking at a subset of the total functionality, it is much more manageable. Table 4-7 contains the options that are most relevant to CPU performance.

Table 4-7   *ps* Command-Line Options

Option	Explanation	
-o <statistic>	This option enables you to specify exactly what process statistics you want to track. The different statistics are specified in a comma-separated list with no spaces.	
	etime	Statistic: Elapsed time is the amount of time since the program began execution.
	time	Statistic: CPU time is the amount of system plus user time the process spent running on the CPU.
	pcpu	Statistic: The percentage of CPU that the process is currently consuming.
	command	Statistic: This is the command name.
	-A	Shows statistics about all processes.
	-u user	Shows statistics about all processes with this effective user ID.
	-U user	Shows statistic about all processes with this user ID.

ps provides myriad different performance statistics in addition to CPU statistics, many of which, such as a process's memory usage, are discussed in subsequent chapters.

4.2.4.2 Example Usage

This example shows a test application that is consuming 88 percent of the CPU and has been running for 6 seconds, but has only consumed 5 seconds of CPU time:

```
[ezolt@wintermute tmp]$ ps -o etime,time,pcpu,cmd 10882
   ELAPSED     TIME %CPU CMD
     00:06 00:00:05 88.0 ./burn
```

In Listing 4.7, instead of investigating the CPU performance of a particular process, we look at all the processes that a particular user is running. This may reveal information about the amount of resources a particular user consumes. In this case, we look at all the processes that the netdump user is running. Fortunately, netdump is a tame user and is only running bash, which is not taking up any of the CPU, and top, which is only taking up 0.5 percent of the CPU.

Listing 4.7

```
[/tmp]$ ps -o time,pcpu,command -u netdump
    TIME %CPU COMMAND
00:00:00  0.0 -bash
00:00:00  0.5 top
```

Unlike time, ps enables us to monitor information about a process currently running. For long-running jobs, you can use ps to periodically check the status of the process (instead of using it only to provide statistics about the program's execution after it has completed).

4.2.5 ld.so (Dynamic Loader)

When a dynamically linked application is executed, the Linux loader, ld.so, runs first. ld.so loads all the application's libraries and connects symbols that the application uses with the functions the libraries provide. Because different libraries were originally linked at different and possibly overlapping places in memory, the linker needs to sort through all the symbols and make sure that each lives at a different place in memory. When a symbol is moved from one virtual address to another, this is called a relocation. It takes time for the loader to do this, and it is much better if it does not need to be done at all. The prelink application aims to do that by rearranging the system libraries of the entire systems so that they do not overlap. An application with a high number of relocations may not have been prelinked.

The Linux loader usually runs without any intervention from the user, and by just executing a dynamic program, it is run automatically. Although the execution of the loader is hidden from the user, it still takes time to run and can potentially slow down an application's startup time. When you ask for loader statistics, the loader shows the amount of work it is doing and enables you to figure out whether it is a bottleneck.

4.2.5.1 CPU Performance-Related Options

The `ld` command is invisibly run for every Linux application that uses shared libraries. By setting the appropriate environment variables, we can ask it to dump information about its execution. The following invocation influences `ld` execution:

```
env LD_DEBUG=statistics,help LD_DEBUG_OUTPUT=filename <command>
```

The debugging capabilities of the loader are completely controlled with environmental variables. Table 4-8 describes these variables.

Table 4-8 *ld* Environmental Variables

Option	Explanation
LD_DEBUG=statistics	This turns on the display of statistics for ld.
LD_DEBUG=help	This displays information about the available debugging statistics.

Table 4-9 describes some of the statistics that `ld.so` can provide. Time is given in clock cycles. To convert this to wall time, you must divide by the processor's clock speed. (This information is available from `cat /proc/cpuinfo`.)

Table 4-9 CPU Specific *ld.so* Output

Column	Explanation
total startup time in dynamic loader	The total amount of time (in clock cycles) spent in the load before the application started to execute.
time needed for relocation	The total amount of time (in clock cycles) spent relocating symbols.
number of relocations	The number of new relocation calculations done before the application's execution began.

Column	Explanation
`number of relocations from cache`	The number of relocations that were precalculated and used before the application started to execute.
`number of relative relocations`	The number of relative relocations.
`time needed to load objects`	The time needed to load all the libraries that an application is using.
`final number of relocations`	The total number of relocations made during an application run (including those made by `dlopen`).
`final number of relocations from cache`	The total number of relocations that were precalculated.

The information provided by `ld` can prove helpful in determining how much time is being spent setting up dynamic libraries before an application begins executing.

4.2.5.2 Example Usage

In Listing 4.8, we run an application with the `ld` debugging environmental variables defined. The output statistics are saved into the `lddebug` file. Notice that the loader shows two different sets of statistics. The first shows all the relocations that happen during startup, whereas the last shows all the statistics after the program closes. These can be different values if the application uses functions such as `dlopen`, which allows shared libraries to be mapped into an application after it has started to execute. In this case, we see that 83 percent of the time spent in the loader was doing allocations. If the application had been prelinked, this would have dropped close to zero.

Listing 4.8

```
[ezolt@wintermute ezolt]$ env LD_DEBUG=statistics LD_DEBUG_OUTPUT=lddebug gcalctool
[ezolt@wintermute ezolt]$ cat lddebug.2647
    2647:
    2647:     runtime linker statistics:
    2647:       total startup time in dynamic loader: 40820767 clock cycles
    2647:             time needed for relocation: 33896920 clock cycles (83.0%)
    2647:                 number of relocations: 2821
```

continues

Listing 4.8 (Continued)

```
2647:              number of relocations from cache: 2284
2647:              number of relative relocations: 27717
2647:              time needed to load objects: 6421031 clock cycles (15.7%)
2647:
2647:    runtime linker statistics:
2647:              final number of relocations: 6693
2647:    final number of relocations from cache: 2284
```

If ld is determined to be the cause of sluggish startup time, it may be possible to reduce the amount of startup time by pruning the number of libraries that an application relies on or running prelink on the system.

4.2.6 gprof

A powerful way to profile applications on Linux is to use the gprof profiling command. gprof can show the call graph of application and sample where the application time is spent. gprof works by first instrumenting your application and then running the application to generate a sample file. gprof is very powerful, but requires application source and adds instrumentation overhead. Although it can accurately determine the number of times a function is called and approximate the amount of time spent in a function, the gprof instrumentation will likely change the timing characteristics of the application and slow down its execution.

4.2.6.1 CPU Performance-Related Options

To profile an application with gprof, you must have access to application source. You must then compile that application with a gcc command similar to the following:

```
gcc -gp -g3 -o app app.c
```

First, you must compile the application with profiling turned on, using gcc's -gp option. You must take care not to strip the executable, and it is even more helpful to turn on symbols when compiling using the -g3 option. Symbol information is necessary to use the source annotation feature of gprof. When you run your instrumented application, an output file is generated. You can then use the gprof command to display the results. The gprof command is invoked as follows:

```
gprof [-p –flat-profile -q --graph --brief -A –annotated-source ] app
```

The options described in Table 4-10 specify what information gprof displays.

Table 4-10 *gprof* Command-Line Options

Option	Explanation
--brief	This option abbreviates the output of gprof. By default, gprof prints out all the performance information and a legend to describe what each metric means. This suppresses the legend.
-p or --flat-profile	This option prints out the total amount of time spent and the number of calls to each function in the application.
-q or --graph	This option prints out a call graph of the profiled application. This shows how the functions in the program called each other, how much time was spent in each of the functions, and how much was spent in the functions of the children.
-A or --annotated-source	This shows the profiling information next to the original source code.

Not all the output statistics are available for a particular profile. Which output statistic is available depends on how the application was compiled for profiling.

4.2.6.2 Example Usage

When profiling an application with gprof, the first step is to compile the application with profiling information. The compiler (gcc) inserts profiling information into the application and, when the application is run, it is saved into a file named gmon.out.

The burn test application is fairly simple. It clears a large area of memory and then calls two functions, a() and b(), which each touch this memory. Function a() touches the memory 10 times as often as function b().

First, we compile the application:

```
[ezolt@wintermute test_app]$ gcc -pg -g3 -o burn_gprof burn.c
```

After we run in it, we can analyze the output. This is shown in Listing 4.9.

Listing 4.9

```
[ezolt@wintermute test_app]$ gprof  --brief -p ./burn_gprof
Flat profile:

Each sample counts as 0.01 seconds.
  %   cumulative   self              self     total
 time   seconds   seconds    calls  s/call   s/call  name
 91.01     5.06     5.06        1     5.06     5.06  a
  8.99     5.56     0.50        1     0.50     0.50  b
```

In Listing 4.9, you can see gprof telling us what we already knew about the application. It has two functions, a() and b(). Each function is called once, and a() takes 10 times (91 percent) the amount of time to complete than b() (8.99 percent). 5.06 seconds of time is spent in the function a(), and .5 seconds is spent in function b().

Listing 4.10 shows the call graph for the test application. The <spontaneous> comment listed in the output means that although gprof did not record any samples in main(), it deduced that main() must have been run, because functions a() and b() both had samples, and main was the only function in the code that called them. gprof most likely did not record any samples in main() because it is a very short function.

Listing 4.10

```
[ezolt@wintermute test_app]$ gprof  --brief -q ./burn_gprof
                 Call graph
```

granularity: each sample hit covers 4 byte(s) for 0.18% of 5.56 seconds

```
index % time   self  children   called    name
                                             <spontaneous>
[1]    100.0   0.00   5.56                   main [1]
                5.06   0.00       1/1           a [2]
                0.50   0.00       1/1           b [3]
-----------------------------------------------------
                5.06   0.00       1/1             main [1]
[2]     91.0   5.06   0.00         1        a [2]
-----------------------------------------------------
                0.50   0.00       1/1             main [1]
[3]      9.0   0.50   0.00         1        b [3]
-----------------------------------------------------


Index by function name

   [2] a                    [3] b
```

Finally, gprof can annotate the source code to show how often each function is called. Notice that Listing 4.11 does not show the time spent in the function; instead, it shows the number of times the function was called. As shown in the previous examples for gprof, a() actually took 10 times as long as b(), so be careful when optimizing. Do not assume that functions that are called a large number of times are actually using the CPU for a large amount of time or that functions that are called a few number of times are necessarily taking a small amount of the CPU time.

Listing 4.11

```
[ezolt@wintermute test_app]$ gprof -A burn_gprof
*** File /usr/src/perf/process_specific/test_app/burn.c:
          #include <string.h>

          #define ITER 10000
          #define SIZE 10000000
          #define STRIDE 10000                    continues
```

Listing 4.11   (Continued)

```
            char test[SIZE];

            void a(void)
    1 -> {
               int i=0,j=0;
               for (j=0;j<10*ITER ; j++)
                 for (i=0;i<SIZE;i=i+STRIDE)
                   {
                      test[i]++;
                   }
            }


            void b(void)
    1 -> {
               int i=0,j=0;
               for (j=0;j<ITER; j++)
                 for (i=0;i<SIZE;i=i+STRIDE)
                   {
                      test[i]++;
                   }
            }



            main()
 ##### -> {

               /* Arbitrary value*/
               memset(test, 42, SIZE);
               a();
               b();
            }
```

```
Top 10 Lines:


    Line        Count


      10            1
      20            1


Execution Summary:


      3      Executable lines in this file
      3      Lines executed
 100.00      Percent of the file executed


      2      Total number of line executions
   0.67      Average executions per line
```

gprof provides a good summary of how many times functions or source lines in an application have been run and how long they took.

4.2.7 oprofile (II)

As discussed in Chapter 2, "Performance Tools: System CPU," you can use oprofile to track down the location of different events in the system or an application. oprofile is a lower-overhead tool than gprof. Unlike gprof, it does not require an application to be recompiled to be used. oprofile can also measure events not supported by gprof. Currently, oprofile can only support call graphs like those that gprof can generate with a kernel patch, whereas gprof can run on any Linux kernel.

4.2.7.1 CPU Performance-Related Options

The oprofile discussion in the section, "System-Wide Performance Tools" in Chapter 2 covers how to start profiling with oprofile. This section describes the parts of oprofile used to analyze the results of process-level sampling.

oprofile has a series of tools that display samples that have been collected. The first tool, opreport, displays information about how samples are distributed to the functions within executables and libraries. It is invoked as follows:

```
opreport [-d --details -f --long-filenames -l --symbols -l] application
```

Table 4-11 describes a few commands that can modify the level of information that opreport provides.

Table 4-11   *opreport* Command-Line Options

Option	Explanation
-d or --details	This shows an instruction-level breakdown of all the collected samples.
-f or --long-filenames	This shows the complete path name of the application being analyzed.
-l or --symbols	This shows how an application's samples are distributed to its symbols. This enables you to see what functions have the most samples attributed to them.

The next command that you can use to extract information about performance samples is opannotate. opannotate can attribute samples to specific source lines or assembly instructions. It is invoked as follows:

```
opannotate [-a --assembly] [-s --source] application
```

The options described in Table 4-12 enable you to specify exactly what information opannotate will provide. One word of caution: because of limitations in the processor hardware counters at the source line and instruction level, the sample attributions may not be on the exact line that caused them; however, they will be near the actual event.

Table 4-12   *opannotate* Command-Line Options

Option	Explanation
-s or --source --	This shows the collected samples next to the application's source code.
-a or --assembly	This shows the samples collected next to the assembly code of the application.
-s and -a	If both -s and -a are specified, opannotate intermingles the source and assembly code with the samples.

When using opannotate and opreport, it is always best to specify the full path name to the application. If you do not, you may receive a cryptic error message (if oprofile cannot find the application's samples). By default, when displaying results, opreport only shows the executable name, which can be ambiguous in a system with multiple executables or libraries with identical names. Always specify the -f option so that opreport shows the complete path to the application.

oprofile also provides a command, opgprof, that can export the samples collected by oprofile into a form that gprof can digest. It is invoked in the following way:

```
opgprof application
```

This command takes the samples of application and generates a gprof-compatible profile. You can then view this file with the gprof command.

4.2.7.2 Example Usage

Because we already looked at oprofile in the section, "System-Wide Performance Tools" in Chapter 2, the examples here show you how to use oprofile to track down a performance problem to a particular line of source code. This section assumes that you have already started the profiling using the opcontrol command. The next step is to run the program that is having the performance problem. In this case, we use the burn program, which is the same that we used in the gprof example. We start our test program as follows:

```
[ezolt@wintermute tmp]$ ./burn
```

After the program finishes, we must dump oprofile's buffers to disk, or else the samples will not be available to opreport. We do that using the following command:

```
[ezolt@wintermute tmp]$ sudo opcontrol -d
```

Next, in Listing 4.12 we ask opreport to tell us about the samples relevant to our test application, /tmp/burn. This gives us an overall view of how many cycles our application consumed. In this case, we see that 9,939 samples were taken for our application. As we dig into the oprofile tools, we will see how these samples are distributed within the burn application.

Listing 4.12

```
[ezolt@wintermute tmp]$ opreport -f /tmp/burn
CPU: PIII, speed 467.731 MHz (estimated)
Counted CPU_CLK_UNHALTED events (clocks processor is not halted) with a
unit mask of 0x00 (No unit mask) count 233865
    9939 100.0000 /tmp/burn
```

Next, in Listing 4.13, we want to see which functions in the burn application had all the samples. Because we are using the CPU_CLK_UNHALTED event, this roughly corresponds to the relative amount of time spent in each function. By looking at the output, we can see that 91 percent of the time was spent in function a(), and 9 percent was spent in function b().

Listing 4.13

```
[ezolt@wintermute tmp]$ opreport -l /tmp/burn
CPU: PIII, speed 467.731 MHz (estimated)
Counted CPU_CLK_UNHALTED events (clocks processor is not halted) with a
unit mask of 0x00 (No unit mask) count 233865
```

```
vma       samples  %           symbol name
08048348 9033      90.9118     a
0804839e 903        9.0882     b
```

In Listing 4.14, we ask opreport to show us which virtual addresses have samples attributed to them. In this case, it appears as if the instruction at address 0x0804838a has 75 percent of the samples. However, it is currently unclear what this instruction is doing or why.

Listing 4.14

```
[ezolt@wintermute tmp]$ opreport -d /tmp/burn
CPU: PIII, speed 467.731 MHz (estimated)
Counted CPU_CLK_UNHALTED events (clocks processor is not halted) with a
unit mask of 0x00 (No unit mask) count 233865
vma       samples  %           symbol name
08048348 9033      90.9118     a
 08048363 4          0.0443
 08048375 431        4.7714
 0804837c 271        3.0001
 0804837e 1          0.0111
 08048380 422        4.6718
 0804838a 6786      75.1245
 08048393 1114      12.3326
 08048395 4          0.0443
0804839e 903         9.0882     b
 080483cb 38         4.2082
 080483d2 19         2.1041
 080483d6 50         5.5371
 080483e0 697       77.1872
 080483e9 99        10.9635
```

Generally, it is more useful to know the source line that is using all the CPU time rather than the virtual address of the instruction that is using it. It is not always easy to figure out the correspondence between a source line and a particular instruction; so, in Listing 4.15, we ask opannotate to do the hard work and show us the samples relative to the original source code (rather than the instruction's virtual address).

Listing 4.15

```
[ezolt@wintermute tmp]$ opannotate --source /tmp/burn
/*
 * Command line: opannotate --source /tmp/burn
 *
 * Interpretation of command line:
 * Output annotated source file with samples
 * Output all files
 *
 * CPU: PIII, speed 467.731 MHz (estimated)
 * Counted CPU_CLK_UNHALTED events (clocks processor is not halted) with
a unit mask of 0x00 (No unit mask) count 233865
 */
/*
 * Total samples for file : "/tmp/burn.c"
 *
 *    9936 100.0000
 */



                  :#include <string.h>
                  :
                  :#define ITER 10000
                  :#define SIZE 10000000
                  :#define STRIDE 10000
                  :
                  :char test[SIZE];
                  :
                  :void a(void)
                  :{ /* a total:    9033 90.9118 */
```

```
                 :   int i=0,j=0;
    8   0.0805  :   for (j=0;j<10*ITER ; j++)
 8603  86.5841  :     for (i=0;i<SIZE;i=i+STRIDE)
                 :       {
  422   4.2472  :          test[i]++;
                 :       }
                 :}
                 :
                 :void b(void)
                 :{ /* b total:     903   9.0882 */
                 :   int i=0,j=0;
                 :   for (j=0;j<ITER; j++)
  853   8.5849  :     for (i=0;i<SIZE;i=i+STRIDE)
                 :       {
   50   0.5032  :          test[i]++;
                 :       }
                 :}
                 :
                 :
                 :main()
                 :{
                 :
                 :   /* Arbitrary value*/
                 :   memset(test, 42, SIZE);
                 :   a();
                 :   b();
                 :}
```

As you can see in Listing 4.15, opannotate attributes most of the samples (86.59 percent) to the for loop in function b(). Unfortunately, this is a portion of the for loop that should not be expensive. Adding a fixed amount to an integer is very fast on modern processors, so the samples that oprofile reported were likely attributed to the wrong source line. The line below, test[i]++;, should be very expensive because it accesses the memory subsystem. This line is where the samples should have been attributed.

oprofile can mis-attribute samples for a few reasons beyond its control. First, the processor does not always interrupt on the exact line that caused the event to occur. This may cause samples to be attributed to instructions near the cause of the event, rather than to the exact instruction that caused the event. Second, when source code is compiled, compilers often rearrange instructions to make the executable more efficient. After a compiler has finished optimizing, code may not execute in the order that it was written. Separate source lines may have been rearranged and combined. As a result, a particular instruction may be the result of more than one source line, or may even be a compiler-generated intermediate piece of code that does not exist in the original source. As a result, when the compiler optimizes the code and generates machine instructions, there may no longer be a one-to-one mapping between the original lines of source code and the generated machine instructions. This can make it difficult or impossible for oprofile (and debuggers) to figure out exactly which line of source code corresponds to each machine instruction. However, oprofile tries to be as close as possible, so you can usually look a few lines above and below the line with the high sample count and figure out which code is truly expensive. If necessary, you can use opannotate to show the exact assembly instructions and virtual addresses that are receiving all the samples. It may be possible to figure out what the assembly instructions are doing and then map it back to your original source code by hand. oprofile's sample attribution is not perfect, but it is usually close enough. Even with these limitations, the profiles provided by oprofile show the approximate source line to investigate, which is usually enough to figure out where the application is slowing down.

4.2.8 Languages: Static (C and C++) Versus Dynamic (Java and Mono)

The majority of the Linux performance tools support analysis of static languages such as C and C++, and all the tools described in this chapter work with applications written in these languages. The tools ltrace, strace, and time work with applications written in dynamic languages such as Java, Mono, Python, or Perl. However, the profiling tools gprof and oprofile cannot be used with these types of applications. Fortunately, most dynamic languages provide non-Linux–specific profiling infrastructures that you can use to generate similar types of profiles.

For Java applications, if the java command is run with the -Xrunhprof command-line option, -Xrunhprof profiles the application. More details are available at http://antprof.sourceforge.net/hprof.html. For Mono applications, if the mono executable is passed the --profile flag, it profiles the application. More details are available at http://www.go-mono.com/performance.html. Perl and Python have similar profile functionality, with Perl's Devel::DProf described at http://www.perl.com/pub/a/2004/06/25/profiling.html, and Python's profiler described at http://docs.python.org/lib/profile.html, respectively.

4.3 Chapter Summary

This chapter covered how to track the CPU performance bottlenecks of individual processes. You learned to determine how an application was spending its time by attributing the time spent to the Linux kernel, system libraries, or even to the application itself. You also learned how to figure out which calls were made to the kernel and system libraries and how long each took to complete. Finally, you learned how to profile an application and determine the particular line of source code that was spending a large amount of time. After mastering these tools, you can start with an application that hogs the CPU and use these tools to find the exact functions that are spending all the time.

Subsequent chapters investigate how to find bottlenecks that are not CPU bound. In particular, you learn about the tools used to find I/O bottlenecks, such as a saturated disk or an overloaded network.

5

Performance Tools: Process-Specific Memory

This chapter covers tools that enable you to diagnose an application's interaction with the memory subsystem as managed by the Linux kernel and the CPU. Because different layers of the memory subsystem have orders of magnitude differences in performance, fixing an application to efficiently use the memory subsystem can have a dramatic influence on an application's performance.

After reading this chapter, you should be able to

* Determine how much memory an application is using (ps, /proc).
* Determine which functions of an application are allocating memory (memprof).
* Profile the memory usage of an application using both software simulation (kcachegrind, cachegrind) and hardware performance counters (oprofile).
* Determine which processes are creating and using shared memory (ipcs).

5.1 Linux Memory Subsystem

When diagnosing memory performance problems, it may become necessary to observe how an application performs at various levels within the memory subsystem. At the top level, the operating system decides how the swap and physical memory are being used. It decides what pieces of an application's address space will be in physical memory, which is called the resident set. Other memory used by the application but not part of the resident set will be swapped to disk. The application decides how much memory it will request from the operating system, and this is called the virtual set. The application can allocate this explicitly by calling `malloc` or implicitly by using a large amount of stack or using a large number of libraries. The application can also allocate shared memory that can be used by itself and other applications. The `ps` performance tool is useful for tracking the virtual and resident set size. The `memprof` performance tool is useful for tracking which code in an application is allocating memory. The `ipcs` tool is useful for tracking shared memory usage.

When an application is using physical memory, it begins to interact with the CPU's cache subsystem. Modern CPUs have multiple levels of cache. The fastest cache is closest to the CPU (also called L1 or Level 1 cache) and is the smallest in size. Suppose, for instance, that the CPU has only two levels of cache: L1 and L2. When the CPU requests a piece of memory, the processor checks to see whether it is already in the L1 cache. If it is, the CPU uses it. If it was not in the L1 cache, the processor generates a L1 cache miss. It then checks in the L2 cache; if the data is in the L2 cache, it is used. If the data is not in the L2 cache, an L2 cache miss occurs, and the processor must go to physical memory to retrieve the information. Ultimately, it would be best if the processor never goes to physical memory (because it finds the data in the L1 or even L2 cache). Smart cache use—rearranging an application's data structures and reducing code size, for example—may make it possible to reduce the number of caches misses and increase performance. `cachegrind` and `oprofile` are great tools to find information about how an application is using the cache and about which functions and data structures are causing cache misses.

5.2 Memory Performance Tools

This section examines the various memory performance tools that enable you to investigate how a given application is using the memory subsystem, including the amount and different types of memory that a process is using, where it is being allocated, and how effectively the process is using the processor's cache.

5.2.1 ps

ps is an excellent command to track a process's dynamic memory usage. In addition to the CPU statistics already mentioned, ps gives detailed information about the amount of memory that the application is using and how that memory usage affects the system.

5.2.1.1 Memory Performance-Related Options

ps has many different options and can retrieve many different statistics about the state of a running application. As you saw in the previous chapter, ps can retrieve information about the CPU that a process is spending, but it also can retrieve information about the amount and type of memory that a process is using. It can be invoked with the following command line:

```
ps [-o vsz,rss,tsiz,dsiz,majflt,minflt,pmem,command] <PID>
```

Table 5-1 describes the different types of memory statistics that ps can display for a given PID.

Table 5-1 *ps* Command-Line Options

Option	Explanation
-o <statistic>	Enables you to specify exactly what process statistics you want to track. The different statistics are specified in a comma-separated list with no spaces.
vsz	Statistic: The virtual set size is the amount of virtual memory that the application is using. Because Linux only allocated physical memory when an application tries to use it, this value may be much greater than the amount of physical memory the application is using.
rss	Statistic: The resident set size is the amount of physical memory the application is currently using.

continues

Table 5-1   *ps* Command-Line Options (Continued)

Option	Explanation
tsiz	Statistic: Text size is the virtual size of the program code. Once again, this isn't the physical size but rather the virtual size; however, it is a good indication of the size of the program.
dsiz	Statistic: Data size is the virtual size of the program's data usage. This is a good indication of the size of the data structures and stack of the application.
majflt	Statistic: Major faults are the number of page faults that caused Linux to read a page from disk on behalf of the process. This may happen if the process accessed a piece of data or instruction that remained on the disk and Linux loaded it seamlessly for the application.
minflt	Statistic: Minor faults are the number of faults that Linux could fulfill without resorting to a disk read. This might happen if the application touches a piece of memory that has been allocated by the Linux kernel. In this case, it is not necessary to go to disk, because the kernel can just pick a free piece of memory and assign it to the application.
pmep	Statistic: The percentage of the system memory that the process is consuming.
command	Statistic: This is the command name.

As mentioned in the preceding chapter, ps is flexible in regards to how you select the group of PIDs for which statistics display. ps —help provides information on how to specify different groups of PIDs.

5.2.1.2 Example Usage

Listing 5.1 shows the burn test application running on the system. We ask ps to tell us information about the memory statistics of the process.

Listing 5.1

```
[ezolt@wintermute tmp]$ ps -o vsz,rss,tsiz,dsiz,majflt,minflt,cmd 10882
  VSZ  RSS TSIZ DSIZ MAJFLT MINFLT CMD
11124 10004    1 11122     66   2465 ./burn
```

As Listing 5.1 shows, the burn application has a very small text size (1KB), but a very large data size (11,122KB). Of the total virtual size (11,124KB), the process has a slightly smaller resident set size (10,004KB), which represents the total amount of physical memory that the process is actually using. In addition, most of the faults generated by burn were minor faults, so most of the memory faults were due to memory allocation rather than loading in a large amount of text or data from the program image on the disk.

5.2.2 /proc/<PID>

The Linux kernel provides a virtual file system that enables you to extract information about the processes running on the system. The information provided by the /proc file system is usually only used by performance tools such as ps to extract performance data from the kernel. Although it is not normally necessary to dig through the files in /proc, it does provide some information that you cannot retrieve with other performance tools. In addition to many other statistics, /proc provides information about a process's use of memory and mapping of libraries.

5.2.2.1 Memory Performance-Related Options

The interface to /proc is straightforward. /proc provides many virtual files that you can cat to extract their information. Each running PID in the system has a subdirectory in /proc. Within this subdirectory is a series of files containing information about that PID. One of these files, status, provides information about the status of a given process PID. You can retrieve this information by using the following command:

```
cat /proc/<PID>/status
```

Table 5-2 describes the memory statistics displayed in the status file.

Table 5-2   /proc/<PID>/status Field Description

Option	Explanation
VmSize	This is the process's virtual set size, which is the amount of virtual memory that the application is using. Because Linux only allocates physical memory when an application tries to use it, this value may be much greater than the amount of physical memory the application is actually using. This is the same as the vsz parameter provided by ps.
VmLck	This is the amount of memory that has been locked by this process. Locked memory cannot be swapped to disk.
VmRSS	This is the resident set size or amount of physical memory the application is currently using. This is the same as the rss statistic provided by ps.
VmData	This is the data size or the virtual size of the program's data usage. Unlike ps dsiz statistic, this does not include stack information.
VmStk	This is the size of the process's stack.
VmExe	This is the virtual size of the executable memory that the program has. It does not include libraries that the process is using.
VmLib	This is the size of the libraries that the process is using.

Another one of the files present in the <PID> directory is the maps file. This provides information about how the process's virtual address space is used. You can retrieve it by using the following command:

```
cat /proc/<PID>/maps
```

Table 5-3 describes the fields shown in the maps file.

Table 5-3   /proc/<PID>/maps Field Description

Option	Explanation
Address	This is the address range within the process where the library is mapped.

Option	Explanation
Permissions	These are the permissions of the memory region, where r = read, w = write, x = execute, s = shared, and p = private (copy on write).
Offset	This is the offset into the library/application where the memory region mapping begins.
Device	This is the device (minor and major number) where this particular file exists.
Inode	This is the inode number of the mapped file.
Pathname	This is the path name of the file that is mapped into the process.

The information that /proc provides can help you understand how an application is allocating memory and which libraries it is using.

5.2.2.2 Example Usage

Listing 5.2 shows the burn test application running on the system. First, we use ps to find the PID (4540) of burn. Then we extract the process's memory statistics using the /proc status file.

Listing 5.2

```
[ezolt@wintermute tmp]$ ps aux | grep burn
ezolt    4540  0.4  2.6 11124 10004 pts/0   T    08:26   0:00 ./burn
ezolt    4563  0.0  0.1  1624   464 pts/0   S    08:29   0:00 grep burn


[ezolt@wintermute tmp]$ cat /proc/4540/status
Name:    burn
State:   T (stopped)
Tgid:    4540
Pid:     4540
PPid:    1514
TracerPid:     0
Uid:     501     501     501     501
```

continues

Listing 5.2   (Continued)

```
Gid:    501      501     501     501
FDSize: 256
Groups: 501 9 502
VmSize:    11124 kB
VmLck:         0 kB
VmRSS:     10004 kB
VmData:     9776 kB
VmStk:         8 kB
VmExe:         4 kB
VmLib:      1312 kB
SigPnd: 0000000000000000
ShdPnd: 0000000000000000
SigBlk: 0000000000000000
SigIgn: 0000000000000000
SigCgt: 0000000000000000
CapInh: 0000000000000000
CapPrm: 0000000000000000
CapEff: 0000000000000000
```

As Listing 5.2 shows, once again we see that the burn application has a very small text size (4KB) and stack size (8KB), but a very large data size (9,776KB) and a reasonably sized library size (1,312KB). The small text size means that the process does not have much executable code, whereas the moderate library size means that it is using a library to support its execution. The small stack size means that the process is not calling deeply nested functions or is not calling functions that use large or many temporary variables. The VmLck size of 0KB means that the process has not locked any pages into memory, making them unswappable. The VmRSS size of 10,004KB means that the application is currently using 10,004KB of physical memory, although it has either allocated or mapped the VmSize or 11,124KB. If the application begins to use the memory that it has allocated but is not currently using, the VmRSS size increases but leaves the VmSize unchanged.

As noted previously, the application's VmLib size is nonzero, so it is using a library. In Listing 5.3, we look at the process's maps to see the exact libraries it is using.

Listing 5.3

```
[ezolt@wintermute test_app]$ cat /proc/4540/maps
08048000-08049000 r-xp 00000000 21:03 393730      /tmp/burn
08049000-0804a000 rw-p 00000000 21:03 393730      /tmp/burn
0804a000-089d3000 rwxp 00000000 00:00 0
40000000-40015000 r-xp 00000000 21:03 1147263     /lib/ld-2.3.2.so
40015000-40016000 rw-p 00015000 21:03 1147263     /lib/ld-2.3.2.so
4002e000-4002f000 rw-p 00000000 00:00 0
4002f000-40162000 r-xp 00000000 21:03 2031811     /lib/tls/libc-2.3.2.so
40162000-40166000 rw-p 00132000 21:03 2031811     /lib/tls/libc-2.3.2.so
40166000-40168000 rw-p 00000000 00:00 0
bfffe000-c0000000 rwxp fffff000 00:00 0
```

As you see in Listing 5.3, the burn application is using two libraries: ld and libc. The text section (denoted by the permission r-xp) of libc has a range of 0x4002f000 through 0x40162000 or a size of 0x133000 or 1,257,472 bytes.

The data section (denoted by permission rw-p) of libc has a range of 40162000 through 40166000 or a size of 0x4000 or 16,384 bytes. The text size of libc is bigger than ld's text size of 0x15000 or 86,016 bytes. The data size of libc is also bigger than ld's text size of 0x1000 or 4,096 bytes. libc is the big library that burn is linking in.

/proc proves to be a useful way to extract performance statistics directly from the kernel. Because the statistics are text based, you can use the standard Linux tools to access them.

5.2.3 memprof

memprof is a graphical memory-usage profiling tool. It shows how a program is allocating memory as it runs. memprof shows the amount of memory your application is consuming and which functions are responsible for the memory consumption. In addition, memprof can show which code paths are responsible for memory usage. For example, if a function foo() allocates no memory, but calls a function bar(), which allocates a large amount of memory, memprof shows you how much foo() itself used and all the functions that foo() called. memprof updates this information dynamically as the application is running.

5.2.3.1 Memory Performance-Related Options

memprof is a graphical application, but has a few command-line options that modify its execution. It is invoked with the following command:

```
memprof [--follow-fork]  [--follow-exec] application
```

memprof profiles the given "application" and creates a graphical display of its memory usage. Although memprof can be run on any application, it can provide more information if the application and the libraries that it relies on are compiled with debugging symbols.

Table 5-4 describes the options that manipulate the behavior of memprof if it is monitoring an application that calls fork or exec. This normally happens when an application launches a new process or executes a new command.

Table 5-4 *memprof* Command-Line Options

Option	Explanation
--follow-fork	This option will cause memprof to launch a new window for the newly forked process.
--follow-exec	This option will cause memprof to continue profiling an application after it has called exec.

Once invoked, memprof creates a window with a series of menus and options that enable you to select an application that you are going to profile.

5.2.3.2 Example Usage

Suppose that I have the example code in Listing 5.4 and I want to profile it. In this application, which I call memory_eater, the function foo() does not allocate any memory, but it calls the function bar(), which does.

Listing 5.4

```
#include <stdlib.h>
void bar(void)
{
  malloc(10000);
}


void foo(void)
{
  int i;
  for (i=0; i<100;i++)
    bar();
}


int main()
{
  foo();
  while(1);
}
```

After compiling this application with the -g3 flag (so that the application has symbols included), we use memprof to profile this application:

```
[ezolt@localhost example]$ memprof ./memory_eater memintercept (3965):
_MEMPROF_SOCKET = /tmp/memprof.Bm1AKu memintercept (3965): New process,
operation = NEW, old_pid = 0
```

memprof creates the application window shown in Figure 5-1. As you can see, it shows memory usage information about the memory_eater application, as well as a series of buttons and menus that enable you to manipulate the profile.

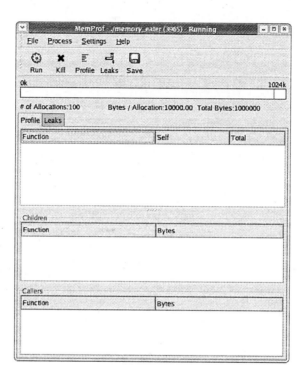

Figure 5-1

If you click the Profile button, memprof shows the memory profile of the application. The first information box in Figure 5-2 shows how much memory each function is consuming (denoted by "self"), as well as the sum of the memory that the function and its children are consuming (denoted by "total"). As expected, the foo() function does not allocate any memory, so its self value is 0, whereas its total value is 100,000, because it is calling a function that does allocate memory.

The children and callers information boxes change as you click different functions in the top box. This way, you can see which functions of an application are using memory.

memprof provides a way to graphically traverse through a large amount of data about memory allocation. It provides an easy way to determine the memory allocation of a given function and each functions that it calls.

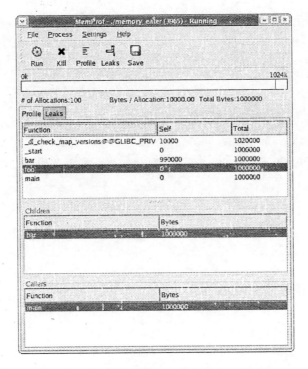

Figure 5-2

5.2.4 valgrind (cachegrind)

valgrind is a powerful tool that enables you to debug tricky memory-management errors. Although valgrind is mainly a developer's tool, it also has a "skin" that can show processor cache usage. valgrind simulates the current processor and runs the application in this virtual processor while tracking memory usage. It can also simulate the processor cache and pinpoint where a program is hitting and missing in the instruction and data caches.

Although very useful, its cache statistics are inexact (because valgrind is only a simulation of the processor rather than an actual piece of hardware). valgrind will not account for cache misses normally caused by system calls to the Linux kernel or cache misses that happen because of context switching. In addition, valgrind runs applications at a much slower speed than a natively executing program. However, valgrind provides a great first approximation of the cache usage of an application. valgrind can be run on any executable; if the program has been compiled with symbols (passed as -g3 to gcc when compiling), however, it will be able to pinpoint the exact line of code responsible for the cache usage.

5.2.4.1 Memory Performance-Related Options

When using valgrind to analyze cache usage for a particular application, there are two phases: collection and annotation. The collection phase starts with the following command line:

```
valgrind --skin=cachegrind application
```

valgrind is a flexible tool that has a few different "skins" that allow it to perform different types of analysis. During the collection phase, valgrind uses the cachegrind skin to collect information about cache usage. The application in the preceding command line represents the application to profile. The collection phase prints summary information to the screen, but it also saves more detailed statistics in a file named cachegrind.out.pid, where pid is the PID of the profiled application as it was running. When the collection phase is complete, the command cg_annoate is used to map the cache usage back to the application source code. cg_annote is invoked in the following way:

```
cg_annotate --pid [--auto=yes|no]
```

cg_annotate takes the information generated by valgrind and uses it to annotate the application that was profiled. The --pid option is required, where pid is the PID of the profile that you are interested in. By default, cg_annotate just shows cache usage at the function level. If you set --auto=yes, cache usage displays at the source-line level.

5.2.4.2 Example Usage

This example shows valgrind (v2.0) running on a simple application. The application clears a large area of memory and then calls two functions, a() and b(), and each touches this memory. Function a() touches the memory ten times as often as function b().

First, as shown in Listing 5.5, we run valgrind on the application using the cachegrind skin.

Listing 5.5

```
[ezolt@wintermute test_app]$  valgrind --skin=cachegrind ./burn
==25571== Cachegrind, an I1/D1/L2 cache profiler for x86-linux.
==25571== Copyright (C) 2002-2003, and GNU GPL'd, by Nicholas Nethercote.
==25571== Using valgrind-2.0.0, a program supervision framework for x86-linux.
==25571== Copyright (C) 2000-2003, and GNU GPL'd, by Julian Seward.
==25571== Estimated CPU clock rate is 468 MHz
==25571== For more details, rerun with: -v
==25571==
==25571==
==25571== I   refs:      11,317,111
==25571== I1  misses:           215
==25571== L2i misses:           214
==25571== I1  miss rate:       0.0%
==25571== L2i miss rate:       0.0%
==25571==
==25571== D   refs:       6,908,012  (4,405,958 rd + 2,502,054 wr)
==25571== D1  misses:     1,412,821  (1,100,287 rd +   312,534 wr)
==25571== L2d misses:       313,810  (    1,276 rd +   312,534 wr)
==25571== D1  miss rate:      20.4% (     24.9% +      12.4%  )
==25571== L2d miss rate:       4.5% (      0.0% +      12.4%  )
==25571==
==25571== L2 refs:        1,413,036  (1,100,502 rd +   312,534 wr)
==25571== L2 misses:        314,024  (    1,490 rd +   312,534 wr)
==25571== L2 miss rate:        1.7% (      0.0% +      12.4%  )
```

In the run of Listing 5.5, the application executed 11,317,111 instructions; this is shown by the I refs statistics. The process had an astonishingly low number of misses in both the L1 (215) and L2 (216) instruction cache, as denoted by an I1 and L2i miss rate of 0.0 percent. The process had a total number of 6,908,012 data references, 4,405,958 were reads and 2,502,054 were writes. 24.9 percent of the reads and 12.4

percent of the writes could not be satisfied by the L1 cache. Luckily, we can almost always satisfy the reads in the L2 data, and they are shown to have a miss rate of 0 percent. The writes are still a problem with a miss rate of 12.4 percent. In this application, memory access of the data is the problem to investigate.

The ideal application would have a very low number of instruction cache and data cache misses. To eliminate instruction cache misses, it may be possible to recompile the application with different compiler options or trim code, so that the hot code does not have to share icache space with the code that is not used often. To eliminate data cache misses, use arrays for data structures rather than linked lists, if possible, and reduce the size of elements in data structures, and access memory in a cache-friendly way. In any event, valgrind helps to point out which accesses/data structures should be optimized. This application run summary shows that data accesses are the main problem.

As shown in Listing 5.5, this command displays cache usage statistics for the overall run. However, when developing an application, or investigating a performance problem, it is often more interesting to see where cache misses happen rather than just the totals during an application's runtime. To determine which functions are responsible for the cache misses, we run cg_annotate, as shown in Listing 5.6. This shows us which functions are responsible for which cache misses. As we expect, the function a() has 10 times (1,000,000) the misses of the function b() (100,000).

Listing 5.6

```
[ezolt@wintermute test_app]$ cg_annotate --25571
--------------------------------------------------------------------------------
I1 cache:        16384 B, 32 B, 4-way associative
D1 cache:        16384 B, 32 B, 4-way associative
L2 cache:        131072 B, 32 B, 4-way associative
Command:         ./burn
Events recorded: Ir I1mr I2mr Dr D1mr D2mr Dw D1mw D2mw
Events shown:    Ir I1mr I2mr Dr D1mr D2mr Dw D1mw D2mw
Event sort order: Ir I1mr I2mr Dr D1mr D2mr Dw D1mw D2mw
Thresholds:      99 0 0 0 0 0 0 0 0
Include dirs:
User annotated:
Auto-annotation: off
```

Ir	I1mr	I2mr	Dr	D1mr	D2mr	Dw	D1mw	D2mw	
11,317,111	215	214	4,405,958	1,100,287	1,276	2,502,054	312,534	312,534	PROGRAM TOTALS

Ir	I1mr	I2mr	Dr	D1mr	D2mr	Dw	D1mw	D2mw	file:function
8,009,011	2	2	4,003,003	1,000,000	989	1,004	0	0	burn.c:a
2,500,019	3	3	6	1	1	2,500,001	312,500	312,500	???:__GI_memset
800,911	2	2	400,303	100,000	0	104	0	0	burn.c:b

Although a per-function breakdown of cache misses is useful, it would be interesting to see which lines within the application are actually causing the cache misses. If we use the --auto option, as demonstrated in Listing 5.7, cg_annotate tells us exactly which line is responsible for each miss.

Listing 5.7

```
[ezolt@wintermute test_app]$ cg_annotate --25571 --auto=yes

----------------------------------------------------------------------

I1 cache:          16384 B, 32 B, 4-way associative
D1 cache:          16384 B, 32 B, 4-way associative
L2 cache:          131072 B, 32 B, 4-way associative
Command:           ./burn
Events recorded:   Ir I1mr I2mr Dr D1mr D2mr Dw D1mw D2mw
Events shown:      Ir I1mr I2mr Dr D1mr D2mr Dw D1mw D2mw
Event sort order:  Ir I1mr I2mr Dr D1mr D2mr Dw D1mw D2mw
Thresholds:        99 0 0 0 0 0 0 0 0
Include dirs:
User annotated:
Auto-annotation:   on
```

continues

Listing 5.7 (Continued)

```
--------------------------------------------------------------------------------
        Ir I1mr I2mr        Dr    D1mr D2mr        Dw    D1mw    D2mw
--------------------------------------------------------------------------------
11,317,111  215  214 4,405,958 1,100,287 1,276 2,502,054 312,534 312,534  PROGRAM TOTALS


--------------------------------------------------------------------------------
        Ir I1mr I2mr        Dr    D1mr D2mr        Dw    D1mw    D2mw  file:function
--------------------------------------------------------------------------------
8,009,011    2    2 4,003,003 1,000,000  989    1,004       0       0  burn.c:a
2,500,019    3    3        6        1      1 2,500,001 312,500 312,500  ???:__GI_memset
  800,911    2    2  400,303  100,000      0      104       0       0  burn.c:b


--------------------------------------------------------------------------------
-- Auto-annotated source: burn.c
--------------------------------------------------------------------------------
        Ir I1mr I2mr        Dr    D1mr D2mr   Dw D1mw D2mw


-- line 2 -----------------------------------------
        .    .    .        .        .    .    .    .    .
        .    .    .        .        .    .    .    .    .  #define ITER 100
        .    .    .        .        .    .    .    .    .  #define SZ 10000000
        .    .    .        .        .    .    .    .    .  #define STRI 10000
        .    .    .        .        .    .    .    .    .
        .    .    .        .        .    .    .    .    .  char test[SZ];
        .    .    .        .        .    .    .    .    .
        .    .    .        .        .    .    .    .    .  void a(void)
        3    0    0        .        .    .    1    0    0  {
        2    0    0        .        .    .    2    0    0    int i=0,j=0;
    5,004    1    1    2,001        0    0    1    0    0    for(j=0;j<10*ITER ; j++)
5,004,000    0    0 2,001,000        0    0 1,000  0    0      for(i=0;i<SZ;i=i+STRI)
        .    .    .        .        .    .    .    .    .      {
3,000,000    1    1 2,000,000 1,000,000  989    .    .    .        test[i]++;
        .    .    .        .        .    .    .    .    .      }
```

```
      2     0     0        2          0   0    .    .   .  }

      .     .     .        .          .   .    .    .   .

      .     .     .        .          .   .    .    .   .  void b(void)

      3     1     1        .          .   .    1    0   0  {

      2     0     0        .          .   .    2    0   0  int i=0,j=0;

    504     0     0      201          0   0    1    0   0  for (j=0;j<ITER; j++)

500,400     1     1  200,100          0   0  100    0   0    for (i=0;i<SZ;i=i+STRI)

      .     .     .        .          .   .    .    .   .      {

300,000     0     0  200,000    100,000   0    .    .   .      test[i]++;

      .     .     .        .          .   .    .    .   .      }

      2     0     0        2          0   0    .    .   .  }

      .     .     .        .          .   .    .    .   .

      .     .     .        .          .   .    .    .   .

      .     .     .        .          .   .    .    .   .  main()

      6     2     2        .          .   .    1    0   0  {

      .     .     .        .          .   .    .    .   .

      .     .     .        .          .   .    .    .   .  /* Arbitrary value*/

      6     0     0        .          .   .    4    0   0  memset(test, 42, SZ);

      1     0     0        .          .   .    1    0   0  a();

      1     0     0        .          .   .    1    0   0  b();

      2     0     0        2          1   1    .    .   .  }

---------------------------------------------------------------------------

Ir I1mr I2mr  Dr D1mr D2mr Dw D1mw D2mw

---------------------------------------------------------------------------

78    3    3 100  100   78  0    0    0  percentage of events annotated
```

As Listing 5.7 shows, we have a line-by-line breakdown of where different cache misses and hits are occurring. We can see that the inner for loops have almost all the data references. As we expect, the for loop in the a() function has ten times those of the b() function.

The different level of detail (program level, function level, and line level) that valgrind/cachegrind provides can give you a good idea of which parts of an application are accessing memory and effectively using the processor caches.

5.2.5 kcachegrind

kcachegrind works intimately with valgrind to provide detailed information about the cache usage of a profiled application. It adds two new pieces of functionality above that of standard valgrind. First, it provides a skin for valgrind, called calltree, that captures both cache and call-tree statistics for a particular application. Second, it provides a graphical exploration the cache performance information and innovative visuals of the data.

5.2.5.1 Memory Performance-Related Options

Similar to valgrind, when using kcachegrind to analyze cache usage for a particular application, there are two phases: collection and annotation. The collection phase starts with the following command line:

```
calltree application
```

The calltree command accepts many different options to manipulate the information to be collected. Table 5-5 shows some of the more important options.

Table 5-5   *calltree* Command-Line Options

Option	Explanation
--help	This provides a brief explanation of all the different collection methods that calltree supports.
-dump-instr=yes|no	This is the amount of memory that has been locked by this process. Locked memory cannot be swapped to disk.
--trace-jump=yes|no	This includes branching information, or information about which path is taken at each branch.

calltree can record many different statistics. Refer to calltree's help option for more details.

During the collection phase, valgrind uses the calltree skin to collect information about cache usage. The application in the preceding command line represents the application to profile. During the collection phase, calltree prints summary information to the screen and, identically to cachegrind, it also saves more detailed statistics in a file named cachegrind.out.pid, where pid is the PID of the profiled application as it was running.

When the collection phase is complete, the command kcachegrind is used to map the cache usage back to the application source code. kcachegrind is invoked in the following way:

```
kcachegrind cachegrind.out.pid
```

kcachegrind displays the cache profiles statistics that have been collected and enables you to navigate through the results.

5.2.5.2 Example Usage

The first step in using kcachegrind is to compile the application with symbols to allow sample-to-source line mappings. This is done with the following command:

```
[ezolt@wintermute test_app]$ gcc -o burn burn.c -g3
```

Next, run calltree against that application, as shown in Listing 5.8. This provides output similar to cachegrind, but, most importantly, it generates a cachegrind.out file, which will be used by kcachegrind.

Listing 5.8

```
[ezolt@wintermute test_app]$ calltree --dump-instr=yes --trace-jump=yes ./burn
==12242== Calltree-0.9.7, a call-graph generating cache profiler for x86-linux.
==12242== Copyright (C) 2002-2004, and GNU GPL'd, by N.Nethercote and J.Weidendorfer.
==12242== Using valgrind-2.0.0, a program supervision framework for x86-linux.
==12242== Copyright (C) 2000-2003, and GNU GPL'd, by Julian Seward.
==12242== Estimated CPU clock rate is 469 MHz
==12242== For more details, rerun with: -v
==12242==
==12242==
```

continues

Listing 5.8   (Continued)

```
==12242== I   refs:      33,808,151
==12242== I1  misses:           216
==12242== L2i misses:           215
==12242== I1  miss rate:       0.0%
==12242== L2i miss rate:       0.0%
==12242==
==12242== D   refs:      29,404,027  (4,402,969 rd + 25,001,058 wr)
==12242== D1  misses:     4,225,324  (1,100,290 rd +  3,125,034 wr)
==12242== L2d misses:     4,225,324  (1,100,290 rd +  3,125,034 wr)
==12242== D1  miss rate:      14.3% (    24.9%   +      12.4%  )
==12242== L2d miss rate:      14.3% (    24.9%   +      12.4%  )
==12242==
==12242== L2 refs:        4,225,540  (1,100,506 rd +  3,125,034 wr)
==12242== L2 misses:      4,225,539  (1,100,505 rd +  3,125,034 wr)
==12242== L2 miss rate:        6.6% (     2.8%   +      12.4%  )
```

When we have the cachegrind.out file, we can start kcachegrind (v.0.54) to analyze the data by using the following command:

```
[ezolt@wintermute test_app]$ kcachegrind cachegrind.out.12242
```

This brings up the window shown in Figure 5-3. The window shows a flat profile of all the cache misses in the left pane. By default, data read misses from the L1 cache are shown.

Next, in Figure 5-4, in the upper-right pane, we can see a visualization of the callee map, or all the functions (a() and b()) that the function in the left pane (main) calls. In the lower-right pane, we can see the application's call graph.

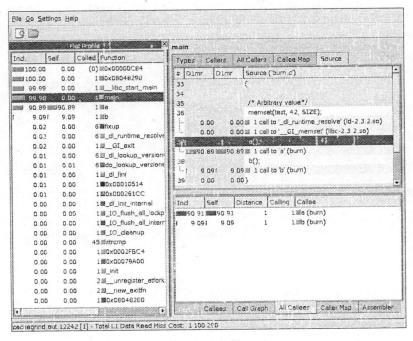

Figure 5-3

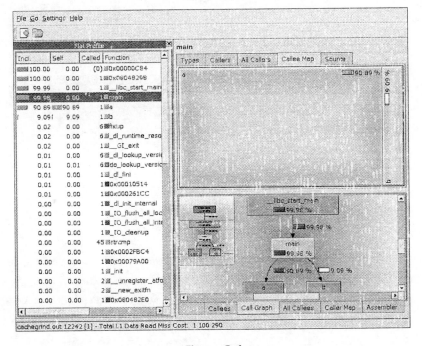

Figure 5-4

Finally, in Figure 5-5, we select a different function to examine in the left pane. We also select a different event to examine (instruction fetches) using the upper-right pane. Finally, we can visualize the loops in the assembly code using the lower-right pane.

These examples barely scratch the surface of what kcachegrind can do, and the best way to learn about it is to try it. kcachegrind is an extraordinarily useful tool for those who like to investigate performance issues visually.

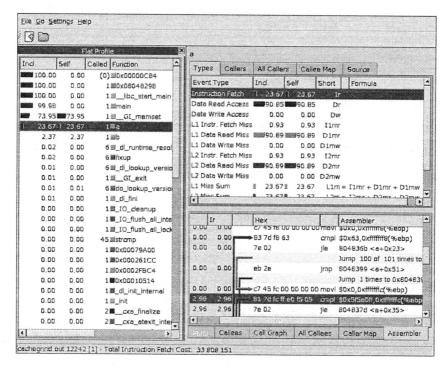

Figure 5-5

5.2.6 oprofile (III)

As you have seen in previous chapters, oprofile is a powerful tool that can help to determine where application time is spent. However, oprofile can also work with the processor's performance counters to provide an accurate view of how it performs. Whereas cachegrind simulates the CPU to find cache misses/hits, oprofile uses the actual CPU performance counters to pinpoint the location of cache misses. Unlike `cachegrind`, `oprofile` does not simulate the processor, so cache effects that it records are real; those caused by the operating system will be visible. In addition, an application analyzed under `oprofile` will run at near native speeds, whereas `cachegrind` takes much longer. However, `cachegrind` is easier to set up and use than `oprofile`, and it can always track the same events no matter what version of x86 processor it runs on. `cachegrind` is a good tool to use when you need a quick and pretty accurate answer, whereas `oprofile` proves useful when you need more accurate statistics or need statistics that `cachegrind` does not provide.

5.2.6.1 Memory Performance-Related Options

This discussion of `oprofile` does not add any new command-line options because they have already been described in section outlining CPU performance. However, one command becomes more important as you start to sample events different from `oprofile`'s defaults. Different processors and architectures can sample different sets of events and `oprofile`'s `op_help` command displays the list of events that your current processor supports.

5.2.6.2 Example Usage

As mentioned previously, the events that `oprofile` can monitor are processor specific, so these examples are run on my current machine, which is a Pentium-III. On the Pentium-III, we can use performance counters exposed by `oprofile` to gather the similar information that was provided by `valgrind` with the `cachegrind` skin. This uses the performance counter hardware rather than software simulation. Using the performance hardware presents two pitfalls. First, we must deal with the underlying hardware limitations of the performance counters. On the Pentium-III, `oprofile` can only measure two events simultaneously, whereas `cachegrind` could measure many types of memory events simultaneously. This means that for `oprofile` to measure the same events as `cachegrind`, we must run the application multiple times and change the events that `oprofile` monitors during each run. The second pitfall is the fact that `oprofile` does not provide an exact count of the events like `cachegrind`, only samples the counters, so we will be able to see where the events most likely occur, but we will not be able to see the exact number. In fact, we will only receive (1/sample rate) number of samples. If an application only causes an event to happen a few times, it might not be recorded at all. Although it can be frustrating to not know the exact number of events when debugging a performance problem, it is usually most important to figure the relative number of samples between code lines. Even though you will not be able to directly determine the total number of events that occurred at a particular source line, you will be able to figure out the line with most events, and that is usually enough to start debugging a performance problem. This inability to retrieve exact event counts is present in every form of CPU sampling and will be present on any processor performance hardware that implements it. However, it is really this limitation that allows this performance hardware to exist at all; without it, the performance monitoring would cause too much overhead.

oprofile can monitor many different types of events, which vary on different processors. This section outlines some of the important events on the Pentium-III for an example. The Pentium-III can monitor the L1 data cache (called the DCU on the Pentium-III) by using the following events (events and descriptions provided by op_help):

```
[ezolt@localhost book]$ op_help
oprofile: available events for CPU type "PIII"


See Intel Architecture Developer's Manual Volume 3, Appendix A and Intel
Architecture Optimization Reference Manual (730795-001)
....
DCU_LINES_IN:       total lines allocated in the DCU
DCU_M_LINES_IN:     number of M state lines allocated in DCU
DCU_M_LINES_OUT:    number of M lines evicted from the DCU
DCU_MISS_OUTSTANDING: number of cycles while DCU miss outstanding
...
```

Notice that we do not have an exact correspondence to what cachegrind provided, which was the number of "reads and writes" to the L1 data cache. However, we can figure out how many cycles of L1 data misses each function had by using the DCU_LINES_IN event. Although this event does not tell us the exact number of misses that each had, it should tell us how much each function missed in the cache relative to each other. The events monitoring the L2 data cache are a little closer, but it still does not have an exact correspondence to what cachegrind was providing. Here are the relevant L2 data cache events for the Pentium-III:

```
[ezolt@localhost book]$ op_help
.....
L2_LD: number of L2 data loads
        Unit masks
        . . . . . . . . . . .
        0x08: (M)odified cache state
        0x04: (E)xclusive cache state
        0x02: (S)hared cache state
        0x01: (I)nvalid cache state
        0x0f: All cache states


L2_ST:  number of L2 data stores
        Unit masks
        . . . . . . . . . . .
        0x08: (M)odified cache state
        0x04: (E)xclusive cache state
        0x02: (S)hared cache state
        0x01: (I)nvalid cache state
        0x0f: All cache states


L2_LINES_IN: number of allocated lines in L2
. . . .
```

The Pentium-III actually supports many more than these, but these are the basic load and store events. (cachegrind calls a load a "read" and a store a "write.") We can use these events to count the number of loads and stores that happened at each source line. We can also use the L2_LINES_IN to show which pieces of code had more L2 cache misses. As mentioned earlier, we will not get an exact value. In addition, on the Pentium-III, both instruction and data share the L2 cache. Any L2 misses could be the result of instruction or data misses. oprofile shows us the cache misses that occurred in the L2 as a result of instructions and data misses, whereas cachegrind helpfully splits it up for us.

On the Pentium-III, there are a similar series of events to monitor the instruction cache. For the L1 instruction cache (what the Pentium-III calls the "IFU"), we can measure the number of reads (or fetches) and misses directly by using the following events:

```
[ezolt@localhost book]$ op_help
...
IFU_IFETCH: number of non/cachable instruction fetches

IFU_IFETCH_MISS: number of instruction fetch misses
...
```

We can also measure the number of instructions that were fetched from the L2 cache by using the following event:

```
[ezolt@localhost book]$ op_help
...
L2_IFETCH: (counter: 0, 1)
        number of L2 instruction fetches (min count: 500)
        Unit masks
        ----------
        0x08: (M)odified cache state
        0x04: (E)xclusive cache state
        0x02: (S)hared cache state
        0x01: (I)nvalid cache state
        0x0f: All cache states
...
```

Unfortunately, as mentioned previously, the processor shares the L2 cache with the instruction and data, so there is no way to distinguish cache misses from data usage and instruction usage. We can use these events to approximate the same information that cachegrind provided.

If it is so difficult to extract the same information, why use oprofile at all? First, oprofile is much lower overhead (< 10 percent) and can be run on production applications. Second, oprofile can extract the exact events that are happening. This is much better than a possibly inaccurate simulator that does not take into account cache usage by the operating system or other applications.

Although these events are available on the Pentium-III, they are not necessarily available on any other processors. Each family of Intel and AMD processors has a different set of events that can be used to reveal different amounts of information about performance of the memory subsystem. op_help shows the events that can be monitored, but it might require reading Intel's or AMD's detailed processor information to understand what they mean.

To understand how you can use oprofile to extract cache information, compare the cache usage statistics of an application using both the virtual CPU of cachegrind and the actual CPU with oprofile. Let's run the burn program that we have been using as an example. Once again, it is an application that executes ten times the number of instructions in function a() as in function b(). It also accesses ten times the amount of data in function a() as in function b(). Here is the output of cachegrind for this demo application:

Ir	I1mr	I2mr	Dr	D1mr	D2mr	Dw	D1mw	D2mw	
883,497,211	215	214	440,332,658	110,000,288	1,277	2,610,954	312,534	312,533	PROGRAM TOTALS

Ir	I1mr	I2mr	Dr	D1mr	D2mr	Dw	D1mw	D2mw	file:function
800,900,011	2	2	400,300,003	100,000,000	989	100,004	0	0	???:a
80,090,011	2	2	40,030,003	10,000,000	0	10,004	0	0	???:b

In the next few examples, I run the data collection phase of oprofile multiple times. I use oprof_start to set up the events for the particular run, and then run the demo application. Because my CPU has only two counters, I have to do this multiple times. This means that different sets of events will be monitored during the different executions of the program. Because my application does not change how it executes from each run, each run should produce similar results. This is not necessarily true for a more complicated application, such as a Web server or database, each of which can dramatically change how it executes based on the requests made to it. However, for the simple test application, it works just fine.

After I collect this sampling information, we use `opreport` to extract the collected information. As shown in Listing 5.9, we query `oprofile` about the amount of data memory references that were made and how many times there was a miss in the L1 data CPU (DCU). As `cachegrind` told us, ten times the number of both memory references and L1 data misses occur in function `a()`.

Listing 5.9

```
[ezolt@wintermute test_app]$ opreport -l ./burn
event:DATA_MEM_REFS,DCU_LINES_IN
CPU: PIII, speed 467.74 MHz (estimated)
Counted DATA_MEM_REFS events (all memory references, cachable and non)
with a unit mask of 0x00 (No unit mask) count 233865
Counted DCU_LINES_IN events (total lines allocated in the DCU) with a
unit mask of 0x00 (No unit mask) count 23386
vma       samples  %          samples  %          symbol name
08048348 3640      90.8864    5598     90.9209    a
0804839e 365        9.1136    559       9.0791    b
```

Now look at Listing 5.10, which shows `opreport` examining similar information for the instruction cache. Notice that the instructions executed in function `a()` are ten times the number as those in function `b()`, as we expect. However, notice that the number of L1 I misses differ from what `cachegrind` predicts. It is most likely that other applications and the kernel are polluting the cache and causing burn to miss in the `icache`. (Remember that `cachegrind` does not take kernel or other application cache usage into account.) This also probably happened with the data cache, but because the number of data cache misses caused by the application were so high, the extra events were lost in the noise.

Listing 5.10

```
[ezolt@wintermute test_app]$ opreport -l ./burn
event:IFU_IFETCH,IFU_IFETCH_MISS
CPU: PIII, speed 467.74 MHz (estimated)
Counted IFU_IFETCH events (number of non/cachable instruction fetches)
with a unit mask of 0x00 (No unit mask) count 233870
```

```
Counted IFU_IFETCH_MISS events (number of instruction fetch misses) with
a unit mask of 0x00 (No unit mask) count 500
vma       samples  %          samples  %          symbol name
08048348 8876       90.9240    14       93.3333    a
0804839e 886         9.0760     1        6.6667    b
```

As you can see when comparing the output of cachegrind and oprofile, using oprofile to gather information about memory information is powerful because oprofile is low overhead and uses the processor hardware directly, but it can be difficult to find events that match those that you are interested in.

5.2.7 ipcs

ipcs is a tool that shows information about the system-wide interprocess communication memory. Processes can allocate system-wide shared memory, semaphores, or memory queues that can be shared by multiple processes running on the system. ipcs is best used to track down which applications are allocating and using large amounts of shared memory.

5.2.7.1 Memory Performance-Related Options

ipcs is invoked with the following command line:

```
ipcs [-t] [-c] [-l] [-u] [-p]
```

If ipcs is invoked without any parameters, it gives a summary of all the shared memory on the system. This includes information about the owner and size of the shared memory segment. Table 5-6 describes options that cause ipcs to display different types information about the shared memory in the system.

Table 5-6   *ipcs* Command-Line Options

Option	Explanation
-t	This shows the time when the shared memory was created, when a process last attached to it, and when a process last detached from it.
-u	This provides a summary about how much shared memory is being used and whether it has been swapped or is in memory.
-l	This shows the system-wide limits for shared memory usage.
-p	This shows the PIDs of the processes that created and last used the shared memory segments.
x	This shows users who are the creators and owners of the shared memory segments.

Because shared memory is used by multiple processes, it cannot be attributed to any particular process. ipcs provides enough information about the state of the system-wide shared memory to determine which processes allocated the shared memory, which processes are using it, and how often they are using it. This information proves useful when trying to reduce shared memory usage.

5.2.7.2 Example Usage

First, in Listing 5.11, we ask ipcs how much of the system memory is being used for shared memory. This is a good overall indication of the state of shared memory in the system.

Listing 5.11

```
[ezolt@wintermute tmp]$ ipcs -u

------ Shared Memory Status --------
segments allocated 21
pages allocated 1585
pages resident  720
```

```
pages swapped    412
Swap performance: 0 attempts      0 successes


------ Semaphore Status --------
used arrays = 0
allocated semaphores = 0


------ Messages: Status --------
allocated queues = 0
used headers = 0
used space = 0 bytes
```

In this case, we can see that 21 different segments or pieces of shared memory have been allocated. All these segments consume a total of 1,585 pages of memory; 720 of these exist in physical memory and 412 have been swapped to disk.

Next, in Listing 5.12, we ask ipcs for a general overview of all the shared memory segments in the system. This indicates who is using each memory segment. In this case, we see a list of all the shared segments. For one in particular, the one with a share memory ID of 65538, the user (ezolt) is the owner. It has a permission of 600 (a typical UNIX permission), which in this case, means that only ezolt can read and write to it. It has 393,216 bytes, and 2 processes are attached to it.

Listing 5.12

```
[ezolt@wintermute tmp]$ ipcs


------ Shared Memory Segments --------
key        shmid    owner    perms     bytes     nattch    status
0x00000000 0        root     777       49152     1          .
0x00000000 32769    root     777       16384     1
0x00000000 65538    ezolt    600       393216    2         dest
0x00000000 98307    ezolt    600       393216    2         dest
0x00000000 131076   ezolt    600       393216    2         dest
0x00000000 163845   ezolt    600       393216    2         dest
```

continues

Listing 5.12   (Continued)

```
0x00000000 196614     ezolt    600       393216      2         dest
0x00000000 229383     ezolt    600       393216      2         dest
0x00000000 262152     ezolt    600       393216      2         dest
0x00000000 294921     ezolt    600       393216      2         dest
0x00000000 327690     ezolt    600       393216      2         dest
0x00000000 360459     ezolt    600       393216      2         dest
0x00000000 393228     ezolt    600       393216      2         dest
0x00000000 425997     ezolt    600       393216      2         dest
0x00000000 458766     ezolt    600       393216      2         dest
0x00000000 491535     ezolt    600       393216      2         dest
0x00000000 622608     ezolt    600       393216      2         dest
0x00000000 819217     root     644       110592      2         dest
0x00000000 589842     ezolt    600       393216      2         dest
0x00000000 720916     ezolt    600       12288       2         dest
0x00000000 786454     ezolt    600       12288       2         dest


------ Semaphore Arrays --------
key          semid     owner     perms     nsems


------ Message Queues --------
key          msqid     owner     perms     used-bytes    messages
```

Finally, we can figure out exactly which processes created the shared memory segments and which other processes are using them, as shown in Listing 5.13. For the segment with shmid 32769, we can see that the PID 1229 created it and 11954 was the last to use it.

Listing 5.13

```
[ezolt@wintermute tmp]$ ipcs -p

------ Shared Memory Creator/Last-op --------
shmid      owner       cpid        lpid
0          root        1224        11954
32769      root        1224        11954
65538      ezolt       1229        11954
98307      ezolt       1229        11954
131076     ezolt       1276        11954
163845     ezolt       1276        11954
196614     ezolt       1285        11954
229383     ezolt       1301        11954
262152     ezolt       1307        11954
294921     ezolt       1309        11954
327690     ezolt       1313        11954
360459     ezolt       1305        11954
393228     ezolt       1321        11954
425997     ezolt       1321        11954
458766     ezolt       1250        11954
491535     ezolt       1250        11954
622608     ezolt       1313        11954
819217     root        1224        11914
589842     ezolt       1432        14221
720916     ezolt       1250        11954
786454     ezolt       1313        11954


------ Message Queues PIDs --------
msqid      owner       lspid       lrpid
```

After we have the PID responsible for the allocation and use, we can use a command such as ps -o command PID to track the PID back to the process name.

If shared memory usage becomes a significant amount of the system total, ipcs is a good way to track down the exact programs that are creating and using the shared memory.

5.2.8 Dynamic Languages (Java, Mono)

As with the CPU performance tools, most of the tools discussed in this chapter support analysis of static languages such as C and C++. Of the tools that we investigated, only ps, /proc, and ipcs work with dynamic languages such as Java, Mono, Python, and Perl. The cache and memory-profiling tools, such as oprofile, cachegrind, and memprof, do not. As with CPU profiling, each of these languages provides custom tools to extract information about memory usage.

For Java applications, if the java command is run with the -Xrunhprof command-line option, it profiles the application's memory usage. You can find more details at http://antprof.sourceforge.net/hprof.html or by running the java command with the -Xrunhprof:help option. For Mono applications, if the mono executable is passed the --profile flag, it also profiles the memory usage of the application. You can find more details about this at http://www.go-mono.com/performance.html. Perl and Python do not appear to have similar functionality.

5.3 Chapter Summary

This chapter presented the various Linux tools that are available to diagnose memory-performance problems. It demonstrated tools that show how much memory an application is consuming (ps, /proc) and which functions within the application are allocating that memory (memprof). It also covered tools that can monitor the effectiveness of the processor and system cache and memory subsystem (cachegrind, kcachegrind and oprofile). Finally, it described a tool that monitors shared memory usage (ipcs). Used together, these tools can track every allocation of memory, the size of these allocations, the functional locations of the allocations in the applications, and how effectively the application is using the memory subsystem when accessing these allocations.

The next chapter moves away from memory to investigate disk I/O bottlenecks.

6

Performance Tools: Disk I/O

This chapter covers performance tools that help you gauge disk I/O subsystem usage. These tools can show which disks or partitions are being used, how much I/O each disk is processing, and how long I/O requests issued to these disks are waiting to be processed.

After reading this chapter, you should be able to

* Determine the amount of total amount and type (read/write) of disk I/O on a system (vmstat).

* Determine which devices are servicing most of the disk I/O (vmstat, iostat, sar).

* Determine how effectively a particular disk is fielding I/O requests (iostat).

* Determine which processes are using a given set of files (lsof).

6.1 Introduction to Disk I/O

Before diving into performance tools, it is necessary to understand how the Linux disk I/O system is structured. Most modern Linux systems have one or more disk drives. If they are IDE drives, they are usually named hda, hdb, hdc, and so on; whereas SCSI drives are usually named sda, sdb, sdc, and so on. A disk is typically split into multiple partitions, where the name of the partition's device is created by adding the partition number to the end of the base device name. For example, the second partition on the first IDE hard drive in the system is usually labeled /dev/hda2. Each individual partition usually contains either a file system or a swap partition. These partitions are mounted into the Linux root file system, as specified in /etc/fstab. These mounted file systems contain the files that applications read to and write from.

When an application does a read or write, the Linux kernel may have a copy of the file stored into its cache or buffers and returns the requested information without ever accessing the disk. If the Linux kernel does not have a copy of the data stored in memory, however, it adds a request to the disk's I/O queue. If the Linux kernel notices that multiple requests are asking for contiguous locations on the disk, it merges them into a single big request. This merging increases overall disk performance by eliminating the seek time for the second request. When the request has been placed in the disk queue, if the disk is not currently busy, it starts to service the I/O request. If the disk is busy, the request waits in the queue until the drive is available, and then it is serviced.

6.2 Disk I/O Performance Tools

This section examines the various disk I/O performance tools that enable you to investigate how a given application is using the disk I/O subsystem, including how heavily each disk is being used, how well the kernel's disk cache is working , and which files a particular application has "open."

6.2.1 vmstat (ii)

As you saw in Chapter 2, "Performance Tools: System CPU," vmstat is a great tool to give an overall view of how the system is performing. In addition to CPU and memory statistics, vmstat can provide a system-wide view of I/O performance.

6.2.1.1 Disk I/O Performance-Related Options and Outputs

While using vmstat to retrieve disk I/O statistics from the system, you must invoke it as follows:

```
vmstat [-D] [-d] [-p partition] [interval [count]]
```

Table 6-1 describes the other command-line parameters that influence the disk I/O statistics that vmstat will display.

Table 6-1   *vmstat* Command-Line Options

Option	Explanation
-D	This displays Linux I/O subsystem total statistics. This option can give you a good idea of how your I/O subsystem is being used, but it won't give statistics on individual disks. The statistics given are the totals since system boot, rather than just those that occurred between this sample and the previous sample.
-d	This option displays individual disk statistics at a rate of one sample per interval. The statistics are the totals since system boot, rather than just those that occurred between this sample and the previous sample.
-p partition	This displays performance statistics about the given partition at a rate of one sample per interval. The statistics are the totals since system boot, rather than just those that occurred between this sample and the previous sample.
interval	The length of time between samples.
count	The total number of samples to take.

If you run vmstat without any parameters other than [interval] and [count], it shows you the default output. This output contains three columns relevant to disk I/O performance: bo, bi, and wa. These statistics are described in Table 6-2.

Table 6-2   *vmstat* I/O Statistics

Statistic	Explanation
bo	This indicates the number of total blocks written to disk in the previous interval. (In vmstat, block size for a disk is typically 1,024 bytes.)

continues

Table 6-2   *vmstat* I/O Statistics (Continued)

Statistic	Explanation
bi	This shows the number of blocks read from the disk in the previous interval. (In vmstat, block size for a disk is typically 1,024 bytes.)
wa	This indicates the amount of CPU time spent waiting for I/O to complete. The rate of disk blocks written per second.

When running with the -D mode, vmstat provides statistical information about the system's disk I/O system as a whole. Information about these statistics is provided in Table 6-3. (Note that more information about these statistics is available in the Linux kernel source package, under Documentation/iostats.txt.)

Table 6-3   *vmstat* Disk I/O Statistics

Statistic	Explanation
disks	The total number of disks in the system.
partitions	The total number of partitions in the system.
total reads	The total number of reads that have been requested.
merged reads	The total number of times that different reads to adjacent locations on the disk were merged to improve performance.
read sectors	The total number of sectors read from disk. (A sector is usually 512 bytes.)
milli reading	The amount of time (in ms) spent reading from the disk.
writes	The total number of writes that have been requested.
merged writes	The total number of times that different writes to adjacent locations on the disk were merged to improve performance.
written sectors	The total number of sectors written to disk. (A sector is usually 512 bytes.)
milli writing	The amount of time (in ms) spent writing to the disk.

Statistic	Explanation
inprogress IO	The total number of I/O that are currently in progress. Note that there is a bug in recent versions (v3.2) of vmstat in which this is incorrectly divided by 1,000, which almost always yields a 0.
milli spent IO	This is the number of milliseconds spent waiting for I/O to complete. Note that there is a bug in recent versions (v3.2) of vmstat in which this is the number of seconds spent on I/O rather than milliseconds.

The -d option of vmstat displays I/O statistics of each individual disk. These statistics are similar to those of the -D option and are described in Table 6-4.

Table 6-4 *vmstat* disk I/O Statistics

Statistic	Explanation
reads: total	The total number of reads that have been requested.
reads: merged	The total number of times that different reads to adjacent locations on the disk were merged to improve performance.
reads: sectors	The total number of sectors read from disk.
reads: ms	The amount of time (in ms) spent reading from the disk.
writes: total	The total number of writes that have been requested for this disk.
writes: merged	The total number of times that different writes to adjacent locations on the disk were merged to improve performance.
writes: sectors	The total number of sectors written to disk. (A sector is usually 512 bytes.)
writes: ms	The amount of time (in ms) spent writing to the disk.
IO: cur	The total number of I/O that are currently in progress. Note that there is a bug in recent versions of vmstat in which this is incorrectly divided by 1,000, which almost always yields a 0.
IO: s	This is the number of seconds spent waiting for I/O to complete.

Finally, when asked to provide partition-specific statistics, vmstat displays those listed in Table 6-5.

Table 6-5 *vmstat* partition I/O Statistics

Statistic	Explanation
reads	The total number of reads that have been requested for this partition.
read sectors	The total number of sectors read from this partition.
writes	The total number of writes that resulted in I/O for this partition.
requested writes	The total number of reads that have been requested for this partition.

The default vmstat output provides a coarse indication of system disk I/O, but a good level. The options provided by vmstat enable you to reveal more details about which device is responsible for the I/O. The primary advantage of vmstat over other I/O tools is that it is present on almost every Linux distribution.

6.2.1.2 Example Usage

The number of I/O statistics that vmstat can present to the Linux user has been growing with recent releases of vmstat. The examples shown in this section rely on vmstat version 3.2.0 or greater. In addition, the extended disk statistics provided by vmstat are only available on Linux systems with a kernel version greater than 2.5.70.

In the first example, shown in Listing 6.1, we are just invoking vmstat for three samples with an interval of 1 second. vmstat outputs the system-wide performance overview that we saw in Chapter 2.

Listing 6.1

```
[ezolt@wintermute procps-3.2.0]$ ./vmstat 1 3
procs -----------memory---------- ---swap-- -----io---- --system-- ----cpu----
 r  b   swpd   free   buff  cache   si   so    bi    bo   in   cs us sy id wa
 1  1      0 197020  81804  29920    0    0   236    25 1017   67  1  1 93  4
 1  1      0 172252 106252  29952    0    0 24448     0 1200  395  1 36  0 63
 0  0      0 231068  50004  27924    0    0 19712    80 1179  345  1 34 15 49
```

Listing 6.1 shows that during one of the samples, the system read 24,448 disk blocks. As mentioned previously, the block size for a disk is 1,024 bytes, so this means that the system is reading in data at about 23MB per second. We can also see that during this sample, the CPU was spending a significant portion of time waiting for I/O to complete. The CPU waits on I/O 63 percent of the time during the sample in which the disk was reading at ~23MB per second, and it waits on I/O 49 percent for the next sample, in which the disk was reading at ~19MB per second.

Next, in Listing 6.2, we ask vmstat to provide information about the I/O subsystem's performance since system boot.

Listing 6.2

```
[ezolt@wintermute procps-3.2.0]$ ./vmstat -D
         3 disks
         5 partitions
     53256 total reads
    641233 merged reads
   4787741 read sectors
    343552 milli reading
     14479 writes
     17556 merged writes
    257208 written sectors
   7237771 milli writing
         0 inprogress IO
       342 milli spent IO
```

In Listing 6.2, vmstat provides I/O statistic totals for all the disk devices in the system. As mentioned previously, when reading and writing to a disk, the Linux kernel tries to merge requests for contiguous regions on the disk for a performance increase; vmstat reports these events as merged reads and merged writes. In this example, a large number of the reads issued to the system were merged before they were issued to the device. Although there were ~640,000 merged reads, only ~53,000 read commands were actually issued to the drives. The output also tells us that a total of 4,787,741 sectors have been read from the disk, and that since system boot, 343,552ms (or 344 seconds) were spent reading from the disk. The same statistics are available for write performance. This view of I/O statistics is a good view of the overall I/O subsystem's performance.

Although the previous example displayed I/O statistics for the entire system, the following example in Listing 6.3 shows the statistics broken down for each individual disk.

Listing 6.3

```
[ezolt@wintermute procps-3.2.0]$ ./vmstat -d 1 3
disk ----------reads----------- ----------writes---------- -------IO-------
       total merged sectors      ms  total merged sectors      ms    cur    s
fd0       0      0       0        0      0      0       0        0      0     0
hde   17099 163180  671517   125006   8279   9925  146304  2831237      0   125
hda       0      0       0        0      0      0       0        0      0     0
fd0       0      0       0        0      0      0       0        0      0     0
hde   17288 169008  719645   125918   8279   9925  146304  2831237      0   126
hda       0      0       0        0      0      0       0        0      0     0
fd0       0      0       0        0      0      0       0        0      0     0
hde   17288 169008  719645   125918   8290   9934  146464  2831245      0   126
hda       0      0       0        0      0      0       0        0      0     0
```

Listing 6.4 shows that 60 (19,059 – 18,999) reads and 94 writes (24,795 – 24,795) have been issued to partition hde3. This view can prove particularly useful if you are trying to determine which partition of a disk is seeing the most usage.

Listing 6.4

```
[ezolt@wintermute procps-3.2.0]$ ./vmstat -p hde3 1 3
hde3          reads    read sectors  writes   requested writes
              18999     191986       24701      197608
              19059     192466       24795      198360
              19161     193282       24795      198360
```

Although vmstat provides statistics about individual disks/partitions, it only provides totals rather than the rate of change during the sample. This can make it difficult to eyeball which device's statistics have changed significantly from sample to sample.

6.2.2 iostat

iostat is like vmstat, but it is a tool dedicated to the display of the disk I/O subsystem statistics. iostat provides a per-device and per-partition breakdown of how many blocks are written to and from a particular disk. (Blocks in iostat are usually sized at 512 bytes.) In addition, iostat can provide extensive information about how a disk is being utilized, as well as how long Linux spends waiting to submit requests to the disk.

6.2.2.1 Disk I/O Performance-Related Options and Outputs

iostat is invoked using the following command line:

```
iostat [-d] [-k] [-x] [device] [interval [count]]
```

Much like vmstat, iostat can display performance statistics at regular intervals. Different options modify the statistics that iostat displays. These options are described in Table 6-6.

Table 6-6 *iostat* Command-Line Options

Option	Explanation
-d	This displays only information about disk I/O rather than the default display, which includes information about CPU usage as well.
-k	This shows statistics in kilobytes rather than blocks.
-x	This shows extended-performance I/O statistics.
device	If a device is specified, iostat shows only information about that device.
interval	The length of time between samples.
count	The total number of samples to take.

The default output of iostat displays the performance statistics described in Table 6-7.

Table 6-7 *iostat* Device Statistics

Statistic	Explanation
tps	Transfers per second. This is the number of reads and writes to the drive/partition per second.
Blk_read/s	The rate of disk blocks read per second.
Blk_wrtn/s	The rate of disk blocks written per second.
Blk_read	The total number of blocks read during the interval.
Blk_wrtn	The total number of blocks written during the interval.

When you invoke iostat with the -x parameter, it displays extended statistics about the disk I/O subsystem. These extended statistics are described in Table 6-8.

Table 6-8 `iostat` Extended Disk Statistics

Statistic	Explanation
rrqm/s	The number of reads merged before they were issued to the disk.
wrqm/s	The number of writes merged before they were issued to the disk.
r/s	The number of reads issued to the disk per second.
w/s	The number of writes issued to the disk per second.
rsec/s	Disk sectors read per second.
wsec/s	Disk sectors written per second.
rkB/s	Kilobytes read from disk per second.
wkB/s	Kilobytes written to disk per second.
avgrq-sz	The average size (in sectors) of disk requests.
avgqu-sz	The average size of the disk request queue.
await	The average time (in ms) for a request to be completely serviced. This average includes the time that the request was waiting in the disk's queue plus the amount of time it was serviced by the disk.
svctm	The average service time (in ms) for requests submitted to the disk. This indicates how long on average the disk took to complete a request. Unlike await, it does not include the amount of time spent waiting in the queue.

iostat is a helpful utility, providing the most complete view of disk I/O performance statistics of any that I have found so far. Although vmstat is present everywhere and provides some basic statistics, iostat is far more complete. If it is available and installed on your system, iostat should be the first tool to turn to when a system has a disk I/O performance problem.

6.2.2.2 Example Usage

Listing 6.5 shows an example iostat run while a disk benchmark is writing a test file to the file system on the /dev/hda2 partition. The first sample iostat displays is the total system average since system boot time. The second sample (and any that would follow) is the statistics from each 1-second interval.

Listing 6.5

```
[ezolt@localhost sysstat-5.0.2]$ ./iostat -d 1 2
Linux 2.4.22-1.2188.nptl (localhost.localdomain)        05/01/2004


Device:            tps    Blk_read/s    Blk_wrtn/s    Blk_read    Blk_wrtn
hda                7.18       121.12        343.87     1344206     3816510
hda1               0.00         0.03          0.00         316          46
hda2               7.09       119.75        337.59     1329018     3746776
hda3               0.09         1.33          6.28       14776       69688
hdb                0.00         0.00          0.00          16           0


Device:            tps    Blk_read/s    Blk_wrtn/s    Blk_read    Blk_wrtn
hda              105.05         5.78      12372.56          16       34272
hda1               0.00         0.00          0.00           0           0
hda2             100.36         5.78      11792.06          16       32664
hda3               4.69         0.00        580.51           0        1608
hdb                0.00         0.00          0.00           0           0
```

One interesting note in the preceding example is that /dev/hda3 had a small amount of activity. In the system being tested, /dev/hda3 is a swap partition. Any activity recorded from this partition is caused by the kernel swapping memory to disk. In this way, iostat provides an indirect method to determine how much disk I/O in the system is the result of swapping.

Listing 6.6 shows the extended output of iostat.

Listing 6.6

```
[ezolt@localhost sysstat-5.0.2]$ ./iostat -x -dk 1 5 /dev/hda2
Linux 2.4.22-1.2188.nptl (localhost.localdomain)        05/01/2004
```

```
Device:      rrqm/s wrqm/s   r/s   w/s rsec/s  wsec/s    rkB/s    wkB/s
avgrq-sz avgqu-sz  await  svctm  %util
hda2         11.22  44.40  3.15  4.20 115.00  388.97    57.50   194.49
68.52      1.75  237.17  11.47    8.43


Device:      rrqm/s wrqm/s   r/s   w/s rsec/s  wsec/s    rkB/s    wkB/s
avgrq-sz avgqu-sz  await  svctm  %util
hda2          0.00 1548.00  0.00 100.00    0.00 13240.00    0.00  6620.00
132.40     55.13  538.60  10.00 100.00


Device:      rrqm/s wrqm/s   r/s   w/s rsec/s  wsec/s    rkB/s    wkB/s
avgrq-sz avgqu-sz  await  svctm  %util
hda2          0.00 1365.00  0.00 131.00    0.00 11672.00    0.00  5836.00
89.10     53.86  422.44   7.63 100.00


Device:      rrqm/s wrqm/s   r/s   w/s rsec/s  wsec/s    rkB/s    wkB/s
avgrq-sz avgqu-sz  await  svctm  %util
hda2          0.00 1483.00  0.00 84.00    0.00 12688.00    0.00  6344.00
151.05     39.69  399.52  11.90 100.00


Device:      rrqm/s wrqm/s   r/s   w/s rsec/s  wsec/s    rkB/s    wkB/s
avgrq-sz avgqu-sz  await  svctm  %util
hda2          0.00 2067.00  0.00 123.00    0.00 17664.00    0.00  8832.00
143.61     58.59  508.54   8.13 100.00
```

In Listing 6.6, you can see that the average queue size is pretty high (~237 to 538) and, as a result, the amount of time that a request must wait (~422.44ms to 538.60ms) is much greater than the amount of time it takes to service the request (7.63ms to 11.90ms). These high average service times, along with the fact that the utilization is 100 percent, show that the disk is completely saturated.

The extended iostat output provides so many statistics that it only fits on a single line in a very wide terminal. However, this information is nearly all that you need to identify a particular disk as a bottleneck.

6.2.3 sar

As discussed in Chapter 2, "Performance Tools: System CPU," sar can collect the performance statistics of many different areas of the Linux system. In addition to CPU and memory statistics, it can collect information about the disk I/O subsystem.

6.2.3.1 Disk I/O Performance-Related Options and Outputs

When using sar to monitor disk I/O statistics, you can invoke it with the following command line:

```
sar -d [ interval [ count ] ]
```

Typically, sar displays information about the CPU usage in a system; to display disk usage statistics instead, you must use the -d option. sar can only display disk I/O statistics with a kernel version higher than 2.5.70. The statistics that it displays are described in Table 6-9.

Table 6-9   sar Device Statistics

Statistic	Explanation
tps	Transfers per second. This is the number of reads and writes to the drive/partition per second.
rd_sec/s	Number of disk sectors read per second.
wr_sec/s	Number of disk sectors written per second.

The number of sectors is taken directly from the kernel, and although it is possible for it to vary, the size is usually 512 bytes.

6.2.3.2 Example Usage

In Listing 6.7, sar is used to collect information about the I/O of the devices on the system. sar lists the devices by their major and minor number rather than their names.

Listing 6.7

```
[ezolt@wintermute sysstat-5.0.2]$ sar -d 1 3
Linux 2.6.5 (wintermute.phil.org)        05/02/04


16:38:28        DEV      tps   rd_sec/s   wr_sec/s
16:38:29       dev2-0    0.00      0.00       0.00
16:38:29      dev33-0  115.15    808.08    2787.88
16:38:29      dev33-64   0.00      0.00       0.00
16:38:29       dev3-0    0.00      0.00       0.00


16:38:29        DEV      tps   rd_sec/s   wr_sec/s
16:38:30       dev2-0    0.00      0.00       0.00
16:38:30      dev33-0  237.00   1792.00       8.00
16:38:30      dev33-64   0.00      0.00       0.00
16:38:30       dev3-0    0.00      0.00       0.00


16:38:30        DEV      tps   rd_sec/s   wr_sec/s
16:38:31       dev2-0    0.00      0.00       0.00
16:38:31      dev33-0  201.00   1608.00       0.00
16:38:31      dev33-64   0.00      0.00       0.00
16:38:31       dev3-0    0.00      0.00       0.00


Average:        DEV      tps   rd_sec/s   wr_sec/s
Average:       dev2-0    0.00      0.00       0.00
Average:      dev33-0  184.62   1404.68     925.75
Average:      dev33-64   0.00      0.00       0.00
Average:       dev3-0    0.00      0.00       0.00
```

sar has a limited number of disk I/O statistics when compared to iostat. However, the capability of sar to simultaneously record many different types of statistics may make up for these shortcomings.

6.2.4 lsof (List Open Files)

lsof provides a way to determine which processes have a particular file open. In addition to tracking down the user of a single file, lsof can display the processes using the files in a particular directory. It can also recursively search through an entire directory tree and list the processes using files in that directory tree. lsof can prove helpful when narrowing down which applications are generating I/O.

6.2.4.1 Disk I/O Performance-Related Options and Outputs

You can invoke lsof with the following command line to investigate which files processes have open:

lsof [-r delay] [+D directory] [+d directory] [file]

Typically, lsof displays which processes are using a given file. However, by using the +d and +D options, it is possible for lsof to display this information for more than one file. Table 6-10 describes the command-line options of lsof that prove helpful when tracking down an I/O performance problem.

Table 6-10 *lsof* Command-Line Options

Option	Explanation
-r delay	This causes lsof to output statistics every delay seconds.
+D directory	This causes lsof to recursively search all the files in the given directory and report on which processes are using them.
+d directory	This causes lsof to report on which processes are using the files in the given directory.

lsof displays the statistics described in Table 6-11 when showing which processes are using the specified files.

Table 6-11 *lsof* File Statistics

Statistic	Explanation
COMMAND	The name of the command that has the file open.
PID	The PID of the command that has the file open.
USER	The user who has the file open.
FD	The file descriptor of the file, or tex for a executable, mem for a memory mapped file.
TYPE	The type of file. REG for a regular file.
DEVICE	Device number in major, minor number.
SIZE	The size of the file.
NODE	The inode of the file.

Although lsof does not show the amount and type of file access that a particular process is doing, it at least displays which processes are using a particular file.

6.2.4.2 Example Usage

Listing 6.8 shows lsof being run on the /usr/bin directory. This run shows which processes are accessing all of the files in /usr/bin.

Listing 6.8

```
[ezolt@localhost manuscript]$ /usr/sbin/lsof -r 2 +D /usr/bin/
COMMAND    PID USER FD   TYPE DEVICE   SIZE   NODE NAME
gnome-ses 2162 ezolt txt    REG    3,2 113800 597490 /usr/bin/gnome-session
ssh-agent 2175 ezolt txt    REG    3,2  61372 596783 /usr/bin/ssh-agent
gnome-key 2182 ezolt txt    REG    3,2  77664 602727 /usr/bin/gnome-keyring-daemon
metacity  2186 ezolt txt    REG    3,2 486520 597321 /usr/bin/metacity
gnome-pan 2272 ezolt txt    REG    3,2 503100 602174 /usr/bin/gnome-panel
nautilus  2280 ezolt txt    REG    3,2 677812 598239 /usr/bin/nautilus
magicdev  2287 ezolt txt    REG    3,2  27008 598375 /usr/bin/magicdev
eggcups   2292 ezolt txt    REG    3,2  32108 599596 /usr/bin/eggcups
```

continues

Listing 6.8   (Continued)

```
pam-panel 2305 ezolt txt    REG    3,2  45672 600140 /usr/bin/pam-panel-icon
gnome-ter 3807 ezolt txt    REG    3,2 289116 596834 /usr/bin/gnome-terminal
less      6452 ezolt txt    REG    3,2 104604 596239 /usr/bin/less
=======
COMMAND    PID  USER  FD  TYPE DEVICE   SIZE   NODE NAME
gnome-ses 2162 ezolt txt    REG    3,2 113800 597490 /usr/bin/gnome-session
ssh-agent 2175 ezolt txt    REG    3,2  61372 596783 /usr/bin/ssh-agent
gnome-key 2182 ezolt txt    REG    3,2  77664 602727 /usr/bin/gnome-keyring-daemon
metacity  2186 ezolt txt    REG    3,2 486520 597321 /usr/bin/metacity
gnome-pan 2272 ezolt txt    REG    3,2 503100 602174 /usr/bin/gnome-panel
nautilus  2280 ezolt txt    REG    3,2 677812 598239 /usr/bin/nautilus
magicdev  2287 ezolt txt    REG    3,2  27008 598375 /usr/bin/magicdev
eggcups   2292 ezolt txt    REG    3,2  32108 599596 /usr/bin/eggcups
pam-panel 2305 ezolt txt    REG    3,2  45672 600140 /usr/bin/pam-panel-icon
gnome-ter 3807 ezolt txt    REG    3,2 289116 596834 /usr/bin/gnome-terminal
less      6452 ezolt txt    REG    3,2 104604 596239 /usr/bin/less
```

In particular, we can see that process 3807 is using the file /usr/bin/gnome-terminal. This file is an executable, as indicated by the txt in the FD column, and the name of the command that is using it is gnome-terminal. This makes sense; the process that is running gnome-terminal must therefore have the executable open. One interesting thing to note is that this file is on the device 3,2, which corresponds to /dev/hda2. (You can figure out the device number for all the system devices by executing ls -la /dev and looking at the output field that normally displays size.) Knowing on which device a file is located can help if you know that a particular device is the source of an I/O bottleneck. lsof provides the unique ability to trace an open file descriptor back to individual processes; although it does not show which processes are using a significant amount of I/O, it does provide a starting point.

6.3 What's Missing?

All the disk I/O tools on Linux provide information about the utilization of a particular disk or partition. Unfortunately, after you determine that a particular disk is a bottleneck, there are no tools that enable you to figure out which process is causing all the I/O traffic.

Usually a system administrator has a good idea about what application uses the disk, but not always. Many times, for example, I have been using my Linux system when the disks started grinding for apparently no reason. I can usually run top and look for a process that might be causing the problem. By eliminating processes that I believe are not doing I/O, I can usually find the culprit. However, this requires knowledge of what the various applications are supposed to do. It is also error prone, because the guess about which processes are not causing the problem might be wrong. In addition, for a system with many users or many running applications, it is not always practical or easy to determine which application might be causing the problem. Other UNIXes support the inblk and oublk parameters to ps, which show you the amount of disk I/O issued on behalf of a particular process. Currently, the Linux kernel does not track the I/O of a process, so the ps tool has no way to gather this information.

You can use lsof to determine which processes are accessing files on a particular partition. After you list all PIDs accessing the files, you can then attach to each of the PIDs with strace and figure out which one is doing a significant amount of I/O. Although this method works, it is really a Band-Aid solution, because the number of processes accessing a partition could be large and it is time-consuming to attach and analyze the system calls of each process. This may also miss short-lived processes, and may unacceptably slow down processes when they are being traced.

This is an area where the Linux kernel could be improved. The ability to quickly track which processes are generating I/O would allow for much quicker diagnosis of I/O performance-related problems.

6.4 Chapter Summary

This chapter presented the Linux disk I/O performance tools used to extract information about system-wide (`vmstat`), device-specific (`vmstat`, `iostat`, `sar`), and file-specific (`lsof`) disk I/O usage. It explained the different types of I/O statistics and how to extract these statistics from Linux using the I/O performance tools. It also discussed some of the significant limitations of the current tools and areas for future growth.

The next chapter examines the tools that enable you to determine the cause of network bottlenecks.

7

Performance Tools: Network

This chapter introduces some of the network performance tools available on Linux. We primarily focus on the tools that analyze the network traffic on a single box rather than network-wide management tools. Although network performance evaluation usually does not make sense in total isolation (that is, nodes do not normally talk to themselves), it is valuable to investigate the behavior of a single system on the network to identify local configuration and application problems. In addition, understanding the characteristics of network traffic on a single system can help to locate other problem systems, or local hardware and applications errors that slow down network performance.

After reading this chapter, you should be able to

* Determine the speed and duplex settings of the Ethernet devices in the system (mii-tool, ethtool).

* Determine the amount of network traffic flowing over each Ethernet interface (ifconfig, sar, gkrellm, iptraf, netstat, etherape).

* Determine the types of IP traffic flowing in to and out of the system (gkrellm, iptraf, netstat, etherape).

* Determine the amount of each type of IP traffic flowing in to and out of the system (gkrellm, iptraf, etherape).

* Determine which applications are generating IP traffic (netstat).

7.1 Introduction to Network I/O

Network traffic in Linux and every other major operating system is abstracted as a series of hardware and software layers. The link, or lowest, layer contains network hardware such as Ethernet devices. When moving network traffic, this layer does not distinguish types of traffic but just transmits and receives data (or frames) as fast as possible.

Stacked above the link layer is a network layer. This layer uses the Internet Protocol (IP) and Internet Control Message Protocol (ICMP) to address and route packets of data from machine to machine. IP/ICMP make their best-effort attempt to pass the packets between machines, but they make no guarantees about whether a packet actually arrives at its destination.

Stacked above the network layer is the transport layer, which defines the Transport Control Protocol (TCP) and User Datagram Protocol (UDP). TCP is a reliable protocol that guarantees that a message is either delivered over the network or generates an error if the message is not delivered. TCP's sibling protocol, UDP, is an unreliable protocol that deliberately (to achieve the highest data rates) does not guarantee message delivery. UDP and TCP add the concept of a "service" to IP. UDP and TCP receive messages on numbered "ports." By convention, each type of network service is assigned a different number. For example, Hypertext Transfer Protocol (HTTP) is typically port 80, Secure Shell (SSH) is typically port 22, and File Transport Protocol (FTP) is typically port 23. In a Linux system, the file /etc/services defines all the ports and the types of service they provide.

The final layer is the application layer. It includes all the different applications that use the layers below to transmit packets over the network. These include applications such Web servers, SSH clients, or even peer-to-peer (P2P) file-sharing clients such as bittorrent.

The lowest three layers (link, network, and transport) are implemented or controlled within the Linux kernel. The kernel provides statistics about how each layer is performing, including information about the bandwidth usage and error count as data flows through each of the layers. The tools covered in this chapter enable you to extract and view those statistics.

7.1.1 Network Traffic in the Link Layer

At the lowest levels of the network stack, Linux can detect the rate at which data traffic is flowing through the link layer. The link layer, which is typically Ethernet, sends information into the network as a series of frames. Even though the layers above may have pieces of information much larger than the frame size, the link layer breaks everything up into frames to send them over the network. This maximum size of data in a frame is known as the maximum transfer unit (MTU). You can use network configuration tools such as `ip` or `ifconfig` to set the MTU. For Ethernet, the maximum size is commonly 1,500 bytes, although some hardware supports jumbo frames up to 9,000 bytes. The size of the MTU has a direct impact on the efficiency of the network. Each frame in the link layer has a small header, so using a large MTU increases the ratio of user data to overhead (header). When using a large MTU, however, each frame of data has a higher chance of being corrupted or dropped. For clean physical links, a high MTU usually leads to better performance because it requires less overhead; for noisy links, however, a smaller MTU may actually enhance performance because less data has to be re-sent when a single frame is corrupted.

At the physical layer, frames flow over the physical network; the Linux kernel collects a number of different statistics about the number and types of frames:

* *Transmitted/received*—If the frame successfully flowed in to or out of the machine, it is counted as a transmitted or received frame.

* *Errors*—Frames with errors (possibly because of a bad network cable or duplex mismatch).

* *Dropped*—Frames that were discarded (most likely because of low amounts of memory or buffers).

* *Overruns*—Frames that may have been discarded by the network card because the kernel or network card was overwhelmed with frames. This should not normally happen.

* *Frame*—These frames were dropped as a result of problems on the physical level. This could be the result of cyclic redundancy check (CRC) errors or other low-level problems.

* *Multicast*—These frames are not directly addressed to the current system, but rather have been broadcast to a series of nodes simultaneously.

　* *Compressed*—Some lower-level interfaces, such as Point-to-Point Protocol
(PPP) or Serial Line Internet Protocol (SLIP) devices compress frames
before they are sent over the network. This value indicates the number
of these compressed frames.

Several of the Linux network performance tools can display the number of frames of
each type that have passed through each network device. These tools often require a
device name, so it is important to understand how Linux names network devices to
understand which name represents which device. Ethernet devices are named ethN,
where eth0 is the first device, eth1 is the second device, and so on. PPP devices are named
pppN in the same manner as Ethernet devices. The loopback device, which is used to
network with the local machine, is named lo.

When investigating a performance problem, it is crucial to know the maximum speed
that the underlying physical layer can support. For example, Ethernet devices commonly
support multiple speeds, such 10Mbps, 100Mbps, or even 1,000Mbps. The underlying
Ethernet cards and infrastructure (switches) must be capable of handling the required
speed. Although most cards can autodetect the highest support speed and set themselves
up appropriately, if a card or switch is misconfigured, performance will suffer. If the
higher speed cannot be used, the Ethernet devices often negotiate down to a slower
speed, but they continue to function. If network performance is much slower than
expected, it is best to verify with tools such as `ethtool` and `mii-tool` that the Ethernet
speeds are set to what you expect.

7.1.2 Protocol-Level Network Traffic

For TCP or UDP traffic, Linux uses the socket/port abstraction to connect two machines.
When connecting to a remote machine, the local application uses a network socket to
open a port on a remote machine. As mentioned previously, most common network
services have an agreed-upon port number, so a given application will be able to connect
to the correct port on the remote machine. For example, port 80 is commonly used for
HTTP. When loading a Web page, browsers connect to port 80 on remote machines.
The Web server of the remote machine listens for connections on port 80, and when a
connection occurs, the Web server sets up the connection for transfer of the Web page.

The Linux network performance tools can track the amount of data that flows over a particular network port. Because port numbers are unique for each service, it is possible to determine the amount of network traffic flowing to a particular service.

7.2 Network Performance Tools

This section describes the Linux network performance tools available to diagnose performance problems. We start with the tools to determine the lowest level of network performance (physical statistics) and add tools that can investigate the layers above that.

7.2.1 mii-tool (Media-Independent Interface Tool)

mii-tool is an Ethernet-specific hardware tool primarily used to configure an Ethernet device, but it can also provide information about the current configuration. This information, such as the link speed and duplex setting, can be useful when tracking down the cause of an under-performing network device.

7.2.1.1 Network I/O Performance-Related Options

mii-tool requires root access to be used. It is invoked with the following command line:

```
mii-tool [-v] [device]
```

mii-tool prints the Ethernet settings for the given device. If no devices are specified, mii-tool displays information about all the available Ethernet devices. If the -v option is used, mii-tool displays verbose statistics about the offered and negotiated network capabilities.

7.2.1.2 Example Usage

Listing 7.1 shows the configuration of eth0 on the system. The first line tells us that the Ethernet device is currently using a 100BASE-T full-duplex connection. The next few lines describe the capabilities of the network card in the machine and the capabilities that the card has detected of the network device on the other end of the wire.

Listing 7.1

```
[root@nohs linux-2.6.8-1.521]#  /sbin/mii-tool -v eth0
eth0: negotiated 100baseTx-FD, link ok
  product info: vendor 00:00:00, model 0 rev 0
  basic mode:   autonegotiation enabled
  basic status: autonegotiation complete, link ok
  capabilities: 100baseTx-FD 100baseTx-HD 10baseT-FD 10baseT-HD
  advertising:  100baseTx-FD 100baseTx-HD 10baseT-FD 10baseT-HD flow-control
  link partner: 100baseTx-FD 100baseTx-HD 10baseT-FD 10baseT-HD
```

mii-tool provides low-level information about how the physical level of the etheRnet device is configured.

7.2.2 ethtool

ethtool provides similar capabilities to mii-tool for configuration and display of statistics for Ethernet devices. However, ethtool is the more powerful tool and contains more configuration options and device statistics.

7.2.2.1 Network I/O Performance-Related Options

ethtool requires root access to be used. It is invoked with the following command line:

```
ethtool [device]
```

ethtool prints out configuration information about the given Ethernet device. If no devices are provided, ethtool prints statistics for all the Ethernet devices in the system. The options to change the current Ethernet settings are described in detail in the ethtool main page.

7.2.2.2 Example Usage

Listing 7.2 shows the configuration of eth0 on the system. Although the device supports many different speed and link settings, it is currently connected to a full-duplex 1,000Mbps link.

Listing 7.2

```
[root@scrffy tmp]# /sbin/ethtool eth0
Settings for eth0:
        Supported ports: [ TP ]
        Supported link modes:   10baseT/Half 10baseT/Full
                                100baseT/Half 100baseT/Full
                                1000baseT/Half 1000baseT/Full
        Supports auto-negotiation: Yes
        Advertised link modes:  10baseT/Half 10baseT/Full
                                100baseT/Half 100baseT/Full
                                1000baseT/Half 1000baseT/Full
        Advertised auto-negotiation: Yes
        Speed: 1000Mb/s
        Duplex: Full
        Port: Twisted Pair
        PHYAD: 0
        Transceiver: internal
        Auto-negotiation: on
        Supports Wake-on: g
        Wake-on: d
        Link detected: yes
```

ethtool is simple to run, and it can quickly provide information about an improperly configured network device.

7.2.3 ifconfig (Interface Configure)

The primary job of ifconfig is to set up and configure the network interfaces in a Linux box. It also provides rudimentary performance statistics about all the network devices in the system. ifconfig is available on almost every Linux machine that uses networking.

7.2.3.1 Network I/O Performance-Related Options

ifconfig is invoked with the following command line:

```
ifconfig [device]
```

If no device is specified, ifconfig shows statistics about all the active network devices. Table 7-1 describes the performance statistics that ifconfig provides.

Table 7-1   Performance-Specific *ifconfig* Statistics

Column	Explanation
RX packets	The number of packets that this device has received.
TX packets	The number of packets that this device has transmitted.
errors	The number of errors when transmitting or receiving.
dropped	The number of dropped packets when transmitting or receiving.
overruns	The number of times the network device did not have enough buffer space to send or receive a packet.
frame	The number of low-level Ethernet frame errors.
carrier	The number of packets discarded because of link media failure (such as a faulty cable).

Although primarily for network configuration, ifconfig provides a reasonable number of statistics that you can use to determine the health and performance of each of the network devices in the system.

7.2.3.2 Example Usage

Listing 7.3 shows the network performance statistics from all the devices in the system. In this case, we have an Ethernet card (eth0) and the loopback (lo) device. In this example, the Ethernet card has received ~790Mb of data and has transmitted ~319Mb.

Listing 7.3

```
[ezolt@wintermute tmp]$ /sbin/ifconfig
eth0      Link encap:Ethernet  HWaddr 00:02:E3:15:A5:03
          inet addr:192.168.0.4  Bcast:192.168.0.255  Mask:255.255.255.0
          UP BROADCAST NOTRAILERS RUNNING  MTU:1500  Metric:1
          RX packets:1047040 errors:0 dropped:0 overruns:0 frame:0
          TX packets:796733 errors:12 dropped:0 overruns:12 carrier:12
          collisions:0 txqueuelen:1000
          RX bytes:829403956 (790.9 Mb)  TX bytes:334962327 (319.4 Mb)
          Interrupt:19 Base address:0x3000


lo        Link encap:Local Loopback
          inet addr:127.0.0.1  Mask:255.0.0.0
          UP LOOPBACK RUNNING  MTU:16436  Metric:1
          RX packets:102 errors:0 dropped:0 overruns:0 frame:0
          TX packets:102 errors:0 dropped:0 overruns:0 carrier:0
          collisions:0 txqueuelen:0
          RX bytes:6492 (6.3 Kb)  TX bytes:6492 (6.3 Kb)
```

The statistics provided by ifconfig represent the cumulative amount since system boot. If you bring down a network device and then bring it back up, the statistics do not reset. If you run ifconfig at regular intervals, you can eyeball the rate of change in the various statistics. You can automate this by using the watch command or a shell script, both of which are described in the next chapter.

7.2.4 ip

Some of the network tools, such as ifconfig, are being phased out in favor of the new command: ip. ip enables you to configure many different aspect of Linux networking, but it can also display performance statistics about each network device.

7.2.4.1 Network I/O Performance-Related Options

When extracting performance statistics, you invoke `ip` with the following command line:

```
ip -s [-s] link
```

If you call `ip` with these options, it prints statistics about all the network devices in the system, including the loopback (`lo`) and simple Internet transition (`sit0`) device. The `sit0` device allows IPv6 packets to be encapsulated in IPv4 packets and exists to ease the transition between IPv4 and IPv6. If the extra `-s` is provided to `ip`, it provides a more detailed list of low-level Ethernet statistics. Table 7-2 describes some of the performance statistics provided by `ip`.

Table 7-2   Network Performance `ip` Output Statistics

Column	Explanation
bytes	The total number of bytes sent or received.
packets	The total number of packets sent or received.
errors	The number of errors that occurred when transmitting or receiving.
dropped	The number of packets that were not sent or received as a result of a lack of resources on the network card.
overruns	The number of times the network did not have enough buffer space to send or receive more packets.
mcast	The number of multicast packets that have been received.
carrier	The number of packets discarded because of link media failure (such as a faulty cable).
collsns	This is the number of collisions that the device experienced when transmitting. These occur when two devices are trying to use the network at the exact same time.

`ip` is a very versatile tool for Linux network configuration, and although its main function is the configuration of the network, you can use it to extract low-level device statistics as well.

7.2.4.2 Example Usage

Listing 7.4 shows the network performance statistics from all the devices in the system. In this case, we have an Ethernet card, the loopback device, and the sit0 tunnel device. In this example, the Ethernet card has received ~820Mb of data and has transmitted ~799Mb.

Listing 7.4

```
[ezolt@nohs ezolt]$ /sbin/ip -s link
1: lo: <LOOPBACK,UP> mtu 16436 qdisc noqueue
    link/loopback 00:00:00:00:00:00 brd 00:00:00:00:00:00
    RX: bytes  packets  errors  dropped overrun mcast
    4460       67       0       0       0       0
    TX: bytes  packets  errors  dropped carrier collsns
    4460       67       0       0       0       0
2: eth0: <BROADCAST,MULTICAST,UP> mtu 1500 qdisc pfifo_fast qlen 1000
    link/ether 00:10:b5:59:2c:82 brd ff:ff:ff:ff:ff:ff
    RX: bytes  packets  errors  dropped overrun mcast
    799273378  920999   0       0       0       0
    TX: bytes  packets  errors  dropped carrier collsns
    820603574  930929   0       0       0       0
3: sit0: <NOARP> mtu 1480 qdisc noop
    link/sit 0.0.0.0 brd 0.0.0.0
    RX: bytes  packets  errors  dropped overrun mcast
    0          0        0       0       0       0
    TX: bytes  packets  errors  dropped carrier collsns
    0          0        0       0       0       0
```

Much like ifconfig, ip provides system totals for statistics since the system has booted. If you use watch (described in the next chapter), you can monitor how these values change over time.

7.2.5 sar

As discussed in previous chapters, sar is one of the most versatile Linux performance tools. It can monitor many different things, archive statistics, and even display information in a format that is usable by other tools. sar does not always provide as much detail as the area-specific performance tools, but it provides a good overview.

Network performance statistics are no different. sar provides information about the link-level performance of the network, as do ip and ifconfig; however, it also provides some rudimentary statistics about the number of sockets opened by the transport layer.

7.2.5.1 Network I/O Performance-Related Options

sar collects network statistics using the following command:

```
sar [-n DEV | EDEV | SOCK | FULL ] [DEVICE]  [interval] [count]
```

sar collects many different types of performance statistics. Table 7-3 describes the command-line options used by sar to display network performance statistics.

Table 7-3   sar Command-Line Options

Option	Explanation
-n DEV	Shows statistics about the number of packets and bytes sent and received by each device.
-n EDEV	Shows information about the transmit and receive errors for each device.
-n SOCK	Shows information about the total number of sockets (TCP, UDP, and RAW) in use.
-n FULL	Shows all the network statistics.
interval	The length of time between samples.
count	The total number of samples to take.

The network performance options that sar provides are described in Table 7-4.

Table 7-4 *sar* Network Performance Statistics

Option	Explanation
rxpck/s	The rate of packets received.
txpck/s	The rate of packets sent.
rxbyt/s	The rate of bytes received.
txbyt/s	The rate of bytes sent.
rxcmp/s	The rate of compressed packets received.
txcmp/s	The rate of compressed packets sent.
rxmcst/s	The rate of multicast packets received.
rxerr/s	The rate of receive errors.
txerr/s	The rate of transmit errors.
coll/s	The rate of Ethernet collisions when transmitting.
rxdrop/s	The rate of received frames dropped due to Linux kernel buffer shortages.
txdrop/s	The rate of transmitted frames dropped due to Linux kernel buffer shortages.
txcarr/s	The rate of transmitted frames dropped due to carrier errors.
rxfram/s	The rate of received frames dropped due to frame-alignment errors.
rxfifo/s	The rate of received frames dropped due to FIFO errors.
txfifo/s	The rate of transmitted frames dropped due to FIFO errors.
totsck	The total number of sockets in use.
tcpsck	The total number of TCP sockets in use.
udpsck	The total number of UDP sockets in use.
rawsck	The total number of RAW sockets in use.
ip-frag	The total number of IP fragments.

Considering all the statistics that sar can gather, it really does provide the most system-level performance statistics in a single location.

7.2.5.2 Example Usage

In Listing 7.5, we examine the transmit and receive statistics of all the network devices in the system. As you can see, the eth0 device is the most active. In the first sample, eth0 is receiving ~63,000 bytes per second (rxbyt/s) and transmitting ~45,000 bytes per second (txbyt/s). No compressed packets are sent (txcmp) or received (rxcmp). (Compressed packets are usually present during SLIP or PPP connections.)

Listing 7.5

```
[ezolt@wintermute sysstat-5.0.2]$ sar -n DEV 1 2
Linux 2.4.22-1.2174.nptlsmp (wintermute.phil.org)        06/07/04


21:22:29   IFACE   rxpck/s   txpck/s   rxbyt/s   txbyt/s   rxcmp/s   txcmp/s   rxmcst/s
21:22:30     lo      0.00      0.00      0.00      0.00      0.00      0.00      0.00
21:22:30   eth0     68.00     65.00  63144.00  45731.00      0.00      0.00      0.00


21:22:30   IFACE   rxpck/s   txpck/s   rxbyt/s   txbyt/s   rxcmp/s   txcmp/s   rxmcst/s
21:22:31     lo      0.00      0.00      0.00      0.00      0.00      0.00      0.00
21:22:31   eth0     80.39     47.06  45430.39  30546.08      0.00      0.00      0.00


Average:   IFACE   rxpck/s   txpck/s   rxbyt/s   txbyt/s   rxcmp/s   txcmp/s   rxmcst/s
Average:     lo      0.00      0.00      0.00      0.00      0.00      0.00      0.00
Average:   eth0     74.26     55.94  54199.50  38063.37      0.00      0.00      0.00
```

In Listing 7.6, we examine the number of open sockets in the system. We can see the total number of open sockets and the TCP, RAW, and UDP sockets. sar also displays the number of fragmented IP packets.

Listing 7.6

```
[ezolt@wintermute sysstat-5.0.2]$ sar -n SOCK 1 2
Linux 2.4.22-1.2174.nptlsmp (wintermute.phil.org)        06/07/04
```

21:32:26	totsck	tcpsck	udpsck	rawsck	ip-frag
21:32:27	373	118	8	0	0
21:32:28	373	118	8	0	0
Average:	373	118	8	0	0

sar provides a good overview of the system's performance. However, when we are investigating a performance problem, we really want to understand what processes or services are consuming a particular resource. sar does not provide this level of detail, but it does enable us to observe the overall system network I/O statistics.

7.2.6 gkrellm

gkrellm is a graphical monitor that enables you to keep an eye on many different system performance statistics. It draws charts of different performance statistics, including CPU usage, disk I/O, and network usage. It can be "themed" to change its appearance, and even accepts plug-ins to monitor events not included in the default release.

gkrellm provides similar information to sar, ip, and ipconfig, but unlike the other tools, it provides a graphical view of the data. In addition, it can provide information about the traffic flowing through particular UDP and TCP ports. This is the first tool that we have seen that can show which services are consuming different amounts of network bandwidth.

7.2.6.1 Network I/O Performance-Related Options

gkrellm is invoked using the following command line:

```
gkrellm
```

None of gkrellm's command-line options configure the statistics that it monitors. You do all configurations graphically after gkrellm is started. To bring up the configuration screen, you can either right-click the gkrellm's title bar and select Configuration, or just press F1 when your cursor is in any area of the window. This brings up a configuration window (see Figure 7-1).

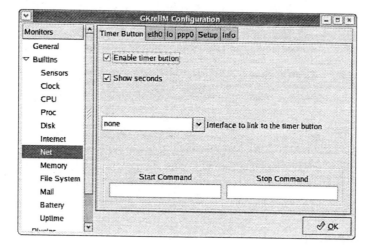

Figure 7-1

Figure 7-2 shows the network configuration window. It is used to configure which statistics and which devices are shown in the final gkrellm output window.

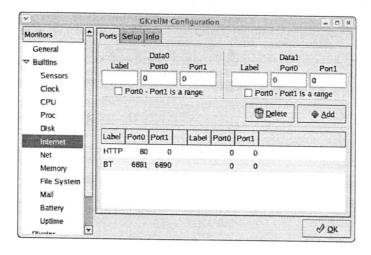

Figure 7-2

You can configure gkrellm to monitor the activity on a particular range of TCP ports. Doing so enables you to monitor the exact ports used by services such as HTTP or FTP and to measure the amount of bandwidth that they are using. In Figure 7-2, we have configured gkrellm to monitor the ports used by the bittorrent (BT) P2P application and the Web server (HTTP).

gkrellm is a flexible and powerful graphical performance-monitoring tool. It enables you to see how the system is currently performing and how its performance changes over time. The most difficult aspect of using gkrellm is reading the small default text. However, the appearance of gkrellm can be easily themed, so presumably, this could be easily fixed.

7.2.6.2 Example Usage

As stated previously, gkrellm can monitor many different types of events. In Figure 7-3, we pruned the output so that only statistics relevant to network traffic and use is displayed.

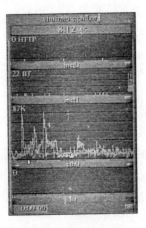

Figure 7-3

As you can see in Figure 7-3, the top two graphs are the bandwidth used for the ports (BT and HTTP) that we set up in the configuration section, and the bottom two graphics are the statistics for each of the network devices (eth0 and lo). There is a small amount of bittorrent (BT) traffic, but no Web server traffic (HTTP). The Ethernet device eth0 had some large activity in the past, but is settling down now. The lighter shade in the eth0 indicates the number of bytes received, and the darker shade indicates the number of bytes transmitted.

gkrellm is a powerful graphical tool that makes it easy to diagnose the status of the system at a glance.

7.2.7 iptraf

iptraf is a real-time network monitoring tool. It provides a large number of modes to monitor network interfaces and traffic. iptraf is a console application, but its user interface is a cursor-based series of menus and windows.

Like the other tools mentioned previously in this chapter, it can provide information about the rate at which each network device is sending frames. However, it can also display information about the type and size of the TCP/IP packet and about which ports are being used for network traffic.

7.2.7.1 Network I/O Performance-Related Options

iptraf is invoked with the following command line:

```
iptraf [-d interface] [-s interface] [-t <minutes>]
```

If iptraf is called with no parameters, it brings up a menu that enables you to select the interface to monitor and type of information that you want to monitor. Table 7-5 describes the command-line parameters that enable you to see the amount of network traffic on a particular interface or network service.

Table 7-5 iptraf Command-Line Options

Option	Explanation
-d interface	Detailed statistics for an interface including receive, transmit, and error rates
-s interface	Statistics about which IP ports are being used on an interface and how many bytes are flowing through them
-t <minutes>	Number of minutes that iptraf runs before exiting

iptraf has many more modes and configuration options. Read its included documentation for more information.

7.2.7.2 Example Usage

iptraf creates a display similar to Figure 7-4 when it is invoked with the following command:

```
[root@wintermute tmp]# iptraf -d eth0 -t 1
```

This command specifies that iptraf should display detailed statistics about Ethernet device eth0 and exit after it has run for 1 minute. In this case, we can see that 186.8kbps are received and 175.5kbps are transmitted by the eth0 network device.

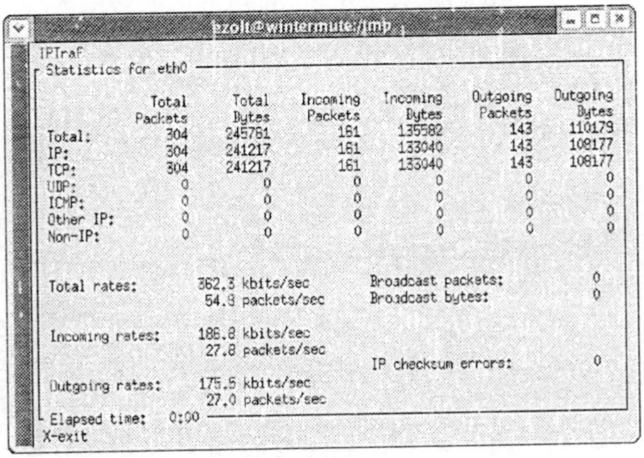

Figure 7-4

The next command, whose results are shown in Figure 7-5, asks iptraf to show information about the amount of network traffic from each UDP or TCP port. iptraf was invoked with the following command:

```
[root@wintermute etherape-0.9.0]# iptraf -s eth0 -t 10
```

Because the TCP or UDP ports of well-known services are fixed, you can use this to determine how much traffic each service is handling. Figure 7-5 shows that 29kb of HTTP data has been sent from eth0 and 25kb has been received.

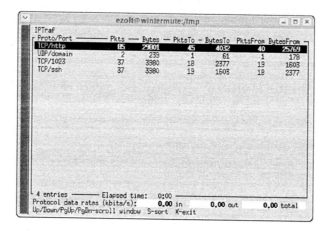

Figure 7-5

Because `iptraf` is a console-based application, it doesn't require an X server or X server libraries. Even though `iptraf` cannot be controlled with a mouse, it is easy to use and configurable.

7.2.8 netstat

`netstat` is a basic network-performance tool that is present on nearly every Linux machine with networking. You can use it to extract information about the number and types of network sockets currently being used and interface-specific statistics regarding the number of UDP or TCP packets flowing to and from the current system. It also enables you to trace the owner of a socket back to a particular process or PID, which can prove useful when trying to determine the application responsible for network traffic.

7.2.8.1 Network I/O Performance-Related Options

`netstat` is invoked with the following command line:

```
netstat [-p] [-c] [-interfaces=<name>] [-s] [-t] [-u] [-w]
```

If netstat is called without any parameters, it shows information about system-wide socket usage and displays information about both Internet and UNIX domain sockets. (UNIX domain sockets are used for interprocess communication on the local machine, but do not indicate network traffic.) To retrieve all the statistics that netstat is capable of displaying, you must run it as root. Table 7-6 describes the command-line options of netstat that modify the types of network statistics that netstat displays.

Table 7-6 *netstat* Command-Line Options

Option	Explanation
-p	Displays the PID/program name responsible for opening each of the displayed sockets
-c	Continually updates the display of information every second
--interfaces=<name>	Displays network statistics for the given interface
--statistics|-s	IP/UDP/ICMP/TCP statistics
--tcp|-t	Shows only information about TCP sockets
--udp|-u	Shows only information about UDP sockets.
--raw|-w	Shows only information about RAW sockets (IP and ICMP)

netstanetstat also accepts some command-line options not described here. See the netstat man page for more details.

7.2.8.2 Example Usage

Listing 7.7 asks netstat to show the active TCP connections and to continually update this information. Every second, netstat displays new TCP network statistics. netstat does not enable you to set the length of time that it will monitor, so it will only stop if it is killed or interrupted (Ctrl-C).

Listing 7.7

```
[root@wintermute ezolt]# netstat -t -c
Active Internet connections (w/o servers)
Proto Recv-Q Send-Q Local Address            Foreign Address          State
tcp       0      0 192.168.0.4:1023          fas.harvard.edu:ssh      ESTABLISHED
tcp       0      0 192.168.0.4:32844         216.239.39.147:http      TIME_WAIT
tcp       0      0 192.168.0.4:32843         216.239.39.147:http      TIME_WAIT
tcp       0      0 192.168.0.4:32853         skaiste.elekta.lt:http   ESTABLISHED
Active Internet connections (w/o servers)
Proto Recv-Q Send-Q Local Address            Foreign Address          State
tcp       0      0 192.168.0.4:1023          fas.harvard.edu:ssh      ESTABLISHED
tcp       0      0 192.168.0.4:32844         216.239.39.147:http      TIME_WAIT
tcp       0      0 192.168.0.4:32843         216.239.39.147:http      TIME_WAIT
tcp       0      0 192.168.0.4:32853         skaiste.elekta.lt:http   ESTABLISHED
```

Listing 7.8 asks netstat to once again print the TCP socket information, but this time, we also ask it to display the program that is responsible for this socket. In this case, we can see that SSH and mozilla-bin are the applications that are initiating the TCP connections.

Listing 7.8

```
[root@wintermute ezolt]# netstat -t -p
Active Internet connections (w/o servers)
Proto Recv-Q Send-Q Local Address       Foreign Address         State        PID/Program name
tcp       0      0 192.168.0.4:1023     fas.harvard.edu:ssh     ESTABLISHED  1463/ssh
tcp       0      0 192.168.0.4:32844    216.239.39.147:http     TIME_WAIT    -
tcp       0      0 192.168.0.4:32843    216.239.39.147:http     TIME_WAIT    -
tcp       0      0 192.168.0.4:32853    skaiste.elekta.lt:http  ESTABLISHED  1291/mozilla-bin
```

Listing 7.9 asks netstat to provide statistics about the UDP traffic that the system has received since boot.

Listing 7.9

```
[root@wintermute ezolt]# netstat -s -u
Udp:
    125 packets received
    0 packets to unknown port received.
    0 packet receive errors
    152 packets sent
```

Listing 7.10 asks netstat to provide information about the amount of network traffic flowing through the eth0 interface.

Listing 7.10

```
[root@wintermute ezolt]# netstat –interfaces=eth0
Kernel Interface table
Iface     MTU Met    RX-OK RX-ERR RX-DRP RX-OVR    TX-OK TX-ERR TX-DRP TX-OVR Flg
eth0      1500  0    52713      0      0      0    13711      1      0      1 BNRU
```

netstat provides a great number of network performance statistics about sockets and interfaces in a running Linux system. It is the only network-performance tool that maps the sockets used back to the PID of the process that is using it, and is therefore very useful.

7.2.9 etherape

etherape (a pun on the Windows-based network tool etherman) provides a visualization of the current network traffic. By default, it observes *all* the network traffic flowing on the network, not just those packets that the current machine is sending or receiving. However, it can be configured to only display network information for the current machine.

etherape is a little rough around the edges (in interface and documentation), but it provides a unique visual insight into how the network is connected, what types of services are being requested, and which nodes are requesting them. It creates a graph whose nodes represent the systems on the network. The nodes that are communicating have lines connecting them that increase in size as more network traffic flows between them. As a particular system's network usage increases, the size of the circle representing that system also increases. The lines connecting the different systems are colored differently depending on the protocols they are using to communicate with each other.

7.2.9.1 Network I/O Performance-Related Options

etherape uses the `libpcap` library to capture the network packets and, as a result, it must be run as root. etherape is invoked using the following command line:

```
etherape [-n] [-i <interface name>]
```

Table 7-7 describes some of the command-line options that change the interface that etherape monitors and whether resolved host names are printed on each node.

Table 7-7   *etherape* Command-Line Options

Option	Explanation
-n, --numeric	Shows only the IP number of the hosts rather than the resolved names
-i, --interface=<interface name>	Specifies the interface that will be monitored

All in all, etherape's documentation is rather sparse. The etherape man page describes a few more command lines that change its appearance and behavior, but the best way to learn it is to try it. In general, etherape is a great way to visualize the network.

7.2.9.2 Example Usage

Figure 7-6 shows etherape monitoring a relatively simple network. If we match up the color of the protocol to the color of the biggest circle, we see that this node is generating a high amount of SSH traffic. From the figure, it can be difficult to determine which node is causing this SSH traffic. Although not pictured, if we double-click the big circle, `etherape` creates a window with statistics pertaining to the node responsible for the traffic. We can use this to investigate each of the generators of network traffic and investigate their node names.

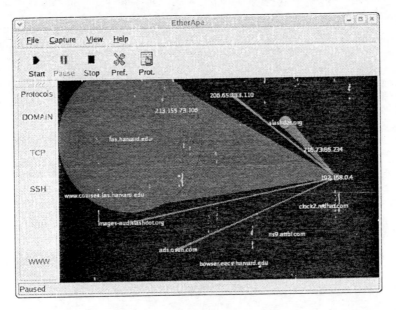

Figure 7-6

`etherape`'s output is periodically updated. As network traffic changes, its graph is updated. It can be fascinating just to watch the network traffic flow and see how it is used and changes over time.

7.3 Chapter Summary

This chapter provided information about how to use the Linux network performance tools to monitor the network traffic flowing through a system all the way from the low-level network interfaces to high-level applications. It introduced tools to query the current physical link settings (`mii-tool`, `ethtool`) and tools that monitor the amount and types of packets flowing through the low-level interfaces (`ifconfig`, `ip`, `sar`, `gkrellm`, `iptraf`, `netstat`, `etherape`). It then presented tools that display the different types of IP traffic (`gkrellm`, `iptraf`, `netstat`, `etherape`) and the amounts of each type of traffic (`gkrellm`, `iptraf`, `etherape`). This chapter then presented a tool (`netstat`) that maps the IP socket usage to the process that is receiving/sending each type of traffic. Finally, a network-visualization tool was presented that visualizes the relationship between the type and amount of data flowing through a network and which nodes it is flowing between (`etherape`).

The next chapters describe some of the common Linux tools that make using performance tools easier. They are not performance tools themselves, but they make using the performance tools more palatable. They can also help to visualize and analyze the results of the tools, as well as automate some of the more repetitive tasks.

8

Utility Tools: Performance Tool Helpers

This chapter provides informatiopn about the utilities available on a Linux system that can enhance the effectiveness and usability of the performance tools. The utility tools are not performance tools themselves, but when used with the performance tools, they can help automate tedious tasks, analyze performance statistics, and create performance tool-friendly applications.

After reading this chapter, you should be able to

* Automate the display and collection of periodic performance data (bash, watch).

* Record all commands and output displayed during a performance investigation (tee, script).

* Import, analyze, and graph performance data (gnumeric).

* Determine the libraries that an application is using (ldd).

* Determine which functions are part of which libraries (objdump).

* Investigate runtime characteristics of an application (gdb).

* Create performance tool/debugging-friendly applications (gcc).

8.1 Performance Tool Helpers

Linux has a rich heritage of tools that can be used together and become greater than the sum of the parts. Performance tools are no different. Although performance tools are useful on their own, combining them with other Linux tools can significantly boost their effectiveness and ease of use.

8.1.1 Automating and Recording Commands

As mentioned in an earlier chapter, one of the most valuable steps in a performance investigation is to save the commands that are issued and results that are generated during a performance investigation. This allows you to review them later and look for new insights. To help with this, Linux provides the `tee` command, which enables you to save tool output to a file, and the `script` command, which records every key press and every output displayed on the screen. This information can be saved and reviewed later or used to create a script to automate test execution.

It is important to automate commands because it reduces the chance of errors and enables you to think about the problem without having to remember all the details. Both the bash shell and the `watch` command enable you to periodically and automatically execute long and complicated command lines after typing them once. After you have the command line correct, `bash` and `watch` can periodically execute the command without the need to retype it.

8.1.2 Graphing and Analyzing Performance Statistics

In addition to the tools for recording and automation, Linux provides powerful analysis tools that can help you understand the implications of performance statistics. Whereas most performance tools generate performance statistics as text output, it is not always easy to see patterns and trends over time. Linux provides the powerful `gnumeric` spreadsheet, which can import, analyze, and graph performance data. When you graph the data, the cause of a performance problem may become apparent, or it may at least open up new areas of investigation.

8.1.3 Investigating the Libraries That an Application Uses

Linux also provides tools that enable you to determine which libraries an application relies on, as well as tools that display all the functions that a given library provides. The ldd command provides the list of all the shared libraries that a particular application is using. This can prove helpful if you are trying to track the number and location of the libraries that an application uses. Linux also provides the objdump command, which enables you to search through a given library or application to display all the functions that it provides. By combining the ldd and objdump commands, you can take the output of ltrace, which only provides the names of the functions that an application calls, and determine which library a given function is part of.

8.1.4 Creating and Debugging Applications

Finally, Linux also provides tools that enable you to create performance-tool-friendly applications, in addition to tools that enable you to interactively debug and investigate the attributes of running applications. The GNU compiler collection (gcc) can insert debugging information into applications that aid oprofile in finding the exact line and source file of a specific performance problem. In addition, the GNU debugger (gdb) can also be used to find information about running applications not available by default to various performance tools.

8.2 Tools

Used together, the following tools can greatly enhance the effectiveness and ease of use of the performance tools described in previous chapters.

8.2.1 bash

bash is the default Linux command-line shell, and you most likely use it every time you interact with the Linux command line. bash has a powerful scripting language that is typically used to create shell scripts. However, the scripting language can also be called from the command line and enables you to easily automate some of the more tedious tasks during a performance investigation.

8.2.1.1 Performance-Related Options

bash provides a series of commands that can be used together to periodically run a particular command. Most Linux users have bash as their default shell, so just logging in to a machine or opening a terminal brings up a bash prompt. If you are not using bash, you can invoke it by typing bash.

After you have a bash command prompt, you can enter a series of bash scripting commands to automate the continuous execution of a particular command. This feature proves most useful when you need to periodically extract performance statistics using a particular command. These scripting options are described in Table 8-1.

Table 8-1 *bash* Runtime Scripting Options

Option	Explanation
while condition	This executes a loop until the condition is false.
do	This indicates the start of a loop.
done	This indicates the end of a loop.

bash is infinitely flexible and is documented in the bash man page. Although bash's complexity can be overwhelming, it is not necessary to master it all to put bash immediately to use.

8.2.1.2 Example Usage

Although some performance tools, such as vmstat and sar, periodically display updated performance statistics, other commands, such as ps and ifconfig, do not. bash can call commands such as ps and ifconfig to periodically display their statistics. For example, in Listing 8.1, we ask bash to do something in a while loop based on the condition true. Because the true command is always true, the while loop will never exit. Next, the commands that will be executed after each iteration start after the do command. These commands ask bash to sleep for one second and then run ifconfig to extract performance information about the eth0 controller. However, because we are only interested in the received packets, we grep output of ifconfig for the string "RX packets". Finally, we issue the done command to tell bash we are done with the loop. Because the true command always returns true, this entire loop will run forever unless we interrupt it with a <Ctrl-C>.

Listing 8.1

```
[ezolt@wintermute tmp]$ while true; do sleep 1; /sbin/ifconfig eth0 | grep
"RX packets" ; done;
                    RX packets:2256178 errors:0 dropped:0 overruns:0 frame:0
                    RX packets:2256261 errors:0 dropped:0 overruns:0 frame:0
                    RX packets:2256329 errors:0 dropped:0 overruns:0 frame:0
                    RX packets:2256415 errors:0 dropped:0 overruns:0 frame:0
                    RX packets:2256459 errors:0 dropped:0 overruns:0 frame:0
. . .
```

With the bash script in Listing 8.1, you see network performance statistics updated every second. The same loop can be used to monitor other events by changing the ifconfig command to some other command, and the amount of time between updates can also be varied by changing the amount of sleep. This simple loop is easy to type directly into the command line and enables you to automate the display of any performance statistics that interest you.

8.2.2 tee

tee is a simple command that enables you to simultaneously save the standard output of a command to a file and display it. tee also proves useful when you want to save a performance tool's output and view it at the same time, such as when you are monitoring the performance statistics of a live system, but also storing them for later analysis.

8.2.2.1 Performance-Related Options

tee is invoked with the following command line:

```
<command> | tee [-a] [file]
```

tee takes the output provided by <command> and saves it to the specified file, but also prints it to standard output. If the -a option is specified, tee appends the output to the file instead of overwriting it.

8.2.2.2 Example Usage

Listing 8.2 shows tee being used to record the output of vmstat. As you can see, tee displays the output that vmstat has generated, but it also saves it in the file /tmp/vmstat_out. Saving the output of vmstat enables us to analyze or graph the performance data at a later date.

Listing 8.2

```
[ezolt@localhost book]$ vmstat 1 5 | tee /tmp/vmstat_out
procs ----------memory--------- ---swap-- -----io---- --system-- ----cpu----
 r  b   swpd   free   buff  cache   si   so    bi    bo   in    cs us sy id wa
 2  0 135832   3648  16112  95236    2    3    15    14   39   194  3  1 92  4
 0  0 135832   4480  16112  95236    0    0     0     0 1007  1014  7  2 91  0
 1  0 135832   4480  16112  95236    0    0     0     0 1002   783  6  2 92  0
 0  0 135832   4480  16112  95236    0    0     0     0 1005   828  5  2 93  0
 0  0 135832   4480  16112  95236    0    0     0     0 1056   920  7  3 90  0
```

tee is a simple command, but it is powerful because it makes it easy to record the output of a given performance tool.

8.2.3 script

The script command is used to save all the input and output generated during a shell session into a text file. This text file can be used later to both replay the executed commands and review the results. When investigating a performance problem, it is useful to have a record of the exact command lines executed so that you can later review the exact tests you performed. Having a record of the executed commands means that you also can easily cut and paste the command lines when investigating a different problem. In addition, it is useful to have a record of the performance results so that you can review them later when looking for new insights.

8.2.3.1 Performance-Related Options

script is a relatively simple command. When run, it just starts a new shell and records all the keystrokes and input and the output generated during the life of the shell into a text file. script is invoked with the following command line:

```
script [-a] [-t] [file]
```

By default, script places all the output into a file called typescript unless you specify a different one. Table 8-2 describes some of the command-line options of script.

Table 8-2 script Command-Line Options

Option	Explanation
-a	Appends the script output to the file instead of overwriting it.
-t	Adds timing information about the amount of time between each output/input. This prints the number of characters displayed and the amount of time elapsed between the display of each group of characters.
file	Name of the output file.

One word of warning: script literally captures every type of output that was sent to the screen. If you have colored or bold output, this shows up as esc characters within the output file. These characters can significantly clutter the output and are not usually useful. If you set the TERM environmental variable to dumb (using setenv TERM dumb for csh-based shells and export TERM=dumb for sh-based shells), applications will not output the escape characters. This provides a more readable output.

In addition, the timing information provided by `script` clutters the output. Although it can be useful to have automatically generated timing information, it may be easier to not use `script`'s timing, and instead just time the important commands with the `time` command mentioned in the previous chapter.

8.2.3.2 Example Usage

As stated previously, we will have more readable `script` output if we set the terminal to dumb. We can do that with the following command:

```
[ezolt@wintermute manuscript]$ export TERM=dumb
```

Next, we actually start the `script` command. Listing 8.3 shows `script` being started with an output file of `ps_output`. `script` continues to record the session until you exit the shell with the `exit` command or a <Ctrl-D>.

Listing 8.3

```
[ezolt@wintermute manuscript]$ script ps_output
Script started, file is ps_output
[ezolt@wintermute manuscript]$ ps
  PID TTY          TIME CMD
 4285 pts/1     00:00:00 bash
 4413 pts/1     00:00:00 ps
[ezolt@wintermute manuscript]$ Script done, file is ps_output
```

Next, in Listing 8.4, we look at the output recorded by `script`. As you can see, it contains all the commands and output that we generated.

Listing 8.4

```
[ezolt@wintermute manuscript]$ cat ps_output
Script started on Wed Jun 16 20:43:35 2004
[ezolt@wintermute manuscript]$ ps
  PID TTY          TIME CMD
```

```
4285 pts/1     00:00:00 bash
4413 pts/1     00:00:00 ps
[ezolt@wintermute manuscript]$
Script done on Wed Jun 16 20:43:41 2004
```

script is a great command to accurately record all interaction during a session. The files that script generates are tiny compared to the size of modern hard drives. Recording a performance investigation session and saving it for later review is always a good idea. At worst, it is a small amount of wasted effort and disk space to record the session. At best, the saved sessions can be looked at later and do not require you to rerun the commands recorded in that session.

8.2.4 watch

By default, the watch command runs a command every second and displays its output on the screen. watch is useful when working with performance tools that do not periodically display updated results. For example, some tools, such as ifconfig and ps, display the current performance statistics and then exit. Because watch periodically runs these commands and displays their output, it is possible to see by glancing at the screen which statistics are changing and how fast they are changing.

8.2.4.1 Performance-Related Options

watch is invoked with the following command line:

```
watch [-d[=cumulative]] [-n sec] <command>
```

If called with no parameters, watch just displays the output of the given command every second until you interrupt it. In the default output, it can often be difficult to see what has changed from screen to screen, so watch provides options that highlight the differences between each output. This can make it easier to spot the differences in output between each sample. Table 8-3 describes the command-line options that watch accepts.

Table 8-3 *watch* Command-Line Options

Option	Explanation
-d[=cumulative]	This option highlights the output that has changed between each sample. If the cumulative option is used, an area is highlighted if it has ever changed, not just if it has changed between samples.
-n sec	The number of seconds to wait between updates.

watch is a great tool to see how a performance statistic changes over time. It is not a complicated tool, but does its job well. It really fills a void when using performance tools that cannot periodically display updated output. When using these tools, you can run watch in a window and glance at it periodically to see how the statistic changes.

8.2.4.2 Example Usage

The first example, in Listing 8.5, shows watch being run with the ps command. We are asking ps to show us the number of minor faults that each process is generating. watch clears the screen and updates this information every 10 seconds. Note that it may be necessary to enclose the command that you want to run in quotation marks so that watch does not confuse the options of the command that you are trying to execute with its own options.

Listing 8.5

```
[ezolt@wintermute ezolt]$ watch  -n 10 "ps -o minflt,cmd"

Every 10s: ps -o minflt,cmd
Wed Jun 16 08:33:21 2004
MINFLT CMD
  1467 bash
    41 watch -n 1 ps -o minflt,cmd
    66 ps -o minflt,cmd
```

watch is a tool whose basic function could easily be written as a simple shell script. However, watch is easier than using a shell script because it is almost always available and just works. Remember that performance tools such as ifconfig or ps display statistics only once, whereas watch makes it easier to follow (with only a glance) how the statistics change.

8.2.5 gnumeric

When investigating a performance problem, the performance tools often generate vast amounts of performance statistics. It can sometimes be problematic to sort through this data and find the trends and patterns that demonstrate how the system is behaving. Spreadsheets in general, and gnumeric in particular, provide three different aspects that make this task easier. First, gnumeric provides built-in functions, such as max, min, average, and standard deviation, which enable you to numerically analyze the performance data. Second, gnumeric provides a flexible way to import the tabular text data commonly output by many performance tools. Finally, gnumeric provides a powerful graphing utility that can visualize the performance data generated by the performance tools. This can prove invaluable when searching for data trends over long periods of time. It is also especially useful when looking for correlations between different types of data (such as the correlation between disk I/O and CPU usage). It is often hard to see patterns in text output, but in graphical form, the system's behavior can be much clearer. Other spreadsheets, such as OpenOffice's oocalc, could also be used, but gnumeric's powerful text importer and graphing tools make it the easiest to use.

8.2.5.1 Performance-Related Options

To use a spreadsheet to assist in performance analysis, just follow these steps:

1. Save performance data into a text file.
2. Import the text file into gnumeric.
3. Analyze or graph the data.

gnumeric can generate many different types of graphs and has many different functions to analyze data. The best way to see gnumeric's power and flexibility is to load some data and experiment with it.

8.2.5.2 Example Usage

To demonstrate the usefulness of the gnumeric, we first have to generate performance data that we will graph or analyze. Listing 8.6 asks vmstat to generate 100 seconds of output and save that information in a text file called vmstat_output. This data will be loaded into gnumeric. The -n option tells vmstat to print only header information once (rather than after every screenful of information).

Listing 8.6

```
[ezolt@nohs ezolt]$ vmstat  -n 1 100 > vmstat_output
```

Next, we start gnumeric using the following command:

```
[ezolt@nohs ezolt]$ gnumeric &
```

This opens a blank spreadsheet where we can import the vmstat data.

Selecting File > Open in gnumeric brings up a dialog (not shown) that enables you to select both the file to open and the type of file. We select Text Import (Configurable) for file type, and we are guided through a series of screens to select which columns of the vmstat_output file map to which columns of the spreadsheet. For vmstat, it is useful to start importing at the second line of text, because the second line contains the names and sizing appropriate for each column. It is also useful to select Fixed-Width for importing the data because that is how vmstat outputs its data. After successfully importing the data, we see the spreadsheet in Figure 8-1.

Next, we graph the data that we have imported. In Figure 8-2, we create a stacked graph of the different CPU usages (us, sys, id, wa). Because these statistics should always total 100 percent (or close to it), we can see which state dominates at each time. In this case, the system is idle most of the time, but it has a big amount of wait time in the first quarter of the graph.

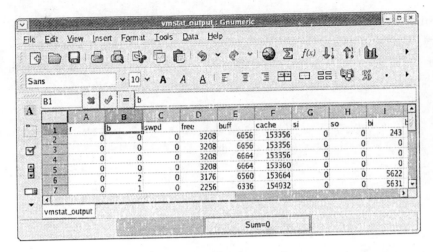

Figure 8-1

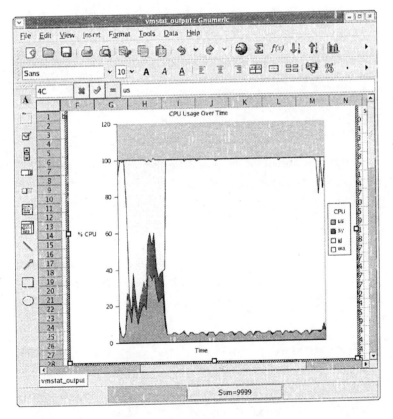

Figure 8-2

Graphs can be a powerful way to see how the performance statistics of a single run of a test change over time. It can also prove useful to see how different runs compare to each other. When graphing data from different runs, be sure to use the same scale for each of the graphs. This allows you to compare and contrast the data more easily.

gnumeric is a lightweight application that enables you to quickly and easily import and graph/analyze vast amounts of performance data. It is a great tool to play around with performance data to see whether any interesting characteristics appear.

8.2.6 ldd

ldd can be used to display which libraries a particular binary relies on. ldd helps track down the location of a library function that an application may be using. By figuring out all the libraries that an application is using, it is possible to search through each of them for the library that contains a given function.

8.2.6.1 Performance-Related Options

ldd is invoked with the following command line:

```
ldd <binary>
```

ldd then displays a list of all the libraries that this binary requires and which files in the system are fulfilling those requirements.

8.2.6.2 Example Usage

Listing 8.7 shows ldd being used on the ls binary. In this particular case, we can see that ls relies on the following libraries: linux-gate.so.1, librt.so.1, libacl.so.1, libselinux.so.1, libc.so.6, libpthread.so.0, ld-linux.so.2, and libattr.so.1.

Listing 8.7

```
[ezolt@localhost book]$ ldd /bin/ls
        linux-gate.so.1 =>  (0x00dfe000)
        librt.so.1 => /lib/tls/librt.so.1 (0x0205b000)
        libacl.so.1 => /lib/libacl.so.1 (0x04983000)
```

```
libselinux.so.1 => /lib/libselinux.so.1 (0x020c0000)
libc.so.6 => /lib/tls/libc.so.6 (0x0011a000)
libpthread.so.0 => /lib/tls/libpthread.so.0 (0x00372000)
/lib/ld-linux.so.2 => /lib/ld-linux.so.2 (0x00101000)
libattr.so.1 => /lib/libattr.so.1 (0x03fa4000)
```

ldd is a relatively simple tool, but it can be invaluable when trying to track down exactly which libraries an application is using and where they are located on the system.

8.2.7 objdump

objdump is a complicated and powerful tool for analyzing various aspects of binaries or libraries. Although it has many other capabilities, it can be used to determine which functions a given library provides.

8.2.7.1 Performance-Related Options

objdump is invoked with the following command line:

```
objdump -T <binary>
```

When object is invoked with the -T option, it displays all the symbols that this library/binary either relies on or provides. These symbols can be data structures or functions. Every line of the objdump output that contains .text is a function that this binary provides.

8.2.7.2 Example Usage

Listing 8.8 shows objdump used to analyze the gtk library. Because we are only interested in the symbols that libgtk.so provides, we use fgrep to prune the output to only those lines that contain .text. In this case, we can see that some of the functions that libgtk.so provides are gtk_arg_values_equal, gtk_tooltips_set_colors, and gtk_viewport_set_hadjustment.

Listing 8.8

```
[ezolt@localhost book]$ objdump -T /usr/lib/libgtk.so | fgrep .text
0384eb60 l    d  .text  00000000
0394c580 g    DF .text  00000209  Base        gtk_arg_values_equal
0389b630 g    DF .text  000001b5  Base        gtk_signal_add_emission_hook_full
0385cdf0 g    DF .text  0000015a  Base        gtk_widget_restore_default_style
03865a20 g    DF .text  000002ae  Base        gtk_viewport_set_hadjustment
03929a20 g    DF .text  00000112  Base        gtk_clist_columns_autosize
0389d9a0 g    DF .text  000001bc  Base        gtk_selection_notify
03909840 g    DF .text  000001a4  Base        gtk_drag_set_icon_pixmap
03871a20 g    DF .text  00000080  Base        gtk_tooltips_set_colors
038e6b40 g    DF .text  00000028  Base        gtk_hseparator_new
038eb720 g    DF .text  0000007a  Base        gtk_hbutton_box_set_layout_default
038e08b0 g    DF .text  000003df  Base        gtk_item_factory_add_foreign
03899bc0 g    DF .text  000001d6  Base        gtk_signal_connect_object_while_alive
....
```

When using performance tools (such as ltrace), which display the library functions an application calls (but not the libraries themselves), objdump helps locate the shared library each function is present in.

8.2.8 GNU Debugger (gdb)

gdb is a powerful application debugger that can help investigate many different aspects of a running application. gdb has three features that make it a valuable tool when diagnosing performance problems. First, gdb can attach to a currently running process. Second, gdb can display a backtrace for that process, which shows the current source line and the call tree. Attaching to a process and extracting a backtrace can be a quick way to find some of the more obvious performance problems. However, if the application is not stuck in a single location, it may be hard to diagnose the problem using gdb, and a system-wide profiler, such as oprofile, is a much better choice. Finally, gdb can map a virtual address back to a particular function. gdb may do a better job of figuring out the location of the virtual address than performance tools. For example, if oprofile gives information about where events occur in relation to a virtual address rather than a function name, gdb can be used to figure out the function for that address.

8.2.8.1 Performance-Related Options

gdb is invoked with the following command line, in which pid is the process that gdb will attach to:

```
gdb -p pid
```

After gdb has attached to the process, it enters an interactive mode in which you can examine the current execution location and runtime variables for the given process. Table 8-4 describes one of the commands that you can use to examine the running process.

Table 8-4 *gdb* Runtime Options

Option	Explanation
bt	This shows the backtrace for the currently executing process.

gdb has many more command-line options and runtime controls that are more appropriate for debugging rather than a performance investigation. See the gdb man page or type help at the gdb prompt for more information.

8.2.8.2 Example Usage

To examine how gdb works, it is useful to demonstrate it on a simple test application. The program in Listing 8.9 just calls function a() from main and spins in an infinite loop. The program will never exit, so when we attach to it with gdb, it should always be executing the infinite loop in function a().

Listing 8.9

```
void a(void)
{
  while(1);
}


main()
{
  a();
}
```

Listing 8.10 launches the application and attaches to its pid with gdb. We ask gdb to generate a backtrace, which shows us exactly what code is currently executing and, what set of function calls leads to the current location. As expected, gdb shows us that we were executing the infinite loop in a(), and that this was called from main().

Listing 8.10

```
[ezolt@wintermute examples]$ ./chew &
[2] 17389
[ezolt@wintermute examples]$ gdb -p 17389
GNU gdb Red Hat Linux (5.3.90-0.20030710.41rh)
Copyright 2003 Free Software Foundation, Inc.
GDB is free software, covered by the GNU General Public License, and you are
welcome to change it and/or distribute copies of it under certain conditions.
Type "show copying" to see the conditions.
There is absolutely no warranty for GDB.  Type "show warranty" for details.
This GDB was configured as "i386-redhat-linux-gnu".
Attaching to process 17389
Reading symbols from /usr/src/perf/utils/examples/chew...done.
Using host libthread_db library
"/lib/tls/libthread_db.so.1".
Reading symbols from /lib/tls/libc.so.6...done.
Loaded symbols for /lib/tls/libc.so.6
```

```
Reading symbols from /lib/ld-linux.so.2...done.
Loaded symbols for /lib/ld-linux.so.2
a () at chew.c:3
3           while(1);
(gdb) bt
#0  a () at chew.c:3
#1  0x0804832f in main () at chew.c:8
```

Finally, in Listing 8.11, we ask gdb to show us where the virtual address 0x0804832F is located, and gdb shows that that address is part of the function main.

Listing 8.11

```
(gdb) x 0x0804832f
0x804832f <main+21>:    0x9090c3c9
```

gdb is an extraordinarily powerful debugger and can be helpful during a performance investigation. It is even helpful after the performance problem has been identified, when you need to determine exactly why a particular code path was taken.

8.2.9 gcc (GNU Compiler Collection)

gcc is the most popular compiler used by Linux systems. Like all compilers, gcc takes source code (such as C, C++, or Objective-C) and generates binaries. It provides many options to optimize the resultant binary, as well as options that make it easier to track the performance of an application. The details of gcc's performance optimization options are not covered in this book, but you should investigate them when trying to increase an application's performance. gcc provides performance optimization options that enable you to tune the performance of compiled binaries using architecture generic optimizations (using -O1, -O2, -O3), architecture-specific optimizations (-march and -mcpu), and feedback-directed optimization (using -fprofile-arcs and -fbranch-probabilities). More details on each of the optimization options are provided in the gcc man page.

8.2.9.1 Performance-Related Options

gcc can be invoked in its most basic form as follows:

```
gcc [-g level] [-pg] -o prog_name source.c
```

gcc has an enormous number of options that influence how it compiles an application. If you feel brave, take a look at them in the gcc man page. The particular options that can help during a performance investigation are shown in Table 8-5.

Table 8-5 *gcc* Command-Line Options

Option	Explanation
-g[1 | 2 | 3]	The -g option adds debugging information to the binary with a default level of 2. If a level is specified, gcc adjusts the amount of debugging information stored in the binary. Level 1 provides only enough information to generate backtraces, but no information on the source-line mappings of particular lines of code. Level 3 provides more information than level 2, such as the macro definitions present in the source.
-pg	This turns on application profiling.

Many performance investigation tools, such as oprofile, require an application to be compiled with debugging information to map performance information back to a particular line of application source code. They will generally still work without the debugging information, but if debugging is enabled, they will provide richer information. Application profiling was described in more detail in a previous chapter.

8.2.9.2 Example Usage

Probably the best way to understand the type of debugging information that gcc can provide is to see a simple example. In Listing 8.12, we have the source for the C application, deep.c, which just calls a series of functions and then prints out the string "hi" a number of times depending on what number was passed in. The application's main function calls function a(), which calls function b() and then prints out "hi".

Listing 8.12

```
void b(int count)
{
  int i;
  for (i=0; i<count;i++)
    {printf("hi\n");}
}

void a(int count)
{
  b(count);
}

int main()
{
  a(10);
}
```

First, as shown in Listing 8.13, we compile the application without any debugging information. We then start the application in the debugger and add a breakpoint to the b() function. When we run the application, it stops at function b(), and we ask for a backtrace. gdb can figure out the backtrace, but it does not know what values were passed between functions or where the function exists in the original source file.

Listing 8.13

```
[ezolt@wintermute utils]$ gcc -o deep deep.c

[ezolt@wintermute utils]$ gdb ./deep
...
(gdb) break b
Breakpoint 1 at 0x804834e
(gdb) run
Starting program: /usr/src/perf/utils/deep
```

Listing 8.13   (Continued)

```
(no debugging symbols found)...(no debugging symbols found)...
Breakpoint 1, 0x0804834e in b ()
(gdb) bt
#0  0x0804834e in b ()
#1  0x08048389 in a ()
#2  0x080483a8 in main ()
```

In Listing 8.14, we compile the same application with debugging information turned on. Now when we run gdb and generate a backtrace, we can see which values were passed to each function call and the exact line of source where a particular line of code resides.

Listing 8.14

```
[ezolt@wintermute utils]$ gcc -g -o deep deep.c
[ezolt@wintermute utils]$ gdb ./deep
..
(gdb) break b
Breakpoint 1 at 0x804834e: file deep.c, line 3.
(gdb) run
Starting program: /usr/src/perf/utils/deep

Breakpoint 1, b (count=10) at deep.c:3
3           for (i=0; i<count;i++)
(gdb) bt
#0  b (count=10) at deep.c:3
#1  0x08048389 in a (count=10) at deep.c:9
#2  0x080483a8 in main () at deep.c:14
```

Debugging information can significantly add to the size of the final executable that gcc generates. However, the information that it provides is invaluable when tracking a performance problem.

8.3 Chapter Summary

This chapter provided a grab bag of Linux utility tools that are useful when investigating a performance problem. It introduced tools such as bash, watch, tee, and script, which automate the display and collection of performance data. It also introduced gnumeric, a tool that can both graph and analyze the results of text-based performance tools. It then investigated ldd and objdump, which can be used to track down which library a function is part of. It then described gdb, a tool that can investigate the execution and runtime information of currently running applications. Finally, this chapter described gcc, a tool that can produce binaries with symbolic debugging information that helps other performance tools, such as oprofile, to map events back to a specific source line.

In the upcoming chapters, we put together all the tools presented so far and solve some real-life performance problems.

9

Using Performance Tools to Find Problems

This chapter contains a method for using the previously presented performance tools together to narrow down the cause of a performance problem.

After reading this chapter, you should be able to

* Start with a misbehaving system and use the Linux performance tools to track down the misbehaving kernel functions or applications.

* Start with a misbehaving application and use the Linux performance tools to track down the misbehaving functions or source lines.

* Track down excess usage of the CPU, memory, disk I/O, and network.

9.1 Not Always a Silver Bullet

This chapter assumes that it is possible to solve a performance problem by changing software. Tuning an application or system to achieve a target performance goal is not always possible. If tuning fails, it may require a hardware upgrade or change. If the capacity of the system is maxed out, performance tuning only helps to a certain extent.

For example, it may be necessary (or even cheaper) to just upgrade the amount of system memory rather than track down which applications are using system memory, and then tune them so that they reduce their usage. The decision to just upgrade the system hardware rather than track down and tune a particular performance problem depends on the problem and is a value judgment of the individual investigating it. It really depends on which option is cheaper, either time-wise (to investigate the problem) or money-wise (to buy new hardware). Ultimately, in some situations, tuning will be the preferred or only option, so that is what this chapter describes.

9.2 Starting the Hunt

After you decide to start optimizing something on Linux, you first have to decide what you are going to optimize. The method used in this chapter covers some of the more common performance problems and an example shows you how to use the previously presented tools together to solve a problem. The next series of sections helps guide you in your discovery of the cause of a performance problem. In many sections you are asked to run various performance tools and jump to different sections in this chapter based on the results. This helps to pinpoint the source of the problem.

As stated in previous chapters, it is a good idea to save the results of each test that you perform. This enables you to review the results later and even to send the results to someone else if the investigation is inconclusive.

Let's get started.

When investigating a problem, it is best to start with a system that has as little unrelated programs running as possible, so close or kill any unneeded applications or processes. A clean system helps eliminate the potentially confusing interference caused by any extraneous applications.

If you have a specific application or program that is not performing as it should, jump to Section 9.3. If no particular application is sluggish and, instead, the entire Linux system is not performing as it should, jump to Section 9.4.

9.3 Optimizing an Application

When optimizing an application, several areas of the application's execution may present a problem. This section directs you to the proper section based on the problem that you are seeing.

Figure 9-1 shows the steps that we will take to optimize the application.

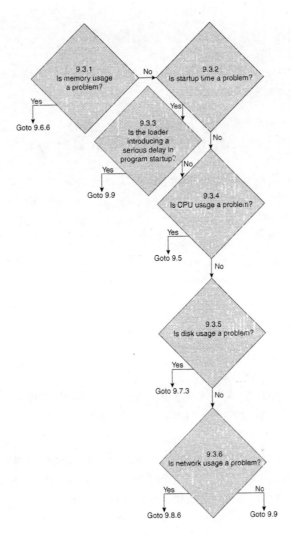

Figure 9-1

To start diagnosing, go to Section 9.3.1.

9.3.1 Is Memory Usage a Problem?

Use top or ps to determine how much memory the application is using. If the application is consuming more memory than it should, go to Section 9.6.6; otherwise, continue to Section 9.3.2.

9.3.2 Is Startup Time a Problem?

If the amount of time that the application takes to start up is a problem, go to Section 9.3.3; otherwise, go to Section 9.3.4.

9.3.3 Is the Loader Introducing a Delay?

To test whether the loader is a problem, set the `ld` environmental variables described in the previous chapters. If the `ld` statistics show a significant delay when mapping all the symbols, try to reduce the number and size of libraries that the application is using, or try to prelink the binaries.

If the loader does appears to be the problem, go to Section 9.9. If it does not, continue on to Section 9.3.4.

9.3.4 Is CPU Usage (or Length of Time to Complete) a Problem?

Use `top` or `ps` to determine the amount of CPU that the application uses. If the application is a heavy CPU user, or takes a particularly long time to complete, the application has a CPU usage problem.

Quite often, different parts of an application will have different performances. It may be necessary to isolate those parts that have poor performance so that their performance statistics are measured by the performance tools without measuring the statistics of those parts that do not have a negative performance impact. To facilitate this, it may be necessary to change an application's behavior to make it easier to profile. If a particular part of the application is performance-critical, when measuring the performance aspects of the total application, you would either try to measure *only* the performance statistics when the critical part is executing or make the performance-critical part run for such a long amount of time that the performance statistics from the uninteresting parts of the application are such a small part of the total performance statistics that they are irrelevant. Try to minimize the work that application is doing so that it only executes the performance-critical functions. For example, if we were collecting performance statistics from the entire run of an application, we would not want the startup and exit procedures to be a significant amount of the total time of the application runtime. In this case, it would be useful to start the application, run the time-consuming part many times, and then exit immediately. This allows the profilers (such as oprofile or gprof) to capture more information about slowly running code rather than parts that are executed but unrelated to the problem (such as launching and exiting). An even better solution is to change the application's source, so when the application is launched, the time-consuming portion is run automatically and then the program exits. This would help to minimize the profile data that does not pertain to the particular performance problem.

If the application's CPU usage is a problem, skip to Section 9.5. If it is not a problem, go to Section 9.3.5.

9.3.5 Is the Application's Disk Usage a Problem?

If the application is known to cause an unacceptable amount of disk I/O, go to Section 9.7.3 to determine what files it is accessing. If not, go to Section 9.3.6.

9.3.6 Is the Application's Network Usage a Problem?

If the application is known to cause an unacceptable amount of network I/O, go to Section 9.8.6.

Otherwise, you have encountered an application performance issue that is not covered in this book. Go to Section 9.9.

9.4 Optimizing a System

Sometimes, it is important to approach a misbehaving system and figure out exactly what is slowing everything down.

Because we are investigating a system-wide problem, the cause can be anywhere from user applications to system libraries to the Linux kernel. Fortunately, with Linux, unlike many other operating systems, you can get the source for most if not all applications on the system. If necessary, you can fix the problem and submit the fix to the maintainers of that particular piece. In the worst case, you can run a fixed version locally. This is the power of open-source software.

Figure 9-2 shows a flowchart of how we will diagnose a system-wide performance problem.

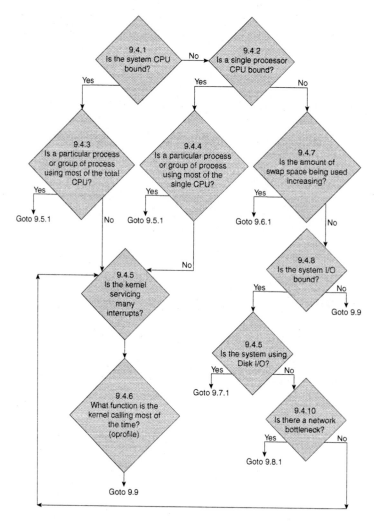

Figure 9-2

Go to Section 9.4.1 to begin the investigation.

9.4.1 Is the System CPU-Bound?

Use top, procinfo, or mpstat and determine where the system is spending its time. If the entire system is spending less than 5 percent of the total time in idle and wait modes, your system is CPU-bound. Proceed to Section 9.4.3. Otherwise, proceed to Section 9.4.2.

9.4.2 Is a Single Processor CPU-Bound?

Although the system as a whole may not be CPU-bound, in a symmetric multiprocessing (SMP) or hyperthreaded system, an individual processor may be CPU-bound.

Use top or mpstat to determine whether an individual CPU has less than 5 percent in idle and wait modes. If it does, one or more CPU is CPU-bound; in this case, go to Section 9.4.4.

Otherwise, nothing is CPU-bound. Go to Section 9.4.7.

9.4.3 Are One or More Processes Using Most of the System CPU?

The next step is to figure out whether any particular application or group of applications is using the CPU. The easiest way to do this is to run top. By default, top sorts the processes that use the CPU in descending order. top reports CPU usage for a process as the sum of the user and system time spent on behalf of that process. For example, if an application spends 20 percent of the CPU in user space code, and 30 percent of the CPU in system code, top will report that the process has consumed 50 percent of the CPU. Sum up the CPU time of all the processes. If that time is significantly less than the system-wide system plus user time, the kernel is doing significant work that is *not* on the behalf of applications. Go to Section 9.4.5.

Otherwise, go to Section 9.5.1 once for each process to determine where it is spending its time.

9.4.4 Are One or More Processes Using Most of an Individual CPU?

The next step is to figure out whether any particular application or group of applications is using the individual CPUs. The easiest way to do this is to run top. By default, top sorts the processes that use the CPU in descending order. When reporting CPU usage for a process, top shows the total CPU and system time that the application uses. For example, if an application spends 20 percent of the CPU in user space code, and 30 percent of the CPU in system code, top will report that the application has consumed 50 percent of the CPU.

First, run top, and then add the last CPU to the fields that top displays. Turn on Irix mode so that top shows the amount of CPU time used per processor rather than the total system. For each processor that has a high utilization, sum up the CPU time of the application or applications running on it. If the sum of the application time is less than 75 percent of the sum of the kernel plus user time for that CPU, it appears as the kernel is spending a significant amount of time on something other than the applications; in this case, go to Section 9.4.5. Otherwise, the applications are likely to be the cause of the CPU usage; for each application, go to Section 9.5.1.

9.4.5 Is the Kernel Servicing Many Interrupts?

It appears as if the kernel is spending a lot of time doing work not on behalf of an application. One explanation for this is an I/O card that is raising many interrupts, such as a busy network card. Run procinfo or cat /proc/interrupts to determine how many interrupts are being fired, how often they are being fired, and which devices are causing them. This may provide a hint as to what the system is doing. Record this information and proceed to Section 9.4.6.

9.4.6 Where Is Time Spent in the Kernel?

Finally, we will find out exactly what the kernel is doing. Run oprofile on the system and record which kernel functions consume a significant amount of time (greater than

10 percent of the total time). Try reading the kernel source for those functions or searching the Web for references to those functions. It might not be immediately clear what exactly those functions do, but try to figure out what kernel subsystem the functions are in. Just determining which subsystem is being used (such as memory, network, scheduling, or disk) might be enough to determine what is going wrong.

It also might be possible to figure out why these functions are called based on what they are doing. If the functions are device specific, try to figure out why the particular device is being used (especially if it also has a high number of interrupts). E-mail others who may have seen similar problems, and possibly contact kernel developers.

Go to Section 9.9.

9.4.7 Is the Amount of Swap Space Being Used Increasing?

The next step is the check whether the amount of swap space being used is increasing. Many of the system-wide performance tools such as `top`, `vmstat`, `procinfo`, and `gnome-system-info` provide this information. If the amount of swap is increasing, you need to figure out what part of the system is using more memory. To do this, go to Section 9.6.1.

If the amount of used swap is not increasing, go to Section 9.4.8.

9.4.8 Is the System I/O-Bound?

While running `top`, check to see whether the system is spending a high percentage of time in the wait state. If this is greater than 50 percent, the system is spending a large amount of time waiting for I/O, and we have to determine what type of I/O this is. Go to Section 9.4.9.

If the system is not spending a large amount of time waiting for I/O, you have reached a problem not covered in this book. Go to Section 9.9.

9.4.9 Is the System Using Disk I/O?

Next, run vmstat (or iostat) and see how many blocks are being written to and from the disk. If a large number of blocks are being written to and read from the disk, this may be a disk bottleneck. Go to Section 9.7.1. Otherwise, continue to Section 9.4.10.

9.4.10 Is the System Using Network I/O?

Next, we see whether the system is using a significant amount of network I/O. It is easiest to run iptraf, ifconfig, or sar and see how much data is being transferred on each network device. If the network traffic is near the capacity of the network device, this may be a network bottleneck. Go to Section 9.8.1. If none of the network devices seem to be passing network traffic, the kernel is waiting on some other I/O device that is not covered in this book. It may be useful to see what functions the kernel is calling and what devices are interrupting the kernel. Go to Section 9.4.5.

9.5 Optimizing Process CPU Usage

When a particular process or application has been determined to be a CPU bottleneck, it is necessary to determine where (and why) it is spending its time.

Figure 9-3 shows the method for investigating a processs CPU usage.

Go to Section 9.5.1 to begin the investigation.

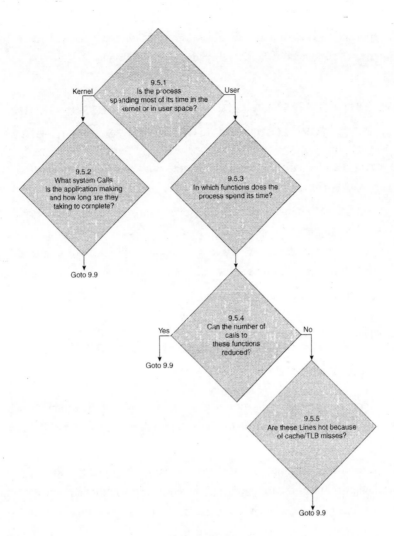

Figure 9-3

9.5.1 Is the Process Spending Time in User or Kernel Space?

You can use the time command to determine whether an application is spending its time in kernel or user mode. oprofile can also be used to determine where time is spent. By profiling per process, it is possible to see whether a process is spending its time in the kernel or user space.

If the application is spending a significant amount of time in kernel space (greater than 25 percent), go to Section 9.5.2. Otherwise, go to Section 9.5.3.

9.5.2 Which System Calls Is the Process Making, and How Long Do They Take to Complete?

Next, run `strace` to see which system calls are made and how long they take to complete. You can also run `oprofile` to see which kernel functions are being called.

It may be possible to increase performance by minimizing the number of system calls made or by changing which systems calls are made on behalf of the program. Some of the system's calls may be unexpected and a result of the application's calls to various libraries. You can run `ltrace` and `strace` to help determine why they are being made.

Now that the problem has been identified, it is up to you to fix it. Go to Section 9.9.

9.5.3 In Which Functions Does the Process Spend Time?

Next, run `oprofile` on the application using the cycle event to determine which functions are using all the CPU cycles (that is, which functions are spending all the application time).

Keep in mind that although `oprofile` shows you how much time was spent in a process, when profiling at the function level, it is not clear whether a particular function is hot because it is called very often or whether it just takes a long time to complete.

One way to determine which case is true is to acquire a source-level annotation from `oprofile` and look for instructions/source lines that should have little overhead (such as assignments). The number of samples that they have will approximate the number of times that the function was called relative to other high-cost source lines. Again, this is only approximate because `oprofile` samples only the CPU, and out-of-order processors can misattribute some cycles.

It is also helpful to get a call graph of the functions to determine how the hot functions are being called. To do this, go to Section 9.5.4.

9.5.4 What Is the Call Tree to the Hot Functions?

Next, you can figure out how and why the time-consuming functions are being called. Running the application with gprof can show the call tree for each function. If the time-consuming functions are in a library, you can use ltrace to see which functions. Finally, you can use newer versions of oprofile that support call-tree tracing. Alternatively, you can run the application in gdb and set a breakpoint at the hot function. You can then run that application, and it will break during every call to the hot function. At this point, you can generate a backtrace and see exactly which functions and source lines made the call.

Knowing which functions call the hot functions may enable you to eliminate or reduce the calls to these functions, and correspondingly speed up the application.

If reducing the calls to the time-consuming functions did not speed up the application, or it is not possible to eliminate these functions, go to Section 9.5.5.

Otherwise, go to Section 9.9.

9.5.5 Do Cache Misses Correspond to the Hot Functions or Source Lines?

Next, run oprofile, cachegrind, and kcache against your application to see whether the time-consuming functions or source lines are those with a high number of cache misses. If they are, try to rearrange or compress your data structures and accesses to make them more cache friendly. If the hot lines do not correspond to high cache misses, try to rearrange your algorithm to reduce the number of times that the particular line or function is executed.

In any event, the tools have told you as much as they can, so go to Section 9.9.

9.6 Optimizing Memory Usage

Often, it is common that a program that uses a large amount of memory can cause other performance problems to occur, such as cache misses, translation lookaside buffer (TLB) misses, and swapping.

Figure 9-4 shows the flowchart of decisions that we will make to figure out how the system memory is being used.

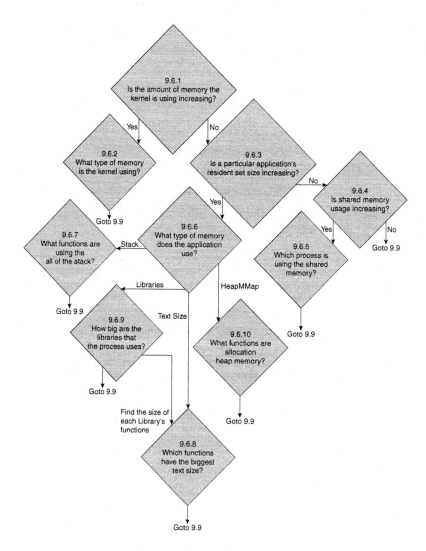

Figure 9-4

Go to Section 9.6.1 to start the investigation.

9.6.1 Is the Kernel Memory Usage Increasing?

To track down what is using the system's memory, you first have to determine whether the kernel itself is allocating memory. Run `slabtop` and see whether the total size of the kernel's memory is increasing. If it is increasing, jump to Section 9.6.2.

If the kernel's memory usage is not increasing, it may be a particular process causing the increase. To track down which process is responsible for the increase in memory usage, go to Section 9.6.3.

9.6.2 What Type of Memory Is the Kernel Using?

If the kernel's memory usage is increasing, once again run slabtop to determine what type of memory the kernel is allocating. The name of the slab can give some indication about why that memory is being allocated. You can find more details on each slab name in the kernel source and through Web searches. By just searching the kernel source for the name of that slab and determining which files it is used in, it may become clear why it is allocated. After you determine which subsystem is allocating all that memory, try to tune the amount of maximum memory that the particular subsystem can consume, or reduce the usage of that subsystem.

Go to Section 9.9.

9.6.3 Is a Particular Process's Resident Set Size Increasing?

Next, you can use top or ps to see whether a particular process's resident set size is increasing. It is easiest to add the rss field to the output of top and sort by memory usage. If a particular process is increasingly using more memory, we need to figure out what type of memory it is using. To figure out what type of memory the application is using, go to Section 9.6.6. If no particular process is using more memory, go to Section 9.6.4.

9.6.4 Is Shared Memory Usage Increasing?

Use ipcs to determine whether the amount of shared memory being used is increasing. If it is, go to Section 9.6.5 to determine which processes are using the memory. Otherwise, you have a system memory leak not covered in this book. Go to Section 9.9.

9.6.5 Which Processes Are Using the Shared Memory?

Use ipcs to determine which processes are using and allocating the shared memory. After the processes that use the shared memory have been identified, investigate the individual processes to determine why the memory is being using for each. For example, look in the application's source code for calls to shmget (to allocate shared memory) or shmat (to attach to it). Read the application's documentation and look for options that explain and can reduce the application's use of shared memory.

Try to reduce shared memory usage and go to Section 9.9.

9.6.6 What Type of Memory Is the Process Using?

The easiest way to see what types of memory the process is using is to look at its status in the /proc file system. This file, cat /proc/<pid>/status, gives a breakdown of the processs memory usage.

If the process has a large and increasing VmStk, this means that the processs stack size is increasing. To analyze why, go to Section 9.6.7.

If the process has a large VmExe, that means that the executable size is big. To figure out which functions in the executable contribute to this size, go to Section 9.6.8. If the process has a large VmLib, that means that the process is using either a large number of shared libraries or a few large-sized shared libraries. To figure out which libraries contribute to this size, go to Section 9.6.9. If the process has a large and increasing VmData, this means that the processs data area, or heap, is increasing. To analyze why, go to Section 9.6.10.

9.6.7 What Functions Are Using All of the Stack?

To figure out which functions are allocating large amounts of stack, we have to use gdb and a little bit of trickery. First, attach to the running process using gdb. Then, ask gdb for a backtrace using bt. Next, print out the stack pointer using info registers esp (on i386). This prints out the current value of the stack pointer. Now type up and print out the stack pointer. The difference (in hex) between the previous stack pointer and the current stack pointer is the amount of stack that the previous function is using. Continue this up the backtrace, and you will be able to see which function is using most of the stack.

When you figure out which function is consuming most of the stack, or whether it is a combination of functions, you can modify the application to reduce the size and number of calls to this function (or these functions). Go to Section 9.9.

9.6.8 What Functions Have the Biggest Text Size?

If the executable has a sizable amount of memory being used, it may be useful to determine which functions are taking up the greatest amount of space and prune unnecessary functionality. For an executable or library compiled with symbols, it is possible to ask nm to show the size of all the symbols and sort them with the following command:

```
nm -S -size-sort
```

With the knowledge of the size of each function, it may be possible to reduce their size or remove unnecessary code from the application.

Go to Section 9.9.

9.6.9 How Big Are the Libraries That the Process Uses?

The easiest way to see which libraries a process is using and their individual sizes is to look at the processs map in the /proc file system. This file, cat /proc/<pid>/map, will shows each of the libraries and the size of their code and data. When you know which libraries a process is using, it may be possible to eliminate the usage of large libraries or use alternative and smaller libraries. However, you must be careful, because removing large libraries may not reduce overall system memory usage.

If any other applications are using the library, which you can determine by running lsof on the library, the libraries will already be loaded into memory. Any new applications that use it do not require an additional copy of the library to be loaded into memory. Switching your application to use a different library (even if it is smaller) actually increases total memory usage. This new library will not be used by any other processes and will require new memory to be allocated. The best solution may be to shrink the size of the libraries themselves or modify them so that they use less memory to store library-specific data. If this is possible, all applications will benefit.

To find the size of the functions in a particular library, go to Section 9.6.8; otherwise, go to Section 9.9.

9.6.10 What Functions Are Allocating Heap Memory?

If your application is written in C or C++, you can figure out which functions are allocating heap memory by using the memory profiler memprof. memprof can dynamically show how memory usage grows as the application is used.

If your application is written in Java, add the -Xrunhprof command-line parameter to the java command line; it gives details about how the application is allocating memory. If your application is written in C# (Mono), add the -profile command-line parameter to the mono command line, and it gives details about how the application is allocating memory.

After you know which functions allocate the largest amounts of memory, it may be possible to reduce the size of memory that is allocated. Programmers often overallocate memory just to be on the safe side because memory is cheap and out-of-bounds errors are hard to detect. However, if a particular allocation is causing memory problems, careful analysis of the minimum allocation makes it possible to significantly reduce memory usage and still be safe. Go to Section 9.9.

9.7 Optimizing Disk I/O Usage

When you determine that disk I/O is a problem, it can be helpful to determine which application is causing the I/O.

Figure 9-5 shows the steps we take to determine the cause of disk I/O usage.

To begin the investigation, jump to Section 9.7.1

Figure 9-5

9.7.1 Is the System Stressing a Particular Disk?

Run iostat in the extended statistic mode and look for partitions that have an average wait (await) greater than zero. await is the average number of milliseconds that requests are waiting to be filled. The higher this number, the more the disk is overloaded. You can confirm this overload by looking at the amount of read and write traffic on a disk and determining whether it is close to the maximum amount that the drive can handle.

If many files are accessed on a single drive, it may be possible to increase performance by spreading out these files to multiple disks. However, it is first necessary to determine what files are being accessed.

Proceed to Section 9.7.2.

9.7.2 Which Application Is Accessing the Disk?

As mentioned in the chapter on disk I/O, this is where it can be difficult to determine which process is causing a large amount of I/O, so we must try to work around the lack of tools to do this directly. By running `top`, you first look for processes that are nonidle. For each of these processes, proceed to Section 9.7.3.

9.7.3 Which Files Are Accessed by the Application?

First, use `strace` to trace all the system calls that an application is making that have to do with file I/O, using `strace -e trace=file`. We can then `strace` using summary information to see how long each call is taking. If certain read and write calls are taking a long time to complete, this process may be the cause of the I/O slowdown. By running `strace` in normal mode, it is possible to see which file descriptors it is reading and writing from. To map these file descriptors back to files on a file system, we can look in the `proc` file system. The files in `/proc/<pid>/fd/` are symbolic links from the file descriptor number to the actual files. An `ls -la` of this directory shows which files this process is using. By knowing which files the process is accessing, it might be possible to reduce the amount of I/O the process is doing, spread it more evenly between multiple disks, or even move it to a faster disk.

After you determine which files the process is accessing, go to Section 9.9.

9.8 Optimizing Network I/O Usage

When you know that a network problem is happening, Linux provides a set of tools to determine which applications are involved. However, when you are connected to external machines, the fix to a network problem is not always within your control.

Figure 9-6 shows the steps that we take to investigate a network performance problem.

To start the investigation, continue to Section 9.8.1.

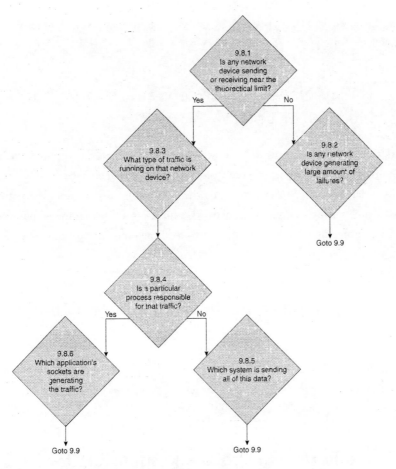

Figure 9-6

9.8.1 Is Any Network Device Sending/Receiving Near the Theoretical Limit?

The first thing to do is to use ethtool to determine what hardware speed each Ethernet device is set to. If you record this information, you then investigate whether any of the network devices are saturated. Ethernet devices and/or switches can be easily mis-configured, and ethtool shows what speed each device believes that it is operating at. After you determine the theoretical limit of each of the Ethernet devices, use iptraf (of even ifconfig) to determine the amount of traffic that is flowing over each interface.

If any of the network devices appear to be saturated, go to Section 9.8.3; otherwise, go to Section 9.8.2.

9.8.2 Is Any Network Device Generating a Large Number of Errors?

Network traffic can also appear to be slow because of a high number of network errors. Use ifconfig to determine whether any of the interfaces are generating a large number of errors. A large number of errors can be the result of a mismatched Ethernet card / Ethernet switch setting. Contact your network administrator, search the Web for people with similar problems, or e-mail questions to one of the Linux networking newsgroups.

Go to Section 9.9.

9.8.3 What Type of Traffic Is Running on That Device?

If a particular device is servicing a large amount of data, use iptraf to track down what types of traffic that device is sending and receiving. When you know the type of traffic that the device is handling, advance to Section 9.8.4.

9.8.4 Is a Particular Process Responsible for That Traffic?

Next, we want to determine whether a particular process is responsible for that traffic. Use netstat with the -p switch to see whether any process is handling the type of traffic that is flowing over the network port.

If an application is responsible, go to Section 9.8.6. If none are responsible, go to Section 9.8.5.

9.8.5 What Remote System Is Sending the Traffic?

If no application is responsible for this traffic, some system on the network may be bombarding your system with unwanted traffic. To determine which system is sending all this traffic, use `iptraf` or `etherape`.

If it is possible, contact the owner of this system and try to figure out why this is happening. If the owner is unreachable, it might be possible to set up `ipfilters` within the Linux kernel to always drop this particular traffic, or to set up a firewall between the remote machine and the local machine to intercept the traffic.

Go to Section 9.9.

9.8.6 Which Application Socket Is Responsible for the Traffic?

Determining which socket is being used is a two-step process. First, we can use `strace` to trace all the I/O system calls that an application is making by using `strace -e trace=file`. This shows which file descriptors the process is reading and writing from. Second, we map these file descriptors back to a socket by looking in the `proc` file system. The files in `/proc/<pid>/fd/` are symbolic links from the file descriptor number to the actual files or sockets. An `ls -la` of this directory shows all the file descriptors of this particular process. Those with `socket` in the name are network sockets. You can then use this information to determine inside the program which socket is causing all the communication.

Go to Section 9.9.

9.9 The End

When you finally arrive here, your problem may or may not be solved, but you will have a lot of information characterizing it. Search the Web and newsgroups for people with similar problems. E-mail them and developers to see how they resolved it. Try a solution and see whether the system's or application's behavior has changed. Every time you try a new solution, jump to Section 9.2 to diagnose the system again, because the application's behavior may change with every fix.

9.10 Chapter Summary

This chapter provided a method for using the Linux performance tools together to track down different types of performance problems. Although it is not possible to capture every type of performance problem that could go wrong, this methodology helps you find some of the more common problems. In addition, if the problem that you face is not covered here, the data that you collect will still be useful because it might open up different areas of investigation.

The next few chapters show this method being used to find performance problems on a Linux system.

10

Performance Hunt 1: A CPU-Bound Application (GIMP)

This chapter contains an example of how to use the Linux performance tools to find and fix performance problems in a CPU-bound application.

After reading this chapter, you should be able to

* Figure out which source lines are using all the CPU in a CPU-bound application.

* Use ltrace and oprofile to figure out how often an application is calling various internal and external functions.

* Look for patterns in the applications source, and search online for information about how an application behaves and possible solutions.

* Use this chapter as a template for tracking down a CPU-related performance problem.

10.1 CPU-Bound Application

In this chapter, we investigate an application that is CPU-bound. It is important to be able to optimize a CPU-bound application because it is one of the most common performance problems.

It is also usually the final frontier for a heavily tuned application.

As the disk and network bottlenecks are removed, the application becomes CPU-bound. In addition, it is often easier to buy faster disks or more memory than to upgrade a CPU, so if a process is CPU-bound, it is an important skill to be able to hunt down and fix a CPU performance problem rather than just buy a new system.

10.2 Identify a Problem

The first step in a performance hunt it to identify a problem to investigate. In this case, I chose to investigate a performance problem that crops up when using GIMP, an open-source image-manipulation program. GIMP can slice and dice various aspects of an image, but it also has a powerful set of filters that can warp and change an image in a variety of ways. These filters can change the appearance of the image based on some complicated algorithms. Typically, the filters take a long time to complete and are very CPU-intensive. One of the filters in particular, Van Gogh (LIC), takes an input image and modifies it so that it looks like a painting done in the style of Van Gogh. This filter takes a particularly long amount of time to complete. When running, the filter uses nearly 100 percent of CPU and takes several minutes to complete. The amount of time to complete depends on the size of the image, the machine's CPU speed, and the values of the parameters passed into the filter. In this chapter, we investigate why this filter is so slow using Linux performance tools and see whether there is any way to speed it up.

10.3 Find a Baseline/Set a Goal

This first step in any performance hunt is to determine the current state of the problem. In the case of the GIMP filter, we need to figure out how much time it takes to run on a particular image. This is our baseline time. Once we have this baseline time, we can then try an optimization and see whether it decreases the execution time. Sometimes, it can be tricky to time how long something takes to execute. It is not as easy as using a stopwatch because the operating system may be scheduling other tasks at the same time that our particularly CPU-intensive job is running. In this case, if other jobs are running in addition to the CPU-intensive one, the amount of wall-clock time could be much greater than the amount of CPU time that the process actually uses. In this case, we are lucky; by looking at top as the filter is running, we can see that the lic process is taking up most of the CPU usage, as shown in Listing 10.1.

Listing 10.1

```
[ezolt@localhost ktracer]$ top

top - 08:24:48 up 7 days,  9:08,  6 users,  load average: 1.04, 0.64, 0.76

  PID USER      PR  NI  VIRT  RES  SHR S %CPU %MEM   TIME+  COMMAND
32744 ezolt     25   0 53696  45m  11m R 89.6 14.6   0:16.00 lic
 2067 root      15   0 69252  21m  17m S  6.0  6.8 161:56.22 X
32738 ezolt     15   0 35292  27m  14m S  2.3  8.7   0:05.08 gimp
```

From this, we can deduce that GIMP actually spawns a separate process to run when running the filter. So when the filter is running, we can then use ps to track how much CPU time the process is using and when it has finished. When we have the PID of the filter using top, we can run the loop in Listing 10.2 and ask ps to periodically observe how much CPU time the filter is using.

Listing 10.2

```
while true ; do sleep 1 ; ps  32744; done
  PID TTY      STAT   TIME COMMAND
32744 pts/0    R      2:46 /usr/local/lib/gimp/2.0/plug-ins/lic -gimp 8 6 -run 0
```

note

> If you need to time an application but do not have a stopwatch, you can use time and cat as a simple stopwatch. Just type time cat when you want to start timing, and then press <Ctrl-D> when you are finished. time shows you how much time has passed.

When running the lic filter on the reference image (which is a fetching picture of my basement) and using the ps method just mentioned to time the filter, we can see from Listing 10.2 that it takes 2 minutes and 46 seconds to run on the entire image. This time is our baseline time. Now that we know the amount of time that the filter takes to run out of the box, we can set our goal for the performance hunt. It is not always clear how to set a reasonable goal for a performance investigation. A reasonable value for a goal can depend on several factors, including the amount of tuning that has already been done on the particular problem and the requirements of the user. It is often best to set the goal based on another quicker-performance application that does a similar thing. Unfortunately, we do not know of any GIMP filters that do similar work, so we have to make a guess. Because a 5 or 10 percent gain in performance is usually a reasonable goal for a relatively untuned piece of code, we'll set a goal of a 10 percent speedup, or a run-time of 2 minutes and 30 seconds.

Now that we have picked our goal, we need a way to guarantee that our performance optimizations are not unacceptably changing the results of the filter. In this case, we will run the original filter on the reference image and save the result into another file. We can then compare the output of our optimized filter to the output of the original filter and see whether the optimizations have changed the output.

10.4 Configure the Application for the Performance Hunt

The next step in our investigation is to set up the application for the performance hunt by recompiling the application with symbols. Symbols allow the performance tools (such as `oprofile`) to investigate which functions and source lines are responsible for all the CPU time that is being spent.

For the GIMP, we download the latest GIMP tarball from its Web site, and then recompile it. In the case of GIMP and much open-source software, the first step in recompilation is running the `configure` command, which generates the makefiles that will be used to build the application. The `configure` command passes any flags present in the `CFLAGS` environmental variable into the makefile. In this case, because we want the GIMP to be built with symbols, we set the `CFLAGS` variable to contain `-g3`. This causes symbols to be included in the binaries that are built. This command is shown in Listing 10.3 and overrides the current value of the `CFLAGS` environmental variable and sets it to `-g3`.

Listing 10.3

```
[root@localhost gimp-2.0.3]# env CFLAGS=-g3 ./configure
```

We then make and install the version of GIMP with all the symbols included, and when we run this version, the performance tools will tell us where time is being spent.

10.5 Install and Configure Performance Tools

The next step in the hunt is to install the performance tools if they are not already installed. Although this might seem like an easy thing to do, it often involves chasing down custom-made packages for a distribution or even recompiling the tools from scratch. In this case, we are going to use oprofile on Fedora Core 2, so we have to track down both the oprofile kernel module, which in Fedora's case, is only included in the symmetric multiprocessing (SMP) kernels and the oprofile package. It also may be interesting to use the ltrace performance tool to see which library functions are called and how often they are being called. Fortunately, ltrace is included in Fedora Core 2, so we do not have to track it down.

10.6 Run Application and Performance Tools

Next, we run the application and take measurements using the performance tools. Because the lic filter is called directly from the GIMP, we have to use tools that can attach and monitor an already running process.

In the case of oprofile, we can start oprofile, run the filter, and then stop oprofile after the filter has been completed. Because the lic filter takes up approximately 90 percent of the CPU when running, the system-wide samples that oprofile collects will be mainly relevant for the lic filter. When lic starts to run, we start oprofile in another window; when lic finishes in that other window, we stop oprofile. The starting and stopping of oprofile is shown in Listing 10.4.

Listing 10.4

```
[root@localhost ezolt]# opcontrol --start
Profiler running.
[root@localhost ezolt]# opcontrol --dump
[root@localhost ezolt]# opcontrol --stop
Stopping profiling.
```

ltrace must be run a little differently. After the filter has been started, ltrace can be attached to the running process. Unlike oprofile, attaching ltrace to a process brings the entire process to a crawl. This can inaccurately inflate the amount of time taken for each library call; however, it provides information about the number of times each call is made. Listing 10.5 shows a listing from ltrace.

Listing 10.5

```
[ezolt@localhost ktracer]$ ltrace -p 32744 -c

% time     seconds  usecs/call     calls      function
------ ----------- ----------- --------- --------------------
 43.61  156.419150         254    614050 rint
 16.04   57.522749         281    204684 gimp_rgb_to_hsl
 14.92   53.513609         261    204684 g_rand_double_range
 13.88   49.793988         243    204684 gimp_rgba_set_uchar
 11.55   41.426779         202    204684 gimp_pixel_rgn_get_pixel
  0.00    0.006287        6287         1 gtk_widget_destroy
  0.00    0.003702        3702         1 g_rand_new
  0.00    0.003633        3633         1 gimp_progress_init
  0.00    0.001915        1915         1 gimp_drawable_get
  0.00    0.001271        1271         1 gimp_drawable_mask_bounds
  0.00    0.000208         208         1 g_malloc
  0.00    0.000110         110         1 gettext
  0.00    0.000096          96         1 gimp_pixel_rgn_init
------ ----------- ----------- --------- --------------------
100.00  358.693497              1432794 total
```

To get the full number of library calls, it is possible to let ltrace run until completion; however, it takes a really long time, so in this case, we pressed <Ctrl-C> after a long period of time had elapsed. This will not always work, because an application may go through different stages of execution, and if you stop it early, you may not have a complete picture of what functions the application is calling. However, this short sample will at least give us a starting point for analysis.

10.7 Analyze the Results

Now that we have used oprofile to collect information about where time is spent when the filter is running, we have to analyze the results to look for ways to change its execution and increase performance.

First, we use oprofile to look at how the entire system was spending time. This is shown in Listing 10.6.

Listing 10.6

```
[root@localhost ezolt]# opreport -f | less

CPU: CPU with timer interrupt, speed 0 MHz (estimated)
Profiling through timer interrupt
          TIMER:0|
  samples|        %|
------------------
    69896 36.9285 /usr/local/lib/libgimp-2.0.so.0.0.3
    44237 23.3719 /usr/local/lib/libgimpcolor-2.0.so.0.0.3
    28386 14.9973 /usr/local/lib/gimp/2.0/plug-ins/lic
    16133  8.5236 /usr/lib/libglib-2.0.so.0.400.0
....
```

As Listing 10.6 shows, 75 percent of the CPU time was spent in the lic process or GIMP-related libraries. Most likely, these libraries are called by the lic process, a fact that we can confirm by combining the information that ltrace gives us with the information from `oprofile`. Listing 10.7 shows the library calls made for a small portion of the run of the filter.

Listing 10.7

```
[ezolt@localhost ktracer]$ ltrace -p 32744 -c
% time     seconds  usecs/call     calls      function
------ ----------- ----------- --------- --------------------
 46.13  101.947798         272    374307 rint
 15.72   34.745099         278    124862 g_rand_double_range
 14.77   32.645236         261    124862 gimp_pixel_rgn_get_pixel
 13.01   28.743856         230    124862 gimp_rgba_set_uchar
 10.36   22.905472         183    124862 gimp_rgb_to_hsl
  0.00    0.006832        6832         1 gtk_widget_destroy
  0.00    0.003976        3976         1 gimp_progress_init
  0.00    0.003631        3631         1 g_rand_new
  0.00    0.001992        1992         1 gimp_drawable_get
  0.00    0.001802        1802         1 gimp_drawable_mask_bounds
  0.00    0.000184         184         1 g_malloc
  0.00    0.000118         118         1 gettext
  0.00    0.000100         100         1 gimp_pixel_rgn_init
------ ----------- ----------- --------- --------------------
100.00  221.006096                873763 total
```

Next, we investigate the information that `oprofile` gives us about where CPU time is being spent in each of the libraries, and see whether the hot functions in the libraries are the same as those that the filter calls. For each of the three top CPU-using images, we ask `opreport` to give us more details about which functions in the library are spending all the time. The results are shown in Listing 10.8 for the `libgimp`, `libgimp-color` libraries, and the `lic` process.

Listing 10.8

```
[/tmp]# opreport -lf /usr/local/lib/libgimp-2.0.so.0.0.3
CPU: CPU with timer interrupt, speed 0 MHz (estimated)
Profiling through timer interrupt
```

```
samples    %           symbol name
27136      38.8234     gimp pixel_rgn_get_pixel
14381      20.5749     gimp drawable_get_tile2
6571        9.4011     gimp tile_unref
6384        9.1336     gimp drawable_get_tile
3921        5.6098     gimp tile_cache_insert
3322        4.7528     gimp tile_ref
3057        4.3736     anonymous symbol from section .plt
2732        3.9087     gimp tile_width
1998        2.8585     gimp tile_height
...


[/tmp]# opreport -lf /usr/local/lib/libgimpcolor-2.0.so.0.0.3
CPU: CPU with timer interrupt, speed 0 MHz (estimated)
Profiling through timer interrupt
samples    %           symbol name
31475      71.1508     gimp rgba_set_uchar
6251       14.1307     gimp bilinear_rgb
2941        6.6483     gimp rgb_multiply
2394        5.4118     gimp rgb_add
466         1.0534     gimp rgba_get_uchar
323         0.7302     gimp rgb_to_hsl
....


[/tmp]# opreport -lf /usr/local/lib/gimp/2.0/plug-ins/lic
CPU: CPU with timer interrupt, speed 0 MHz (estimated)
Profiling through timer interrupt
samples    %           symbol name
11585      40.8124     getpixel
5185       18.2660     lic_image
4759       16.7653     peek
3287       11.5797     filter
1698        5.9818     peekmap
1066        3.7554     anonymous symbol from section .plt
```

continues

Listing 10.8   (Continued)

```
316     1.1132  compute_lic
232     0.8173  rgb_to_hsl
111     0.3910  grady
106     0.3734  gradx
41      0.1444  poke
....
```

As you can see by comparing the output of ltrace in Listing 10.8, and the oprofile output in Listing 10.9, the lic filter is repeatedly calling the library functions that are spending all the time.

Next, we investigate the source code of the lic filter to determine how it is structured, what exactly its hot functions are doing, and how the filter calls the GIMP library functions. The lic function that generated the most samples is the getpixel function, shown by the opannotate output in Listing 10.9. opannotate shows the number of samples, followed by the total percentage of samples in a column to the left of the source. This enables you to look through the source and see which exact source lines are hot.

Listing 10.9

```
opannotate --source /usr/local/lib/gimp/2.0/plug-ins/lic
....
                :static void
                :getpixel (GimpPixelRgn *src_rgn,
                :          GimpRGB      *p,
                :          gdouble      u,
                :          gdouble      v)
    428  1.5961 :{ /* getpixel total:   11198 41.7587 */
                : register gint x1, y1, x2, y2;
                : gint width, height;
                : static GimpRGB pp[4];
                :
     98  0.3655 : width = src_rgn->w;
     72  0.2685 : height = src_rgn->h;
```

```
                :
1148   4.2810 :   x1 = (gint)u;
1298   4.8404 :   y1 = (gint)v;
                :
 603   2.2487 :   if (x1 < 0)
   1   0.0037 :     x1 = width - (-x1 % width);
                :   else
1605   5.9852 :     x1 = x1 % width;
                :
  87   0.3244 :   if (y1 < 0)
                :     y1 = height - (-y1 % height);
                :   else
1264   4.7136 :     y1 = y1 % height;
                :
1358   5.0641 :   x2 = (x1 + 1) % width;
1379   5.1425 :   y2 = (y1 + 1) % height;
                :
 320   1.1933 :   peek (src_rgn, x1, y1, &pp[0]);
 267   0.9957 :   peek (src_rgn, x2, y1, &pp[1]);
 285   1.0628 :   peek (src_rgn, x1, y2, &pp[2]);
 244   0.9099 :   peek (src_rgn, x2, y2, &pp[3]);
                :
 706   2.6328 :   *p = gimp_bilinear_rgb (u, v, pp);
  35   0.1305 :}
...
```

There are a few interesting things to note about the get_pixel function. First, it calls the gimp_bilinear_rgb function, which is one of the hot functions in the GIMP libraries. Second, it calls the peek function four times. If the get_pixel call is executed many times, the peek function is executed four times as much. Using opannotate to look at the peek function (shown in Listing 10.10), we can see that it calls gimp_pixel_rgn_get_pixel and gimp_rgba_set_uchar, which are top functions for libgimp and libgimp-color respectively.

Listing 10.10

```
           :static void
           :peek (GimpPixelRgn *src_rgn,
           :          gint          x,
           :          gint          y,
           :          GimpRGB       *color)
    481  1.7937 :{ /* peek total:    4485 16.7251 */
           :  static guchar data[4] = { 0, };
           :
   1373  5.1201 :  gimp_pixel_rgn_get_pixel (src_rgn, data, x, y);
   2458  9.1662 :  gimp_rgba_set_uchar (color, data[0], data[1], data[2],
data[3]);
    173  0.6451 :}
```

Although it is not quite clear exactly what the filter is doing or what the library calls are used for, there are a few curious points. First, peek sounds like a function that would retrieve pixels from the image so that the filter can process them. We can check this hunch shortly. Second, most of the time spent in the filter does not appear to be spent running a mathematical algorithm on the image data. Instead of spending all the CPU time running calculations based on the values of the pixels, this filter appears to spend most of the time retrieving pixels to be manipulated. If this is really the case, perhaps it can be fixed.

10.8 Jump to the Web

Now that we have found which GIMP functions are used for much of the time, we have to figure out exactly what these functions are and possibly optimize their use.

First, we search the Web for pixel_rgn_get_pixel and try to determine what it does. After a few false starts, the following link and information revealed in Listing 10.11 confirm our suspicions about what pixel_rgn_get_pixel does.

Listing 10.11

"There are calls for pixel_rgn_get_ pixel, row, col, and rect, which grab data from the image and dump it into a buffer that you've pre-allocated. And there are set calls to match. Look for "Pixel Regions" in gimp.h." (from http://gimp-plug-ins.sourceforge.net/doc/Writing/html/sect-image.html)

In addition, the information in Listing 10.12 suggests that it is a good idea to avoid using pixel_rgn_get_ calls.

Listing 10.12

"Note that these calls are relatively slow, they can easily be the slowest thing in your plug-in. Do not get (or set) pixels one at a time using pixel_rgn_[get!set]_pixel if there is any other way. " (from http://www.home.unix-ag.org/simon/gimp/guadec2002/gimp-plugin/html/imagedata.html)

In addition, the Web search yields information about the gimp_rgb_set_uchar function by simply turning up the source for the function. As shown in Listing 10.13, this call just packs the red, green, and blue values into a GimpRGB structure that represents a single color.

Listing 10.13

```
void
gimp_rgb_set_uchar (GimpRGB *rgb,
                    guchar   r,
                    guchar   g,
                    guchar   b)
{
  g_return_if_fail (rgb != NULL);

  rgb->r = (gdouble) r / 255.0;
  rgb->g = (gdouble) g / 255.0;
  rgb->b = (gdouble) b / 255.0;
}
```

Information gleaned from the Web confirms our suspicion: The `pixel_rgn_get_pixel` function is a way to extract image data from the image, and `gimp_rgba_set_uchar` is just a way to take the color data returned by `pixel_rgn_get_pixel` and put it into the `GimpRGB` data structure.

Not only do we see how these functions are used, other pages also hint that they may not be the best functions to use if we want the filter to perform at its peak. One Web page (http://www.home.unix-ag.org/simon/gimp/guadec2002/gimp-plugin/html/efficientaccess.html) suggests that it may be possible to increase performance by using the GIMP image cache. Another Web site (http://gimp-plug-ins.sourceforge.net/doc/Writing/html/sect-tiles.html) suggests that it might be possible to increase performance by rewriting the filter to access the image data more efficiently.

10.9 Increase the Image Cache

The Web sites explain that GIMP manages images in a slightly counterintuitive fashion. Instead of storing the image in a big array, GIMP instead breaks the image up into a series of tiles. These tiles are 64×64 wide. When a filter wants to access a particular pixel of the image, GIMP loads the appropriate tile, and then finds and returns the pixel value. Each call to retrieve a particular pixel can be slow. If this process is done repeatedly for each pixel, this can dramatically slow down performance as GIMP reloads the tile that it will use to retrieve the pixel values. Fortunately, GIMP provides a way to cache the old tile values and use the cache values rather than reload the tiles at each time. This should increase performance. The amount of cache that GIMP provides can be controlled by using the `gimp_tile_cache_ntiles` call. This call is currently used inside the `lic` and sets the cache to twice as many tiles as the image is wide.

Even though this might seem like enough cache, the GIMP might possibly still need more. The simple way to test this is to increase the cache to a very large value and see whether that improves performance. So, in this case, we increase the amount of cache to 10 times the amount that is normally used. After increasing this value and rerunning the filter, we receive a time of 2 minutes and 40 seconds. This is an increase of 6 seconds, but we have not reached our goal of 2 minutes and 30 seconds. This says that we must look in other areas to increase the performance.

10.10   Hitting a (Tiled) Wall

In addition to using the tile cache, the Web pages suggest a better way to increase the performance of get_pixel. By accessing the pixel information directly (without a call to gimp_pixel_rgn_get_pixel), it is possible to dramatically increase the performance of the pixel access.

GIMP can provide a way for the filter programmer to directly access the tiles of an image. The filter can then access the image data as if it were accessing a data array, instead of requiring a call into a GIMP library. However, there is a catch. When you have direct access to the pixel data, it is only for the current tile. GIMP will then iterate over all the tiles in the image, allowing you to ultimately have access to all the pixels in the image, but you cannot access them all simultaneously. It is only possible to look at the pixels from a single tile, and this is incompatible with how lic accesses data. When the lic filter is generating a new pixel at a particular location, it calculates its new value based on the values of the pixels that surround it. Therefore, when generating new pixels on the edge of a tile, the lic filter requires pixel data from all the pixels around it. Unfortunately, these pixels may be on the previous tile or the next tile in the image. Because this pixel information is not available, the image filter will not work with this optimized access method.

10.11   Solving the Problem

Because we have determined that the reading of pixel values is taking a significant amount of time, there is yet another solution that may solve the problem. We have to start looking at how the filter runs. As it generates the new image, it repeatedly asks for the same pixel. Because the new pixel value is based on the pixels that surround it, during the course of running the filter on the image, each pixel can be accessed by each of its nine neighbors. This means that each pixel in the image will be read by each of its neighbors and, as a result, it is read at least nine times.

Because the calls to the GIMP library are expensive, we would only like to do them once for each pixel rather than nine times. It is possible to optimize access to the image by reading the entire image into a local array when the filter starts up, and then accessing this local array as the filter runs, rather than calling the GIMP library routines each time we want to access the data. This method should significantly reduce the overhead for looking up the pixel data. Instead of a couple of function calls for each data access, we just access our local array. On filter initialization, the array is allocated with `malloc` and filled with the pixel data. This is shown in Listing 10.14.

Listing 10.14

```
int g_image_width, g_image_height;
GimpRGB *g_cached_image;


void cache_image(GimpPixelRgn *src_rgn,int width,int height)
{
  static guchar data[4];
  int x,y;
  GimpRGB *current_pixel;

  g_image_width = width;
  g_image_height = height;

  g_cached_image = malloc(sizeof(GimpRGB)*width*height);
  current_pixel = g_cached_image;

  /* Malloc */
  for (y = 0; y < height; y++)
    {
      for (x = 0; x < width; x++)
        {
          gimp_pixel_rgn_get_pixel (src_rgn, data, x, y);
          gimp_rgba_set_uchar (current_pixel, data[0], data[1], data[2],
data[3]);
          current_pixel++;
        }
    }
```

In addition, the peek routine has been rewritten just to access this local array rather than call into the GIMP library functions. This is shown in Listing 10.15.

Listing 10.15

```
static void peek (GimpPixelRgn *src_rgn,
      gint          x,
      gint          y,
      GimpRGB       *color)
{
  *color = g_cached_image[y*g_image_width + x];
}
```

So, does it work? When we run the filter using the new method, runtime has decreased to 56 seconds! This is well within our goal of 2 minutes and 30 seconds, and it is a significant boost in performance.

The performance, though impressive, did not come for free. We made one of the classic trade-offs in performance engineering: We increased performance at the expense of memory usage. For example, when a 1280×1024 image is used with this filter, we require 5 additional megabytes of memory. For very big images, it may not be practical to cache this data; for reasonably sized images, however, a 5MB increase in memory usage seems like a good sacrifice for a filter that is more than two times as fast.

10.12 Verify Correctness?

After we have an optimization that has significantly reduced the filter's runtime, it is necessary to verify that the output image it produces is the same for both the optimized and the unoptimized filter. After loading up the original reference image and comparing it to the newly generated image, I used GIMP to take the difference of the two images. If the reference and optimized image are identical, all the pixels should be zero (black). However, the different image was not perfectly black. Visually, it looked black, but upon closer inspection (using the GIMP color picker), some of the pixels were nonzero. This means that the reference and optimized images are different.

This would normally be a cause for concern, because this might indicate that optimization changed the behavior of the filter. However, a closer examination of the filter's source code showed several places where random noise was used to slightly jitter the image before the filter was run. Any two runs of the filter would be different, so the optimization was likely not to blame. Because the differences between the two images were so visually small, we can assume that the optimization did not introduce any problems.

10.13 Next Steps

We exceeded our goal of 10 percent performance increase in the lic filter, so in that sense, we are done with the optimization process. However, if we want to continue to increase performance, we have to reprofile the filter when using the new optimizations. It is important to reprofile the application after each performance optimization is applied and to not rely on old profiles when continuing to optimize the application. The application's runtime behavior can change dramatically after each optimization. If you do not profile after every optimization, you run the risk of chasing a performance problem that no longer exists.

10.14 Chapter Summary

In this chapter, we determined why an application (the GIMP filter lic) was CPU-bound. We figured out the base runtime of the application, set a goal for optimization, and saved a reference image to verify that our optimizations did not change the behavior of the application. We used the Linux CPU performance tools (oprofile and ltrace) to investigate exactly why the application was CPU-bound. We then used the Web to understand how the application worked and to figure out different ways to optimize it. We tried a few different optimizations, but ultimately, we chose the classic performance trade-off of increased memory usage for reduced CPU usage.

We beat our optimization goal, and then verified that our optimization did not change the output of the application.

Whereas this chapter focused on optimizing a single application's runtime, the next chapter presents a performance hunt that concentrates on reducing the amount of latency when interacting with X Windows. Reducing latency can be tricky, because a single event often sets off a nonobvious set of other events. The hard part is figuring out what events are being called and how long each of them are taking.

## 11

Performance Hunt 2: A Latency-Sensitive Application (nautilus)

This chapter contains an example of how to use the Linux performance tools to find and fix a performance problem in a latency-sensitive application.

After reading this chapter, you should be able to

* Use `ltrace` and `oprofile` to figure out where latency is being generated in a latency-sensitive application.
* Use `gdb` to generate a stack trace for each call to a "hot" function.
* Use performance tools to determine where time is spent for an application that uses many different shared libraries.
* Use this chapter as a template to find the cause of high latency in a latency-sensitive application.

11.1 A Latency-Sensitive Application

In this chapter, we investigate an application that is sensitive to slow latency. Latency can be thought of as the time it takes for an application to respond to different external or internal events. An application with a latency performance problem often does not hog the CPU for long periods of time; instead, it only uses a small amount of CPU time to respond to different events. However, the response to the particular events is not swift enough. When fixing a latency performance problem, we need to reduce the latency in response to the various events and figure out what parts of the application are slowing down the response. As you will see, tracking down a latency problem requires a slightly different tactic than tracking down a CPU-intensive problem.

11.2 Identify a Problem

As with the performance problem in the preceding chapter, we have to define what we will investigate and try to overcome it. In this case, we will optimize the time to open a pop-up menu when using the nautilus file manager for the GNOME desktop. In nautilus, pop-up menus are opened by right-clicking anywhere in a nautilus file management window. In this particular case, we will be investigating the performance of the pop-up menus that appear when we right-click the background of an open window rather than when we right-click a particular file or folder.

Why should we optimize this? Even though the amount of time to open a pop-up may be less than a second, it is still slow enough that users can perceive the lag between when they right-click the mouse and when the menu shows up. This sluggish pop-up gives the GNOME user the impression that the computer is running slowly. People notice a slight delay, and it can make interaction with nautilus annoying or give the impression that the desktop is slow.

This particular performance problem is different from the GIMP problem of the preceding chapter. First, the core components of the desktop (in this case, GNOME) are typically more complicated and interlocked than a typical desktop application. The components typically rely on a variety of subsystems and shared libraries to do their work. Whereas the GIMP was a relatively self-contained application, making it easier to profile and recompile when necessary, the GNOME desktop is made up of many different interlocking components. The components may require multiple processes and shared libraries, each performing a different task on behalf of the desktop. nautilus, in particular, is linked to 72 different shared libraries. Tracking down exactly which piece of code is spending time, how much it is spending, and why it is spending it, can be a daunting task.

The significant second difference of this performance investigation from the GIMP investigation is that the times we are trying to reduce are on the order of milliseconds rather than seconds or minutes. When the times are so small, it can be difficult to make sure that the profiling data that you are capturing is actually the result of the event that you are trying to measure rather than just the noise around trying to stop and start the profiling tools. However, this short time period also makes it practical to trace all aspects of what the application does for the interesting period of time.

11.3 Find a Baseline/Set a Goal

As with the previous hunt, the first step is to determine the current state of the problem. To make our lives a little easier, and to avoid some of the profiling problems mentioned in the preceding section, we are going to cheat a little and make the pop-up menu problem look more similar to the long-running CPU-intensive tasks that we measured before. The amount of time that it takes for a single pop-up to appear is in the millisecond range, which makes it hard to accurately measure it with our performance profiling tools. As mentioned previously, it will be difficult to start them and stop them in the proper amount of time and guarantee that we are only measuring what we are interested in (that is, the CPU time spent to open up the actual menu). Here is where we cheat. Instead of opening up the menu just one time, we will open up the menu 100 times in rapid succession. This way, the total amount of time spent opening menus will increase by a factor of 100. This enables us to use our profiling tools to capture information about how the menu is executing.

Because right-clicking 100 times would be tedious, and a human (unless very well trained) could not reliably open up a pop-up menu 100 times in a repeatable manner, we must automate it. To reliably open up the pop-up menu 100 times, we rely on the xautomation package. The xautomation package is available at http://hoopajoo.net/projects/xautomation.html. It can send arbitrary X Window events to the X server, mimicking a user. After downloading the xautomation tar file, unzipping and compiling it, we can use it to automate the right mouse click.

Unlike with the GIMP, we cannot simply measure the amount of CPU time used by nautilus to evaluate the time needed to create 100 pop-up menus. This is mainly because nautilus does not start immediately before a menu is opened and end immediately after. We are going to use wall-clock time to see how much time it takes to complete this task. This requires that the system not have any other things running while we run the test.

Listing 11.1 shows the shell script of xautomation commands that are used to open 100 pop-up menus in the nautilus file browser. When we run the test, we have to make sure that we have oriented the nautilus window so that none of the clicks actually opens a pop-up menu on a folder, and that instead all the pop-ups occur on the background. This is important because the code paths for the different pop-up menus could be radically different.

Listing 11.1

```
#!/bin/bash
for i in `seq 1 100`;
do
       echo $i
       ./xte 'mousemove 100 100' 'mouseclick 3' 'mouseclick 3'
       ./xte 'mousemove 200 100' 'mouseclick 3' 'mouseclick 3'
done
```

The commands in Listing 11.1 move the cursor to position (100,100) on the X screen, and click the right mouse button (button 3). This brings up a menu. Then they click the right mouse button again, and this closes the menu. They then move to X position (100,100), and repeat the process.

Next, we use time to see how much the script of these 100 iterations takes to complete. This is our baseline time. When we do our optimizations, we will check them against this time to see whether they have improved. This baseline time for the stock Fedora 2 version of nautilus on my laptop is 26.5 seconds.

Finally, we have to pick a goal for our optimization path. One easy way to do this is to find an application that already has fast pop-up menus and see how long it takes for it to bring up a pop-up menu 100 times. A perfect example of this is xterm, which has nice snappy menus. Although the menus are not as complicated as those in nautilus, they should at least be considered an upper bound on how fast menus can be.

The pop-up menus on xterm work a little bit differently, so we have to slightly change the script to create 100 pop-ups. When xterm creates a pop-up, it requires that the left control key is depressed, so we have to slightly modify our automation script. This script is shown in Listing 11.2.

Listing 11.2

```
#!/bin/bash
for i in `seq 1 100`;
do
    echo $i
    ./xte 'keydown Control_L' 'mousemove 100 100' 'mouseclick 3' 'mouseclick 3'

    ./xte 'keydown Control_L' 'mousemove 200 100' 'mouseclick 3' 'mouseclick 3' done
```

When running xterm and timing the pop-up menu creation, xterm takes ~9.2 seconds to complete the script. nautilus has signficant (almost 17 seconds) room for improvement. It is probably unreasonable to expect the creation of nautilus's complex pop-up menus to be the same speed as those of xterm, so let's be conservative and set a goal of 10 percent, or 3 seconds. Hopefully, we will be able to do much better than this, or at least figure out why it is not possible to speed it up any more.

11.4 Configure the Application for the Performance Hunt

The next step in the investigation is to set up the application for the performance hunt. Whereas with GIMP we recompiled the application immediately, we are going to take a different approach with nautilus. It may be hard to figure out exactly which pieces need to be recompiled because it relies on so many different shared libraries. Instead of recompiling, we are going to download and install the debugging information for each of the applications and libraries. For Fedora and Enterprise Linux, Red Hat provides a set of debuginfo rpms that contain all the symbol information and sources that were generated by the compiler when the application was complied. Each binary package or library has a corresponding debuginfo rpm that contains the debugging information. This allows Red Hat to ship the binaries without the disk-space–consuming debugging information. However, it allows developers, or those investigating performance problems, to download the appropriate debuginfo packages and use them. In this case, Red

Hat's version of `oprofile` will also recognize the `debuginfo` packages and pick up the symbols when profiling both an application, such a nautilus, and a library, such as `gtk`. In this case, we are going to download the `debuginfo` for `gtk`, nautilus, glib, and the kernel. If `oprofile` finds a library that contributes a significant amount of cycles, but does not allow you to analyze the libraries (`opreport` prints out "no symbols"); this indicates that no debugging information is installed for the library. We can download and install the appropriate `debuginfo` package for the library, and then `oprofile` will have access to the debugging information and will then be able to map the events back to the original functions and source lines.

11.5 Install and Configure Performance Tools

The next step in the hunt is to install the performance tools we need to investigate the problem. As we did in the performance hunt for the GIMP, we will install both `oprofile` and `ltrace`. In this case, we will also download and install `gdb` (if it is not already installed). `gdb` enables us to look at some of the dynamic aspects of the running application.

11.6 Run Application and Performance Tools

Next, we run the application and take measurements using the performance tools. Because we already suspect that a complex interaction of many different processes and libraries might be the cause of the problem, we are going to start with `oprofile` and see what it has to say.

Because we only want `oprofile` to measure events that occur while we are opening the pop-up menus, we are going to use the command line shown in Listing 11.3 to start and stop the profiling immediately before and immediately after we run our script (named `script.sh`) that opens and closes 100 pop-up menus.

Listing 11.3

```
opcontrol —start ; ./script.sh ; opcontrol -stop
```

Running opreport after that profiling information has been collected gives us the information shown in Listing 11.4.

Listing 11.4

```
CPU: CPU with timer interrupt, speed 0 MHz (estimated)
Profiling through timer interrupt
          TIMER:0|
   samples|      %|
. . . . . . . . . . . . . . . . .
     3134 27.1460 /usr/lib/libgobject-2.0.so.0.400.0
     1840 15.9376 /usr/lib/libglib-2.0.so.0.400.0
     1303 11.2863 /lib/tls/libc-2.3.3.so
     1048  9.0775 /lib/tls/libpthread-0.61.so
      900  7.7956 /usr/lib/libgtk-x11-2.0.so.0.400.0
      810  7.0160 /usr/X11R6/bin/Xorg
      719  6.2278 /usr/lib/libgdk-x11-2.0.so.0.400.0
      334  2.8930 /usr/lib/libpango-1.0.so.0.399.1
      308  2.6678 /lib/ld-2.3.3.so
      298  2.5812 /usr/X11R6/lib/libX11.so.6.2
      228  1.9749 /usr/lib/libbonoboui-2.so.0.0.0
      152  1.3166 /usr/X11R6/lib/libXft.so.2.1.2
```

As you can see, time is spent in many different libraries. Unfortunately, it is not at all clear which application is responsible for making those calls. In particular, we have no idea which processes have called the libgobject library. Fortunately, oprofile provides a way to record the shared libraries' functions that an application uses during a run. Listing 11.5 shows how to configure oprofile's sample collection to separate the samples by library, which means that oprofile will attribute the samples collected in shared libraries to the programs that called them.

Listing 11.5

```
opcontrol -p library; opcontrol ---reset
```

After we rerun our test (using the commands in Listing 11.3), opreport splits up the library samples per application, as shown in Listing 11.6.

Listing 11.6

```
[root@localhost menu_work]# opreport  -f

CPU: CPU with timer interrupt, speed 0 MHz (estimated)
Profiling through timer interrupt
          TIMER:0|
  samples|       %|
------------------
     8172 61.1311 /usr/bin/nautilus
              TIMER:0|
      samples|      %|
      ----------------
         3005 36.7719 /usr/lib/libgobject-2.0.so.0.400.0
         1577 19.2976 /usr/lib/libglib-2.0.so.0.400.0
          826 10.1077 /lib/tls/libpthread-0.61.so
          792  9.6916 /lib/tls/libc-2.3.3.so
          727  8.8962 /usr/lib/libgtk-x11-2.0.so.0.400.0
          391  4.7846 /usr/lib/libgdk-x11-2.0.so.0.400.0
          251  3.0715 /usr/lib/libpango-1.0.so.0.399.1
          209  2.5575 /usr/lib/libbonoboui-2.so.0.0.0
          140  1.7132 /usr/X11R6/lib/libX11.so.6.2
           75  0.9178 /usr/X11R6/lib/libXft.so.2.1.2
           54  0.6608 /usr/lib/libpangoxft-1.0.so.0.399.1
           23  0.2814 /usr/lib/libnautilus-private.so.2.0.0
          ....
```

If we drill down into the libgobject and libglib libraries, we can see exactly which functions are being called, as shown in Listing 11.7.

Listing 11.7

```
[root@localhost menu_work]# opreport  -lf /usr/lib/libgobject-
2.0.so.0.400.0
...


CPU: CPU with timer interrupt, speed 0 MHz (estimated)
Profiling through timer interrupt
samples  %        image name              app name
symbol name
394      11.7753  /usr/lib/libgobject-2.0.so.0.400.0 /usr/bin/nautilus-
g_type_check_instance_is_a
248       7.4118  /usr/lib/libgobject-2.0.so.0.400.0 /usr/bin/nautilus-
g_bsearch_array_lookup_fuzzy
208       6.2164  /usr/lib/libgobject-2.0.so.0.400.0 /usr/bin/nautilus-
g_signal_emit_valist
162       4.8416  /usr/lib/libgobject-2.0.so.0.400.0 /usr/bin/nautilus-
signal_key_cmp
147       4.3933  /usr/lib/libgobject-2.0.so.0.400.0 /usr/bin/nautilus-
signal_emit_unlocked_R
137       4.0944  /usr/lib/libgobject-2.0.so.0.400.0 /usr/bin/nautilus-
__i686.get_pc_thunk.bx
90        2.6898  /usr/lib/libgobject-2.0.so.0.400.0 /usr/bin/nautilus-
g_type_value_table_peek
85        2.5403  /usr/lib/libgobject-2.0.so.0.400.0 /usr/bin/nautilus-
type_check_is_value_type_U


...


opreport  -lf /usr/lib/libglib-2.0.so.0.400.0


CPU: CPU with timer interrupt, speed 0 MHz (estimated)
Profiling through timer interrupt
```

continues

Listing 11.7   (Continued)

```
samples    %         image name              app name
symbol name
385       18.0075  /usr/lib/libglib-2.0.so.0.400.0 /usr/bin/nautilus-
g_hash_table_lookup
95         4.4434  /usr/lib/libglib-2.0.so.0.400.0 /usr/bin/nautilus-
g_str_hash
78         3.6483  /usr/lib/libglib-2.0.so.0.400.0 /usr/bin/nautilus-
g_data_set_internal
78         3.6483  /usr/lib/libglib-2.0.so.0.400.0 /usr/bin/nautilus-
g_pattern_ph_match
70         3.2741  /usr/lib/libglib-2.0.so.0.400.0 /usr/bin/nautilus-
__i686.get_pc_thunk.bx
...
```

From the oprofile output, we can see that nautilus spends a significant amount of time in the libgobject library and, in particular, in the g_type_check_instance_is_a function. However, it is unclear what function within the nautilus file manager called these functions. In fact, the functions may not even be called directly from nautilus, instead being made by other shared library calls that nautilus is making.

We next use ltrace, the shared library tracer, to try to figure out which library calls are the most expensive and ultimately what is calling the g_type_check_instance_is_a function. Because we are concerned primarily about which functions nautilus is calling, rather than the exact timing information, it is only necessary to open a pop-up menu once rather than 100 times. Because ltrace will catch every single shared library call for a single run, if we create 100 pop-up menus, ltrace would just show the same profile information 100 times.

This procedure for capturing shared library usage information is similar to how we did it for the GIMP. We first start nautilus as normal. Then before we open up a pop-up menu, we attach to the nautilus process using the following ltrace command:

```
ltrace -c -p <pid_of_nautilus>.
```

We right-click in the nautilus background to bring up the menu, and then immediately kill the ltrace process with a <Ctrl-C>. After tracing the pop-up, we get the summary table shown in Listing 11.8.

Listing 11.8

```
[ezolt@localhost menu_work]$ ltrace -c -p 2196
% time     seconds  usecs/call     calls      function
......  ...........  ...........  .........  ....................
32.75   0.109360      109360          1  bonobo_window_add_popup
25.88   0.086414         257        335  g_cclosure_marshal_VOID__VOID
14.98   0.050011         145        344  g_cclosure_marshal_VOID__OBJECT
 8.85   0.029546       29546          1  eel_pop_up_context_menu
 5.25   0.017540         604         29  gtk_widget_destroy
 5.22   0.017427        1340         13  g_cclosure_marshal_VOID__POINTER
 2.96   0.009888          41        241  g_free
 0.93   0.003101        3101          1  gtk_widget_get_ancestor
 0.45   0.001500        1500          1  gtk_widget_show
 0.45   0.001487         495          3  nautilus_icon_container_get_type
 0.43   0.001440          41         35  g_type_check_instance_cast
 0.38   0.001263        1263          1  nautilus_file_list_free
 0.34   0.001120        1120          1  gtk_widget_get_screen
 0.29   0.000978          46         21  gdk_x11_get_xatom_by_name
 0.25   0.000845          42         20  g_object_unref
 0.11   0.000358          89          4  g_type_check_class_cast
 0.09   0.000299          42          7  g_type_check_instance_is_a
 0.09   0.000285          40          7  g_cclosure_marshal_VOID__ENUM
 0.06   0.000187          37          5  strcmp
 0.04   0.000126         126          1  g_cclosure_marshal_VOID__STRING
 0.03   0.000093          93          1  gtk_menu_get_type
 0.03   0.000087          43          2  bonobo_window_get_type
 0.02   0.000082          82          1  nautilus_icon_container_get_selection
 0.02   0.000082          41          2  gtk_bin_get_type
 0.02   0.000081          40          2  gtk_widget_get_type
 0.02   0.000080          80          1  gtk_menu_set_screen
 0.02   0.000072          72          1  g_signal_connect_object
 0.02   0.000071          71          1  nautilus_file_set_boolean_metadata
 0.01   0.000041          41          1  nautilus_file_list_ref
 0.01   0.000040          40          1  eel_g_list_exactly_one_item
 0.01   0.000038          38          1  nautilus_icon_container_set_keep_aligned
......  ...........  ...........  .........  ....................
100.00  0.333942                   1085  total
```

We can see something interesting in this table. `ltrace` shows a completely different function at the top of the list than `oprofile` did. This is mainly because `oprofile` and `ltrace` measure slightly different things. `oprofile` shows how much time is spent in actual functions, but none of the children. `ltrace` just shows how much time it takes for an external library call to complete. If that library function in turn calls other functions, `ltrace` does not record their individual timings. In fact, it currently does not even detect or display that these other library calls happened.

In this particular case, the function that `oprofile` says is the hottest function of `libgobject` (that is, `g_type_check_instance_is_a`) barely shows up on the `ltrace` profile at all. Even though this function is part of a shared library, the calls to it are not shown in the `ltrace` output. `ltrace` is not able to show the cross-library calls, and it is also not able to show calls that are made internally to the library. `ltrace` can only track when an external library or application calls into a shared library. When a library calls a function internally, `ltrace` cannot trace that the call has been made. In this case, all the functions that are prefixed with `g_` are actually part of the `libgobject` library. If any of them call `g_type_check_instance_is_a`, `ltrace` will not be able to detect it.

The most significant information that `ltrace` gives us is a set of a few library calls that our application makes that we can investigate. We can figure out where the library is being called, and possibly why all the time is being spent in that library call.

11.7 Compile and Examine the Source

So now that we have some idea about which calls the application is taking all of the time, we will download the source and compile it. Until now, all of our analysis was possible using the binary packages that Red Hat provides. However, now we need to dive into the source code to examine why the hot functions are called and then, when we figure out why, make changes in the source to alleviate the performance problem. As we did for GIMP, when we recompile, we generate debugging symbols by setting CFLAGS to -g before we call the configure script.

In this case, we downloaded and installed Red Hat's source rpm for nautilus, which places the source of nautilus in /usr/src/redhat/SOURCES/. By using Red Hat's source package, we have the exact source and patches that Red Hat used to create the binary in the package. It is important to investigate the source that was used to create the binaries that we have been investigating, because another version may have different performance characteristics. After we extract the source, we can begin to figure out where the bonobo_window_add_popup call is made. We can search all the source files in the nautilus directory using the commands in Listing 11.9.

Listing 11.9

```
[nautilus ]$ find -type f | xargs grep bonobo_window_add_popup

./src/file-manager/fm-directory-view.c: bonobo_window_add_popup\
(get_bonobo_window (view), menu, popup_path);
```

Fortunately, it appears as if bonobo_window_add_popup is only called from a single function, create_popup_menu, as shown in Listing 11.10.

Listing 11.10

```
static GtkMenu *create_popup_menu (FMDirectoryView *view,
                                   const char *popup_path)
{
  GtkMenu *menu;

  menu = GTK_MENU (gtk_menu_new ());
  gtk_menu_set_screen (menu, gtk_widget_get_screen (GTK_WIDGET (view)));

  gtk_widget_show (GTK_WIDGET (menu));

  bonobo_window_add_popup (get_bonobo_window (view), menu, popup_path);

  g_signal_connect_object (menu, "hide",
                           G_CALLBACK (popup_menu_hidden),
                           G_OBJECT (view),
                           G_CONNECT_SWAPPED);
      return menu;
}
```

In turn, this function is called by two other functions: `fm_directory_view_pop_` `up_background_context_menu` and `fm_directory_view_pop_up_selection_context_` `menu`. By adding a `printf` to each of the functions, we can determine which one is called when we right-click a window. We then recompile nautilus, launch it, and then right-click the background of the window. nautilus prints out `fm_directory_view_pop_up_` `background_context_menu`, so we know that this is the function that is called when opening a pop-up menu in the background of the window. The source code for this function is shown in Listing 11.11.

Listing 11.11

```
void fm_directory_view_pop_up_background_context_menu (FMDirectoryView
*view, GdkEventButton *event)
{
g_assert (FM_IS_DIRECTORY_VIEW (view));

/* Make the context menu items not flash as they
        * update to proper disabled,
 * etc. states by forcing menus to update now.
 */
update_menus_if_pending (view);
eel_pop_up_context_menu
(create_popup_menu (view, FM_DIRECTORY_VIEW_POPUP_PATH_BACKGROUND),
                    EEL_DEFAULT_POPUP_MENU_DISPLACEMENT,
                    EEL_DEFAULT_POPUP_MENU_DISPLACEMENT, event);
}
```

Now that we have narrowed down exactly where the menu pop-ups are created and displayed, we can begin to figure out exactly which pieces are taking all the time and which pieces are ultimately calling the `g_type_check_instance_is_a` function that oprofile says is the hot function.

11.8 Using gdb to Generate Call Traces

The two different tools for retrieving information about which functions our application was calling gave us different information about which functions were the hot functions. We theorized that the high-level functions that ltrace reported were calling the low-level function that operofile was reporting. It would be nice to have a performance tool that could show us exactly which functions were calling g_type_check_instance_is_a to verify this theory.

Although no Linux performance tool shows us exactly which functions are calling a particular function, gprof should be able to present this callback information, but this requires recompiling the application and all the libraries that it relies on with the -pg flag to be effective. For nautilus, which relies on 72 shared libraries, this can be a daunting and infeasible task, so we have to look for another solution. Newer versions of oprofile can also provide this type of information, but because oprofile only samples periodically, it will still not be able to account for every call to any given function.

Fortunately, we can creatively use gdb to extract that information. Using gdb to trace the application greatly slows down the run; however, we do not really care whether the trace takes a long time. We are interested in finding the number of times that a particular function is called rather than the amount of time it is called, so it is acceptable for the run to take a long time. Luckily, the creation of the pop-up menu is in the millisecond range; even if it is 1,000 times slower with gdb, it still only takes about 15 minutes to extract the full trace. The value of the information outweighs our wait to retrieve it.

In particular, to find which functions are calling g_type_check_instance_is_a, we are going to use a few different features of gdb. First, we use gdb's ability to set a breakpoint at that function. Then we use gdb's ability to generate a backtrace with bt at that breakpoint. These two features are really all that we need to figure out which functions are calling this g_type_check_instance_is_a, but manually recording the information and continuing would be tedious. We would need to type bt ; cont after each time gdb breaks in the function.

To solve this, use another one of gdb's features. gdb can execute a given set of commands when it hits a breakpoint. By using the command command, we can tell gdb to execute bt; cont every time it hits the breakpoint in our function. So now the backtrace displays automatically, and the application continues running every time it hits g_type_check_instance_is_a.

Now we have to isolate when the trace actually runs. We could just set up the breakpoint in g_type_check_instance_is_a at the start of the nautilus execution, and gdb would show tracing information when it is called by any function. Because we only care about those functions that are called when we are creating a pop-up menu, we want to limit that tracing to only when pop-ups are being created. To do this, we set another breakpoint at the beginning and end of the fm_directory_view_pop_up_background_context_menu function. When we reach the first breakpoint, we turn on the backtracing in g_type_check_instance_is_a; when we reach the second breakpoint, we exit the debugger. This limits the backtrace information to that which is generated when we are creating a pop-up menu. Finally, we want to be able to save this backtrace information for post-processing. We can use gdb's ability to log its output to a file to save the information for later. The commands passed into gdb to extract this information are shown in Listing 11.12.

Listing 11.12

```
# Prevent gdb from stopping after a screenful of output
set height 0
# Turn on output logging to a file (default: gdb.txt)
set logging on
# Turn off output to the screen
set logging redirect on
# Stop when a popup menu is about to be created
break fm-directory-view.c:5730
# Start the application
run
# When we've stopped at the preceding breakpoint, setup
# the breakpoint in g_type_check_instance_is_a
break g_type_check_instance_is_a
# When we reach the breakpoint, print a backtrace and exit
command
bt
cont
end
```

```
# break after the popup was created and exit gdb
break fm-directory-view.c:5769
command
quit
end
# continue running
cont
```

When running these gdb commands and opening a pop-up menu, gdb churns away for several minutes and creates a 33MB file containing all the backtrace information for functions that called the g_type_check_instance_is_a function. A sample of one is shown in Listing 11.13.

Listing 11.13

```
Breakpoint 2, g_type_check_instance_is_a (type_instance=0x9d2b720,
iface_type=164410736) at gtype.c:31213121      if (!type_instance ||
!type_instance->g_class)
#1  0x08099f09 in fm_directory_view_pop_up_background_context_menu
(view=0x9d2b720, event=0x9ceb628)
    at fm-directory-view.c:5731
#2  0x080a2911 in icon_container_context_click_background_callback
(container=0x80c5a2b, event=0x9ceb628,
    icon_view=0x9d2b720) at fm-icon-view.c:2141
#3  0x00da32be in g_cclosure_marshal_VOID__POINTER (closure=0x9d37620,
return_value=0x0, n_param_values=2,
    param_values=0xfef67320, invocation_hint=0xfef67218,
marshal_data=0x0) at gmarshal.c:601
#4  0x00d8e160 in g_closure_invoke (closure=0x9d37620,
return_value=0x9d2b720, n_param_values=164804384,
    param_values=0x9d2b720, invocation_hint=0x9d2b720) at gclosure.c:437
#5  0x00da2195 in signal_emit_unlocked_R (node=0x9d33140, detail=0,
instance=0x9d35130, emission_return=0x0,
    instance_and_params=0xfef67320) at gsignal.c:2436
#6  0x00da1157 in g_signal_emit_valist (instance=0x9d35130, signal_id=0,
detail=0, var_args=0xfef674b0 "") at gsignal.c:2195

....
```

Although this information is very detailed, it is not exactly in an easy-to-digest format. It would be better if each backtrace were on a single line, with each function separated by arrows. It would also be nice to get rid of the backtrace information above the call to fm_directory_view_pop_up_background_context_menu, because we know that every one of the calls will have that same backtrace information. We can use the python program, slice.py, shown in Listing 11.14 to do exactly that. The program takes the verbose output file generated by gdb and creates a nicely formatted call trace of every function that called fm_directory_view_pop_up_background_context_menu.

Listing 11.14

```
#!/usr/bin/python
import sys
import string
funcs = ""
stop_at = "fm_directory_view_pop_up_background_context_menu"
for  line  in sys.stdin:
    parsed = string.split(line)
    if (line[:1] == "#"):
        if (parsed[0] == "#0"):
            funcs = parsed[1]
        elif (parsed[3] == stop_at):
            print funcs
            funcs = ""
        else:
            funcs = parsed[3] + "->" + funcs
```

When we run the gdb.txt file into this python program using the command line shown in Listing 11.15, we have a more consolidated output, an example of which is shown in Listing 11.16.

Listing 11.15

```
cat gdb.txt | ./slice.py > backtrace.txt
```

Listing 11.16

```
....
create_popup_menu->gtk_widget_show->g_object_notify->g_type_check_
instance_is_a
create_popup_menu->gtk_widget_show->g_object_notify->g_object_ref->g_
type_check_instance_is_a
create_popup_menu->gtk_widget_show->g_object_notify->g_object_
notify_queue_add->g_param_spec_get_redirect_target->g_type_check_
instance_is_a
create_popup_menu->gtk_widget_show->g_object_notify->g_object_notify_
queue_add->g_param_spec_get_redirect_target->g_type_check_instance_is_a
create_popup_menu->gtk_widget_show->g_object_notify->g_object_unref->g_
type_check_instance_is_a
create_popup_menu->gtk_widget_show->g_object_unref->g_type_check_
instance_is_a
...
```

Because the output lines are long, they have been wrapped when displayed in this book; in the text file, however, there is one backtrace per line. Each line ends with the g_type_check_instance_is_a function. Because each backtrace spans only one line, we can extract information about the backtraces using some common Linux tools, such as wc, which we can use to count the number of lines in a particular file.

First, let's look at how many calls have been made to the g_type_check_instance_is_a function. This is the same as the number of backtraces and, hence, the number of lines in the backtrace.txt file. Listing 11.17 shows the wc command being called on our pruned backtrace file. The first number indicates the number of lines in the file.

Listing 11.17

```
[ezolt@localhost menu_work]$ wc backtrace.txt
  6848   6848 3605551 backtrace.txt
```

As you can see, the function has been called 6,848 times just to create the pop-up menu. Next, let's see how many of those functions are made on behalf of bonobo_window_add_popup. This is shown in Listing 11.18.

Listing 11.18

```
[ezolt@localhost menu_work]$ grep bonobo_window_add_popup backtrace.txt | wc
    6670    6670 3558590
```

bonobo_window_add_popup is responsible for 6,670 of the calls to our hot function. Looking at the backtrace.txt file reveals few of these are direct calls; most are made from other functions that it calls. From this, it appears as if the bonobo_window_ add_popup is indeed responsible for much of the CPU time that is being spent. However, we still have to confirm that this is the case.

11.9 Finding the Time Differences

Now that we have narrowed down which functions do the work of creating the menu, we want to figure out which pieces are taking up all the time and which pieces are relatively lightweight. A great way to do that, without using any performance tools at all, is to just disable pieces of code and see how it changes performance. Even though this causes nautilus to function incorrectly, it will at least indicate which of the functions are taking all the time.

We first have to start by taking a baseline, because the binaries we are testing have been compiled with different flags than those provided by Red Hat. We time the scripts as we did before. In this case, a run of 100 iterations takes 30.5 seconds on the version that we have compiled ourselves. Next, we comment out the eel_pop_up_context_menu call. This shows us how much time it took nautilus to detect the mouse click and decide that a context menu needed to be created. Even if we completely optimize away all the commands in these functions, we will not be able to run any faster than this. In this case, it takes 7.6 seconds to run all 100 iterations. Next, we comment out bonobo_window_ add_popup to see how much time it costs us to actually call the function that ltrace says is taking the most amount of time. If we comment out bonobo_window_add_popup, the 100 iterations take 21.9 seconds to complete. This says that if we optimize away the bonobo_window_add_popup, it can shave ~8 seconds off the total run, which is nearly a 25 percent improvement.

11.10 Trying a Possible Solution

So, as we have seen, bonobo_window_add_popup is an expensive function that must be called every time we want to create a pop-up menu. If we are repeatedly calling it with the same parameters, it may be possible to cache the value it returns from the initial call and use that every time after that instead of repeatedly calling that expensive function. Listing 11.19 shows an example of a rewritten function to do just that.

Listing 11.19

```
void
fm_directory_view_pop_up_background_context_menu (FMDirectoryView *view,
                              GdkEventButton *event)
{
    /* Primitive Cache */
    static FMDirectoryView *old_view = NULL;
    static GtkMenu *old_menu = NULL;

    g_assert (FM_IS_DIRECTORY_VIEW (view));

    /* Make the context menu items not flash as they update to proper disabled,
     * etc. states by forcing menus to update now.
     */
    if ((old_view != view)  || view->details->menu_states_untrustworthy)
        {
            update_menus_if_pending (view);
            old_view = view;
            old_menu = create_popup_menu(view, FM_DIRECTORY_VIEW_POPUP_PATH_BACKGROUND);
        }

    eel_pop_up_context_menu (old_menu,
        EEL_DEFAULT_POPUP_MENU_DISPLACEMENT,
        EEL_DEFAULT_POPUP_MENU_DISPLACEMENT,
        event);
}
```

In this case, we remember the menu that was generated last time. If we are past it in the same view, and we do not believe that the menu for that view has changed, we just use the same menu that we used last time instead of creating a new one. This is not a sophisticated technique, and it will break down if the user does not open a pop-up menu in the same directory repeatedly. For example, if the user opens a pop-up in directory 1, and then opens one in directory 2, if the user then opens a pop-up in directory 1, nautilus will still create a new menu. It is possible to create a simple cache that stores menus as they are created. When opening a menu, the first check is to see whether these views already have menus in the cache. If they do, the cached menus could be viewed; otherwise, new ones could be created. This cache would be especially useful for some special directories, such as the desktop, computer, or home directory where the user will most likely open a pop-up menu more than once. After applying this proposed solution and timing it with the 100 iterations, the time has dropped to 24.0 seconds. This is a ~20 percent performance improvement, and close to the theoretical improvement that we would get if we did not create the menu at all (21.9 seconds). Creating pop-up menus in various directories worked as expected. The patch did not appear to break anything.

Note, however, that right now, this is just a test solution. It would have to be presented to the nautilus developers to confirm that it did not break any functionality and is suitable for inclusion. However, through the course of the hunt, we have determined what functions are slow, tracked down where they are called, and created a possible solution that objectively improves performance. It is also important to note that the improvement was objective; that is, we have hard data to prove that the new method is faster, rather than simply subjective (i.e., just saying that it feels snappier). Most developers would love to have this kind of performance bug report.

11.11 Chapter Summary

In this chapter, we determined why a particular component of an application had high latency (pop-up menus in nautilus). We figured out how to automate the creation of the pop-up menus (xautomation) and extend the amount of time that nautilus spent creating pop-up means (100 iterations). We used `oprofile` to figure out in which function nautilus was spending all of its time. We then used `ltrace` and `gdb` to determine which shared library calls were responsible for making all the calls. After we figured out which library calls were high cost, we tried to reduce or limit the number of times they were called. In this case, we stored a pointer to a new menu when it was allocated and used it later to avoid unneeded reallocations. We created a proposed patch and then ran our performance test against it to see whether performance improved. Performance improved, and functionality did not appear to be affected. The next step is to submit the patch to the nautilus developers for comment. Whereas this chapter focused on optimizing a single application's latency, the next chapter presents a performance hunt that concentrates on solving a system-level performance problem. This type of hunt can often involve investigating many different areas of the system, including hardware (disk, network, and memory) and software (applications, shared libraries, and the Linux kernel).

12

Performance Hunt 3: The System-Wide Slowdown (prelink)

This chapter contains an example of how to use the Linux performance tools to find and fix a performance problem that affects the entire system rather than a specific application.

After reading this chapter, you should be able to

* Track down which individual process is causing the system to slow down.

* Use strace to investigate the performance behavior of a process that is not CPU-bound.

* Use strace to investigate how an application is interacting with the Linux kernel.

* Submit bug reports that describe a performance problem so that an author or maintainer has enough information to fix the problem.

12.1 Investigating a System-Wide Slowdown

In this chapter, we investigate a system-wide slowdown. Initially, we will notice that the system is behaving slowly, and we will use the Linux performance tools to pinpoint the exact cause. This sort of problem happens quite often. As a user or system administrator, you may sometimes notice the Linux machine becoming sluggish or taking a long time to complete a task. It is valuable to be able to figure out why the machine is slowing down.

12.2 Identify a Problem

Once again, our first step is to identify the exact problem that we will investigate. In this case, we are going to investigate a periodic slowdown that occurs when I use my Fedora Core 2 desktop. Typically, the desktop performance is reasonable, but occasionally, the disk starts grinding and, as a result, menus and applications take forever to open. After a while, the disk grinding subsides, and then the desktop behavior goes back to normal. In this chapter, we figure out exactly what is causing this problem, and why.

This type of problem is different from the problems in the two previous chapters, because we initially have absolutely no idea what part of the system is causing the problem. When investigating the GIMP's and nautilus's performance, we knew which application was responsible for the problem. In this case, we just have a misbehaving system, and the performance problem could theoretically be in any part of the system. This type of situation is common. When confronted with it, it is important to use the performance tools to actually track down the cause of the problem rather than just guess the cause and try a solution.

12.3 Find a Baseline/Set a Goal

Once again, the first step is to determine the current state of the problem.

However, in this case, it is not so easy to do. We do not know when the problem will begin or how long it will last, so we cannot really set a baseline without more investigation. As far as a goal, ideally we would like the problem to disappear completely, but the problem might be caused by essential OS functions, so eliminating it entirely might not be possible.

First, we need to do a little more investigation into why this problem is happening to figure out a reasonable baseline. The initial step is to run top as the slowdown is happening. This gives us a list of processes that may be causing the problem, or it may even point at the kernel itself.

In this case, as shown in Listing 12.1, we run top and ask it to show only nonidle processes (by pressing <I> as top runs).

Listing 12.1

```
top - 12:03:40 up 12 min,  7 users,  load average: 1.35, 0.98, 0.53
Tasks:  86 total,   2 running,  84 sleeping,   0 stopped,   0 zombie
Cpu(s):  2.3% us,  5.0% sy,  1.7% ni,  0.0% id, 91.0% wa,  0.0% hi,  0.0% si
Mem:    320468k total,   317024k used,    3444k free,    24640k buffers
Swap:   655192k total,        0k used,  655192k free,   183620k cached

  PID USER      PR  NI  VIRT  RES  SHR S %CPU %MEM   TIME+  COMMAND
 5458 root      34  19  4920 1944 2828 R  1.7  0.6  0:01.13 prelink
 5389 ezolt     17   0  3088  904 1620 R  0.7  0.3  0:00.70 top
```

The top output in Listing 12.1 has several interesting properties. First, we notice that no process is hogging the CPU; both nonidle tasks are using less than 2 percent of the total CPU time. Second, the system is spending 91 percent waiting for I/O to happen. Third, the system is not using any of the swap space, so the grinding disk is NOT caused by swapping. Finally, an unknown process, prelink, is running when the problem happens. It is unclear what this prelink command is, so we will remember that application name and investigate it later.

Our next step is to run vmstat to see what the system is doing. Listing 12.2 shows the result of vmstat and confirms what we saw with top. That is, ~90 percent of the time the system is waiting for I/O. It also tells us that the disk subsystem is reading in about 1,000 blocks a second of data. This is a significant amount of disk I/O.

Listing 12.2

```
[ezolt@localhost ezolt]$ vmstat 1 10
procs ----------memory---------- ---swap-- -----io---- --system-- ----cpu----
  r  b   swpd   free   buff  cache   si   so    bi    bo   in    cs us sy id wa
  0  1      0   2464  24568 184992    0    0   689    92 1067   337  5  4 45 46
  0  1      0   2528  24500 185060    0    0  1196     0 1104  1324  6 10  0 84
  0  1      0   3104  24504 184276    0    0   636   684 1068   967  3  7  0 90
  0  1      0   3160  24432 184348    0    0  1300     0 1096  1575  4 10  0 86
  0  2      0   3488  24336 184444    0    0  1024     0 1095  1498  5  9  0 86
  0  1      0   2620  24372 185188    0    0   980     0 1096  1900  6 12  0 82
  0  1      0   3704  24216 184304    0    0  1480     0 1120   500  1  7  0 92
  0  1      0   2296  24256 185564    0    0  1384   684 1240  1349  6  8  0 86
  2  1      0   3320  24208 184572    0    0   288     0 1211  1206 63  7  0 30
  0  1      0   3576  24148 184632    0    0  1112     0 1153   850 19  7  0 74
```

Now that we know that the disk is being heavily used, the kernel is spending a significant amount of time waiting for I/O, and an unknown application, prelink, is running, we can begin to figure out exactly what the system is doing.

We do not know for certain that prelink is causing the problem, but we suspect that it is. The easiest way to determine whether prelink is causing the disk I/O is to "kill" the prelink process and see whether the disk usage goes away. (This might not be possible on a production machine, but since we are working on a personal desktop we can be more fast and loose.) Listing 12.3 shows the output of vmstat, where halfway through this output, we killed the prelink process. As you can see, the blocks read in drop to zero after prelink is killed.

Listing 12.3

```
procs ----------memory---------- ---swap-- -----io---- --system-- ----cpu----
 r  b   swpd   free   buff  cache   si   so    bi    bo   in    cs us sy id wa
 0  1 122208   3420  13368  84508    0    0  1492   332 1258  1661 15 11  0 74
 0  1 122516   3508  13404  85780    0  308  1188   308 1134  1163  5  7  0 88
 0  2 123572   2616  13396  86860    0 1056  1420  1056 1092   911  4  6  0 90
 0  1 126248   3064  13356  86656    0 2676   316  2676 1040   205  1  2  0 97
 0  2 126248   2688  13376  87156    0    0   532   528 1057   708  2  5  0 93
 0  0 126248   3948  13384  87668    0    0   436     4 1043   342  3  3 43 51
 1  0 126248   3980  13384  87668    0    0     0     0 1154   426  3  1 96  0
 0  0 126248   3980  13384  87668    0    0     0     0 1139   422  2  1 97  0
12  0 126248   4020  13384  87668    0    0     0     0 1023   195  9  0 91  0
```

Because prelink looks like the guilty application, we can start investigating exactly what it is and why it is run. In Listing 12.4, we ask rpm to tell us which files are part of the package that prelink is part of.

Listing 12.4

```
[root@localhost root]# rpm -qlf 'which prelink'
/etc/cron.daily/prelink
/etc/prelink.conf
/etc/rpm/macros.prelink
/etc/sysconfig/prelink
/usr/bin/execstack
/usr/sbin/prelink
/usr/share/doc/prelink-0.3.2
/usr/share/doc/prelink-0.3.2/prelink.pdf
/usr/share/man/man8/execstack.8.gz
/usr/share/man/man8/prelink.8.gz
```

First, we note that the prelink package has a cron job that runs daily. This explains why the performance problem occurs periodically. Second, we note that prelink has a man page and documentation that describe its function. The man page describes `prelink` as an application that can prelink executables and libraries so that their startup times decrease. (It is just a little ironic that an application that is meant to boost performance is slowing down our system.) The `prelink` application can be run in two modes. The first mode causes all of the specified executables and libraries to be prelinked even if it has already been done. (This is specified by the `--force` or `-f` option). The second mode is a quick mode, where `prelink` just checks the `mtimes` and `ctimes` of the libraries and executables to see whether anything has changed since the last prelinking. (This is specified by the `--quick` or `-q` option.) Normally, `prelink` writes all the `mtimes` and `ctimes` of the prelinked executable to its own cache. It then uses that information in quick mode to avoid prelinking those executables that have already been linked.

Examining the `cron` entry from the `prelink` package shows that, by default, the Fedora system uses `prelink` in both modes. It calls `prelink` in the full mode every 14 days. However, for every day between that, `prelink` runs in the quick mode.

Timing `prelink` in both full and quick mode tells us how slow the worst case is (full prelinking) and how much performance increases when using the quick mode. We have to be careful when timing `prelink`, because different runs may yield radically different times. When running an application that uses a significant amount of disk I/O, it is necessary to run it several times to get an accurate indication of its baseline performance. The first time a disk-intensive application is run, much of the data from its I/O is loaded into the cache. The second time the application is run, performance is much greater, because the data it is using is in the disk caches, and it does not need to read from the disk. If you use the first run as the baseline, you can be misled into believing that performance has increased after a performance tweak when the real cause of the performance boost was the warm caches. By just running the application several times, you can warm up the caches and get an accurate baseline. Listing 12.5 shows the results of `prelink` in both modes after it has been run several times.

Listing 12.5

```
[root@localhost root]# time prelink -f -a
....
real    4m24.494s
user    0m9.552s
sys     0m14.322s
```

```
[root@localhost root]# time prelink -q -a
....
real    3m18.136s
user    0m3.187s
sys     0m3.663s
```

The first fact to note from Listing 12.5 is that the quick mode is not all that quicker than the full mode. This is suspicious and needs more investigation. The second fact reinforces what top reported. prelink spends only a small amount of CPU time; the rest is spent waiting for disk I/O.

Now we have to pick a reasonable goal. The PDF file that was installed in the prelink package describes the process of prelinking. It also says that the full mode should take several minutes, and the quick mode should take several seconds. As a goal, let's try to reduce the quick mode's time to under a minute. Even if we could optimize the quick mode, we would still have significant disk grinding every 14 days, but the daily runs would be much more tolerable.

12.4 Configure the Application for the Performance Hunt

The next step in the investigation is to set up the application for the performance hunt. prelink is a small and self-contained application. In fact, it does not even use any shared libraries. (It is statically linked.) However, it is a good idea to recompile it with all the symbols so that we can examine it in the debugger (gdb) if we need to. Again, this tool uses the configure command to generate the makefiles. We must download the source to prelink and recompile it with symbols. We can once again download the source rpms for prelink from Red Hat. The source will be installed in /usr/src/redhat/SOURCES. Once we unpack prelink's source code, we compile it as shown in Listing 12.6.

Listing 12.6

```
env CFLAGS=-g3 ./configure
gmake
```

After `prelink` is configured and compiled, we can use the binary we compiled to investigate the performance problems.

12.5 Install and Configure Performance Tools

The next step in the hunt is to install the performance tools. In this case, neither `ltrace` nor `oprofile` will be of help. `oprofile` is used to profile applications that use a significant amount of CPU time, and because `prelink` uses only about 3 percent of the CPU when running, `oprofile` will not help us. Because the `prelink` binary is statically linked and does not use any shared libraries, `ltrace` will also not help us. However, `strace`, the system call tracer, may help, so we need to install that.

12.6 Run Application and Performance Tools

Now we can finally begin to analyze the performance characteristics of the different modes of `prelink`. As you just saw, `prelink` does not spend much time using the CPU; instead, it spends all of its time on disk I/O. Because `prelink` must call the kernel for disk I/O, we should be able to trace its execution using the `strace` performance tool. Because the quick mode of `prelink` does not appear to be that much faster than the standard `full-run` mode, we compare both runs using `strace` to see whether any suspicious behavior shows up.

At first, we ask `strace` to trace the slower full run of `prelink`. This is the run that creates the initial cache that is used when `prelink` is running in quick mode. Initially, we ask `strace` to show us the summary of the system calls that `prelink` made and see how long each took to complete. The command to do this is shown in Listing 12.7.

Listing 12.7

```
[root@localhost prelink]# strace -c -o af_sum  /usr/sbin/prelink -af
....
/usr/sbin/prelink: /usr/libexec/autopackage/luau-downloader.bin: Could
not parse '/usr/libexec/autopackage/luau-downloader.bin: error while
loading shared libraries: libuau.so.2: cannot open shared object file: No
such file or directory'
...
/usr/sbin/prelink: /usr/lib/mozilla-1.6/regchrome: Could not parse
'/usr/lib/mozilla-1.6/regchrome: error while loading shared libraries:
libxpcom.so: cannot open shared object file: No such file or directory'
...
```

Listing 12.7 is also a sample of prelink's output. prelink is struggling when trying to prelink some of the system executables and libraries. This information becomes valuable later, so remember it.

Listing 12.8 shows the summary output file that the strace command in Listing 12.7 generated.

Listing 12.8

```
[root@localhost prelink] # cat af_sum
execve("/usr/sbin/prelink", ["/usr/sbin/prelink", "-af"], [/* 31 vars
*/]) = 0
```

% time	seconds	usecs/call	calls	errors	syscall
77.87	151.249181	65	2315836		read
11.93	23.163231	55	421593		pread
3.59	6.976880	63	110585		pwrite
1.70	3.294913	17	196518		mremap
1.02	1.977743	32	61774		lstat64
0.97	1.890977	40	47820	1	open
0.72	1.406801	249	5639		vfork
0.35	0.677946	11	59097		close
...					
100.00	194.230415		3351032	5650	total

As you can see in Listing 12.8, a significant amount of time is spent in the read system call. This is expected. prelink needs to figure out what shared libraries are linked into the application, and this requires that part of the executable be read in to be analyzed. The prelink documentation mentions that when generating the list of libraries that an application requires, that application is actually started by the dynamic loader in a special mode, and then the information is read from the executable using a pipe. This is why pread is also high in the profile. In contrast, we would expect the quick version to have very few of these calls.

To see how the profile of the quick version is different, we run the same strace command on the quick version of prelink. We can do that with the strace command shown in Listing 12.9.

Listing 12.9

```
[root@localhost prelink]# strace -c -o aq_sum /usr/sbin/prelink -aq
```

Listing 12.10 shows the strace profile of prelink running in quick mode.

Listing 12.10

```
[root@localhost prelink] # cat aq_sum
execve("/usr/sbin/prelink", ["/usr/sbin/prelink", "-aq"], [/* 31 vars*/]) = 0
% time     seconds  usecs/call     calls    errors syscall
------ ----------- ----------- --------- --------- -----------------
 47.42   3.019337          70     43397           read
 26.74   1.702584          28     59822           lstat64
 10.35   0.658760         163      4041           getdents64
  5.52   0.351326          30     11681           pread
  3.26   0.207800          21      9678         1 open
  1.99   0.126593          21      5980        10 stat64
  1.98   0.126243          12     10155           close
  0.62   0.039335         165       239           vfork
....
------ ----------- ----------- --------- --------- -----------------
100.00   6.367230                154681       250 total
```

As expected, Listing 12.10 shows that the quick mode executes a significant number of lstat64 system calls. These are the system calls that return the mtime and ctime for each executable. prelink looks in its cache to compare the saved mtime and ctime with the executable's current mtime and ctime. If the executable has changed, it starts to prelink it; if it has not changed, it continues to the next executable. The fact that prelink calls lstat64 a large number of times is a good sign, because that means that prelink's cache is working. However, the fact that prelink still calls read a large number of times is a bad sign. The cache should remember that the executables have already been prelinked and should not try to analyze them. We have to figure out why prelink is trying to analyze them. The easiest way to do that is to run strace in normal mode. strace will show all the system calls that prelink makes, and will hopefully clarify which files are being read and explain why read is being called so often. Listing 12.11 shows the command strace used on the quick prelink.

Listing 12.11

```
[root@localhost prelink]# strace -o aq_run  /usr/sbin/prelink -aq
```

The output of strace is a 14MB text file, aq_run. Browsing through it shows that prelink uses lstat64 to check many of the libraries and executables. However, it reveals a few different types cases where read() is used. The first, shown in Listing 12.12, is where prelink reads a file that is a shell script. Because this shell script is not a binary ELF file, it can't be prelinked.

These shell scripts were unchanged since the original full-system prelink was run, so it would be nice if prelink's cache would record the fact that this file cannot be prelinked. If the ctime and mtime do not change, prelink should not even try to read them. (If it was a shell script during the last full prelink and we haven't touched it, it still cannot be prelinked.)

Listing 12.12

```
[root@localhost prelink] # cat aq_run
...
open("/bin/unicode_stop", O_RDONLY|O_LARGEFILE) = 5
read(5, "#!/bin/sh\n# stop u", 18)      = 18
```

continues

Listing 12.12   (Continued)

```
close(5)                             = 0
....
open("/bin/unicode_start", O_RDONLY|O_LARGEFILE) = 5
read(5, "#!/bin/bash\n# Enab", 18)       = 18
close(5)                             = 0
....
```

Next, in Listing 12.13, we watch as prelink tries to operate on a statically linked application. Because this application does not rely on any shared libraries, it makes no sense to try to prelink it. The initial run of prelink should have caught the fact that this application could not be prelinked and stored that information in the prelink cache. In quick mode, it should not have even tried to prelink this binary.

Listing 12.13

```
[root@localhost prelink] # cat aq_run
...
open("/bin/ash.static", O_RDONLY|O_LARGEFILE) = 5

read(5, "\177ELF\1\1\1\0\0\0\0\0\0\0\0\0\2\0", 18) = 18
fcntl64(5, F_GETFL)                 = 0x8000 (flags
O_RDONLY|O_LARGEFILE)
pread(5, "\177ELF\1\1\1\0\0\0\0\0\0\0\0\0", 16, 0) = 16
pread(5, "\177ELF\1\1\1\0\0\0\0\0\0\0\0\0", 16, 0) = 16
pread(5, "\177ELF\1\1\1\0\0\0\0\0\0\0\0\0\2\0\3\0\1\0\0\0\0\201\4"...,
52, 0) = 52
pread(5, "\177ELF\1\1\1\0\0\0\0\0\0\0\0\0\2\0\3\0\1\0\0\0\0\201\4"...,
52, 0) = 52
pread(5, "\1\0\0\0\0\0\0\0\0\200\4\10\0\200\4\10\320d\7\0\320d\7"...,
128, 52) = 128
pread(5, "\0\0\0\0\0\0\0\0\0\0\0\0\0\0\0\0\0\0\0\0\0\0\0\0\0\0\0"...,
920, 488632) = 920
close(5)
...
```

Finally, in Listing 12.14, we see prelink reading a binary that it had trouble prelinking in the original full system run. We saw an error regarding this binary in the original prelink output. When it starts to read this file, it pulls in other libraries and begins to operate on each of those and their dependencies. This triggers an enormous amount of reading.

Listing 12.14

```
[root@localhost prelink] # cat aq_run

...

lstat64("/usr/lib/mozilla-1.6/regchrome", {st_mode=S_IFREG|0755, st_size=14444,

...}) = 0

open("/usr/lib/mozilla-1.6/regchrome", O_RDONLY|O_LARGEFILE) = 6

read(6, "\177ELF\1\1\1\0\0\0\0\0\0\0\0\0\2\0", 18) = 18

fcntl64(6, F_GETFL)                    = 0x8000 (flags O_RDONLY|O_LARGEFILE)

pread(6, "\177ELF\1\1\1\0\0\0\0\0\0\0\0\0", 16, 0) = 16

...

open("/usr/lib/mozilla-1.6/libldap50.so", O_RDONLY|O_LARGEFILE) = 6

read(6, "\177ELF\1\1\1\0\0\0\0\0\0\0\0\0\3\0", 18) = 18

close(6)                    = 0

lstat64("/usr/lib/mozilla-1.6/libgtkxtbin.so", {st_mode=S_IFREG|0755, st_size=14268, ...}) = 0

open("/usr/lib/mozilla-1.6/libgtkxtbin.so", O_RDONLY|O_LARGEFILE) = 6

read(6, "\177ELF\1\1\1\0\0\0\0\0\0\0\0\0\3\0", 18) = 18

close(6)                    = 0

lstat64("/usr/lib/mozilla-1.6/libjsj.so", {st_mode=S_IFREG|0755, st_size=96752,

...}) = 0

open("/usr/lib/mozilla-1.6/libjsj.so", O_RDONLY|O_LARGEFILE) = 6

read(6, "\177ELF\1\1\1\0\0\0\0\0\0\0\0\0\3\0", 18) = 18

close(6)                    = 0

lstat64("/usr/lib/mozilla-1.6/mozilla-xremote-client", {st_mode=S_IFREG|0755, st_size=12896, ...}) = 0

lstat64("/usr/lib/mozilla-1.6/regxpcom", {st_mode=S_IFREG|0755, st_size=55144, ...}) = 0

lstat64("/usr/lib/mozilla-1.6/libgkgfx.so", {st_mode=S_IFREG|0755, st_size=143012, ...}) = 0

open("/usr/lib/mozilla-1.6/libgkgfx.so", O_RDONLY|O_LARGEFILE) = 6

read(6, "\177ELF\1\1\1\0\0\0\0\0\0\0\0\0\3\0", 18) = 18

close(6)                    = 0

...
```

Optimizing this case is tricky. Because this binary was not actually the problem (rather the library that it was linking to, libxpcom.so), we cannot just mark the executable as bad in the cache. However, if we store the errant library name libxpcom.so with the failing executable, it may be possible to check the times of the binary and the library, and only try to prelink again if one of them has changed.

12.7 Simulating a Solution

The information revealed by strace shows that prelink is spending a lot of time trying to open and analyze binaries that it cannot possibly prelink. The best way to test whether caching of nonprelinkable binaries could improve prelink's performance is to modify prelink so that it adds all these unprelinkable binaries to its initial cache. Unfortunately, adding code to cache these "unprelinkable" binaries could be a complicated process that involves a good amount of knowledge about the internals of the prelink application. An easier method is to simulate the cache by replacing all the unprelinkable binaries with a known prelinkable binary. This causes all the formerly unprelinkable binaries to be ignored when quick mode is run. This is exactly what would happen if we had a working cache, so we can use it to estimate the performance increase we would see if prelink were able to cache and ignore unprelinkable binaries.

To start the experiment, we copy all the files in /usr/bin/ to the sandbox directory and run prelink on this directory. This directory includes normal binaries, and shell scripts, and other libraries that cannot be prelinked. We then run prelink on the sandbox directory and tell it to create a new cache rather than rely on the system cache. This is shown in Listing 12.15.

Listing 12.15

```
/usr/sbin/prelink -C new_cache -f sandbox/
```

Next, in Listing 12.16, we time how long it takes the quick mode of prelink to run. We had to run this multiple times until it gave a consistent result. (The first run warmed the cache for each of the succeeding runs.) The baseline time in Listing 12.16 is .983 seconds. We have to beat this time for our optimization (improving the cache) to be worth investigating.

Listing 12.16

```
time /usr/sbin/prelink -C new_cache -q sandbox/
real    0m0.983s
user    0m0.597s
sys     0m0.386s
```

Next, in Listing 12.17, we run strace on this prelink command. This is to record which files prelink opens in the sandbox directory.

Listing 12.17

```
strace -o strace_prelink_sandbox /usr/sbin/prelink -C new_cache -q
sandbox/
```

Next we create a new directory, sandbox2, into which we once again copy all the binaries in the /usr/bin directory. However, we overwrite all the files that prelink "opened" in the preceding strace output with a known good binary, less, which can be prelinked. We copy the less on to all the problem binaries rather than just deleting them, so that both sandboxes contain the same number of files. After we set up the second sandbox, we run the full version of prelink on this new directory using the command in Listing 12.18.

Listing 12.18

```
[root@localhost prelink]#/usr/sbin/prelink -C new_cache2 -f sandbox2/
```

Finally, we time the run of the quick mode and compare it to our baseline.

Again, we had to run it several times, where the first time warmed the cache. In Listing 12.19, we can see that we did, indeed, see a performance increase. The time to execute the prelink dropped from ~.98 second to ~.29 seconds.

Listing 12.19

```
[root@localhost prelink]# time /usr/sbin/prelink -C new_cache2 -q
sandbox2/
real    0m0.292s
user    0m0.158s
sys     0m0.134s
```

Next, we compare the strace output of the two different runs to verify that the number of reads did, in fact, decrease. Listing 12.20 shows the strace summary information from sandbox, which contained binaries that prelink could not link.

Listing 12.20

```
execve("/usr/sbin/prelink", ["/usr/sbin/prelink", "-C", "new_cache",
"-q", "sandbox/"], [/* 20 vars */]) = 0
% time     seconds  usecs/call     calls    errors syscall
------ ----------- ----------- --------- --------- ----------------
 62.06    0.436563          48      9133           read
 13.87    0.097551          15      6504           lstat64
  6.20    0.043625          18      2363        10 stat64
  5.62    0.039543          21      1922           pread
  3.93    0.027671         374        74           vfork
  1.78    0.012515           9      1423           getcwd
  1.65    0.011594         644        18           getdents64
  1.35    0.009473          15       623         1 open
  0.90    0.006300           8       770           close
.....
100.00    0.703400               24028        85 total
```

Listing 12.21 shows the strace summary from sandbox where prelink could link all the binaries.

Listing 12.21

```
execve("/usr/sbin/prelink", ["/usr/sbin/prelink", "-C", "new_cache2",
"-q", "sandbox2/"], [/* 20 vars */]) = 0
% time     seconds  usecs/call     calls    errors syscall
------ ----------- ----------- --------- --------- ----------------
54.29    0.088766          15      5795           lstat64
26.53    0.043378          19      2259        10 stat64
 8.46    0.013833           8      1833           getcwd
 6.95    0.011363         631        18           getdents64
 2.50    0.004095        2048         2           write
 0.37    0.000611         611         1           rename
 0.26    0.000426          39        11         1 open
...
100.00   0.163515                  9973        11 total
```

As you can see from the differences in Listing 12.20 and Listing 12.21, we have dramatically reduced the number of reads done in the directory. In addition, we have significantly reduced the amount of time required to prelink the directory. Caching and avoiding unprelinkable executables looks like a promising optimization.

12.8 Reporting the Problem

Because we have found a problem and potential solution in a pretty low-level piece of system software, it is a good idea to work with the author to resolve the problem. We must at least submit a bug report so that the author knows that a problem exists. Submitting the tests we used to discover the problem helps him to reproduce the problem and hopefully fix it. In this case, we will add a bug report to Red Hat's bugzilla (bugzilla.redhat.com) tracking system. (Most other distributions have similar bug tracking systems.) Our bug report describes the problem that we encountered and the possible solution that we discovered.

When arriving at bugzilla, we first search for bug reports in prelink to see whether anyone else has reported this problem. In this case, no one has, so we enter the bug report in Listing 12.22 and wait for the author or maintainer to respond and possibly fix the bug.

Listing 12.22

From Bugzilla Helper:

User-Agent: Mozilla/5.0 (X11; U; Linux i686; en-US; rv:1.6)
Gecko/20040510

Description of problem:
When running in quick mode, prelink does not cache the fact that some
binaries can not be prelinked.   As a result it rescans them every time ,
even if prelink is running in quick mode.   This causes the disk to grind
and dramatically slows down the whole system.

There are 3 types of executables that it retries during quick mode:

1) Static Binaries

2) Shell Scripts

3) Binaries that rely on unprelinkable binaries. (Such as OpenGL)

For 1&2, it would be nice if prelink cached that fact that these
executables can not be prelinked, and then in quick mode check their
ctime & mtime, and don't even try to read them if it already knows that
they can't be prelinked.

For 3, it would be nice if prelink recorded which libraries are causing
the prelink to fail (Take the OpenGL case for example), and record that
with the binary in the cache. If that library or the binary's ctime &
mtime haven't changed, then don't even try to prelink it.   If things have
really changed, it will be picked up on the next run of "prelink -af".

Version-Release number of selected component (if applicable):
prelink-0.3.2-1

How reproducible:
Always

Steps to Reproduce:

1.Run prelink -a -f on a directory with shell scripts & other executables that can not be prelinked.

2. Strace "prelink -a -q", and look for the "reads".

3. Examine strace's output, and you'll see all of the reads that take place.

Actual Results: Shell script:

```
open("/bin/unicode_stop", O_RDONLY|O_LARGEFILE) = 5
read(5, "#!/bin/sh\n# stop u", 18)      = 18
close(5)                                = 0
....
```


Static Binary:

```
open("/bin/ash.static", O_RDONLY|O_LARGEFILE) = 5
read(5, "\177ELF\1\1\1\0\0\0\0\0\0\0\0\0\2\0", 18) = 18
fcntl64(5, F_GETFL)                     = 0x8000 (flags
O_RDONLY|O_LARGEFILE)
pread(5, "\177ELF\1\1\1\0\0\0\0\0\0\0\0\0", 16, 0) = 16
pread(5, "\177ELF\1\1\1\0\0\0\0\0\0\0\0\0", 16, 0) = 16
pread(5, "\177ELF\1\1\1\0\0\0\0\0\0\0\0\0\2\0\3\0\1\0\0\0\0\201\4"...,
52, 0) = 52
pread(5, "\177ELF\1\1\1\0\0\0\0\0\0\0\0\0\2\0\3\0\1\0\0\0\0\201\4"...,
52, 0) = 52
pread(5, "\1\0\0\0\0\0\0\0\200\4\10\0\200\4\10\320d\7\0\320d\7"...,
128, 52) = 128
pread(5, "\0\0\0\0\0\0\0\0\0\0\0\0\0\0\0\0\0\0\0\0\0\0\0\0\0\0\0\0\0"...,
920, 488632) = 920
close(5)
```


Un-prelinkable executable:

```
lstat64("/usr/lib/mozilla-1.6/regchrome", {st_mode=S_IFREG|0755,
st_size=14444,
...}) = 0
```

continues

Listing 12.22   (Continued)

```
open("/usr/lib/mozilla-1.6/regchrome", O_RDONLY|O_LARGEFILE) = 6
read(6, "\177ELF\1\1\1\0\0\0\0\0\0\0\0\0\0\2\0", 18) = 18
fcntl64(6, F_GETFL)                    = 0x8000 (flags
O_RDONLY|O_LARGEFILE)
pread(6, "\177ELF\1\1\1\0\0\0\0\0\0\0\0\0\0\0", 16, 0) = 16
...
open("/usr/lib/mozilla-1.6/libldap50.so", O_RDONLY|O_LARGEFILE) = 6
read(6, "\177ELF\1\1\1\0\0\0\0\0\0\0\0\0\0\3\0", 18) = 18
close(6)                               = 0
lstat64("/usr/lib/mozilla-1.6/libgtkxtbin.so", {st_mode=S_IFREG|0755,
st_size=14268, ...}) = 0
open("/usr/lib/mozilla-1.6/libgtkxtbin.so", O_RDONLY|O_LARGEFILE) = 6
read(6, "\177ELF\1\1\1\0\0\0\0\0\0\0\0\0\0\3\0", 18) = 18
close(6)                               = 0
lstat64("/usr/lib/mozilla-1.6/libjsj.so", {st_mode=S_IFREG|0755,
st_size=96752,
...}) = 0
open("/usr/lib/mozilla-1.6/libjsj.so", O_RDONLY|O_LARGEFILE) = 6
read(6, "\177ELF\1\1\1\0\0\0\0\0\0\0\0\0\0\3\0", 18) = 18
close(6)                               = 0
lstat64("/usr/lib/mozilla-1.6/mozilla-xremote-client",
{st_mode=S_IFREG|0755, st_size=12896, ...}) = 0
lstat64("/usr/lib/mozilla-1.6/regxpcom", {st_mode=S_IFREG|0755,
st_size=55144, ...}) = 0
lstat64("/usr/lib/mozilla-1.6/libgkgfx.so", {st_mode=S_IFREG|0755,
st_size=143012, ...}) = 0
open("/usr/lib/mozilla-1.6/libgkgfx.so", O_RDONLY|O_LARGEFILE) = 6
read(6, "\177ELF\1\1\1\0\0\0\0\0\0\0\0\0\0\3\0", 18) = 18
close(6)                               = 0
...
```

Expected Results: All of these should have been simple lstat checks
rather than actual reads of the executables.

Additional info:

Even if the author or maintainer never replies, it is still a good idea to enter the problem in the bug-tracking database. The problem and possible solution will be recorded, and some enthusiastic programmer may come along and fix the problem.

12.9 Testing the Solution

Because we have not solved the problem in the prelink code, but instead reported a bug, we cannot test the fixed prelink time against our original baseline immediately. However, if the author or maintainer is able to implement the proposed changes, or even find a better way to optimize things, we will be able to check out the performance of the updated version when it arrives.

12.10 Chapter Summary

In this chapter, we started with a misbehaving system and used performance tools to pinpoint which subsystem was used excessively (the disk subsystem as shown by vmstat) and which component caused the problem (prelink). We then investigated the prelink application to determine why it used so much disk I/O (using strace). We discovered in prelink's documentation a cached mode that should dramatically reduce disk I/O. We investigated the performance of the cached mode and found that it did not eliminate disk I/O as much as it should, because it was trying to prelink files that could not be prelinked. We then simulated a cache that avoided trying to prelink files that could not be prelinked and verified that it significantly reduced the amount of disk I/O and runtime of prelink in quick mode. Finally, we submitted a bug report to the author of prelink in the hopes that the author will recognize the problem and fix it. This chapter was the last chapter of Linux performance hunts.

In the next chapter, the final chapter, we look at the higher-level picture of Linux performance and performance tools. We review methodologies and tools covered in this book and look at some of the areas of Linux performance tools that are ripe for improvement.

13

Performance Tools: What's Next?

This chapter contains musings about the current state of Linux performance tools, what still needs to improved, and why Linux is currently a great platform to do performance investigation.

After reading this chapter, you should be able to

* Understand the holes in the Linux performance toolbox, and understand some of the ideal solutions
* Understand the benefits of Linux as a platform for performance investigation

13.1 The State of Linux Tools

This book tours the current Linux performance tools, how to use them individually, and how to use them together to solve performance problems. As with every aspect of Linux, these performance tools are constantly evolving, so when investigating a problem, it is always a good idea to review the man page or documentation of a performance tool to determine whether its usage has changed. The fundamental functions of the performance tools rarely change, but new features are commonly added, so it is helpful to review the latest release notes and documentation for a given tool.

13.2 What Tools Does Linux Still Need?

As we toured some of the Linux performance tools, we saw some holes in the overall performance-investigation functionality. Some of these holes are the result of kernel limitations, and some exist just because no one has written a tool to solve the problem. However, filling some of these holes would make it dramatically easier to track down and fix Linux performance problems.

13.2.1 Hole 1: Performance Statistics Are Scattered

One glaring hole is that Linux has no single tool that provides all relevant performance statistics for a particular process. ps was meant to fill this hole in the original UNIX, and on Linux, it is pretty good but it does not cover all the statistics that other commercial UNIX implementations provide. Some statistics are invaluable in tracking down performance problems—for example, inblk (I/O blocks read in) and oublk (I/O blocks written out), which indicate the amount of disk I/O a process is using; vcsw (voluntary context switches) and invcsw (involuntary context switches), which often indicate a process was context-switched off the CPU; msgrcv (messages received on pipes and sockets) and msgsnd (messages sent on pipes and sockets), which show the amount of network and pipe I/O an application is using. An ideal tool would add all these statistics and combine the functionality of many performance tools presented so far (including oprofile, top, ps, strace, ltrace, and the /proc file system) into a single application. A user should be able point this single application at a process and extract all the important performance statistics. Each statistic would be updated in real time, enabling a user to debug an application as it runs. It would group statistics for a single area of investigation in the same location.

For example, if I were investigating memory usage, it would show exactly how memory was being used in the heap, in the stack, by libraries, shared memory, and in mmap. If a particular memory area was much higher than I expected, I could drill down, and this performance tool would show me exactly which functions allocated the memory. If I were investigating CPU usage, I would start with overall statistics, such as how much time is spent in system time versus user time, and how many system calls a particular process is making, but then I would be able to drill down into either the system or user time and see exactly which functions are spending all the time and how often they are being called. A smart shell script that used the appropriate preexisting tools to gather and combine this information would go a long way to achieving some of this functionality, but fundamental changes in the behavior of some of the tools would be necessary to completely realize this vision.

13.2.2 Hole 2: No Reliable and Complete Call Tree

The next performance tool hole is the fact that there is currently no way to provide a complete call tree of a program's execution. Linux has several incomplete implementations. oprofile provides call-tree generation, but it is based on sampling, so it will not catch every call that is made. gprof supports call trees, but it will not be able to profile the full application unless every library that a particular process calls is also complied with profile support. This most promising tool, valgrind, has a skin called calltree, described in the section, "5.2.5 kcachegrind," in Chapter 5, "Performance Tools: Process-Specific Memory ," which has a goal of providing a completely accurate call tree. However, it is still in development and does not work on all binaries.

This call-tree tool would be useful even if it dramatically slowed down application performance as it runs. A common way of using this would be to run oprofile to figure out which functions in an application are "hot," and then run the call-tree program to figure out why the application called them. The oprofile step would provide an accurate view of the application's bottlenecks when it runs at full speed, and the call tree, even if it runs slowly, would show how and why the application called those functions. The only problem would be if the program's behavior was timing sensitive and it would change if it was run slowly (for example, something that relied on network or disk I/O). However, many problems exist that are not timing sensitive, and an accurate call-tree mechanism would go a long way to fixing these.

13.2.3 Hole 3: I/O Attribution

The final and biggest hole in Linux right now is that of I/O attribution. Right now, Linux does not provide a good way to track down which applications are using the highest amounts of disk or even network I/O.

An ideal tool would show, in real time, the amount of input and output bytes of disk and network I/O that a particular process is using. The tool would show the statistics as raw bandwidth, as well as a percentage of the raw I/O that the subsystem is capable of. In addition, users would also be able to split up the statistics, so that they could see the same statistics for each individual network and disk device.

13.3 Performance Tuning on Linux

Even with the holes just mentioned, Linux is still an ideal place to find and fix performance problems. It was written for developers by developers and, as a result, it is very friendly to the performance investigator. Linux has a few characteristics that make it a great platform to track down performance problems.

13.3.1 Available Source

First, a developer has access to most (if not all) source code for the entire system. This is invaluable when tracking down a problem that appears to exist outside of your code. On a commercial UNIX or other operating systems where source is not available, you might have to wait for a vendor to investigate the problem, and you have no guarantee that he will fix it if it is his problem. However, on Linux, you can investigate the problem yourself and figure out exactly why the performance problem is happening. If the problem is outside your application, you can fix it and submit a patch, or just run with a fixed version. If, by reading the source of the Linux code, you realize that the problem is in your code, you can then fix the problem. In either case, you can fix it immediately and are not gated by waiting for someone else.

13.3.2 Easy Access to Developers

The second advantage of Linux is that it is relatively easy to find and contact the developers of a particular application or library. In contrast to most other proprietary operating systems, where it is difficult to figure out which engineer is responsible for a given piece of code, Linux is much more open. Usually, the names or contact information of the developers for a particular piece of software are with the software package. Access to the developers allows you to ask questions about how a particular piece of code behaves, what slow-running code intends to do, and whether a given optimization is safe to perform. The developers are usually more than happy to help with this.

13.3.3 Linux Is Still Young

The final reason that Linux is a great platform on which to optimize performance is because it is still young. Features are still being developed, and Linux has many opportunities to find and fix straightforward performance bugs. Because most developers focus on adding functionality, performance issues can be left unresolved. An ambitious performance investigator can find and fix many of the small performance problems in the ever-developing Linux. These small fixes go beyond a single individual and benefit the entire Linux community.

13.4 Chapter Summary

In this chapter, we investigated a few of the areas where the set of Linux performance tools has shortcomings and proposed some ideal solutions. We also discussed why Linux is a good platform on which to try performance investigation and optimization.

It is up to you, the reader, to change Linux performance for the better. The opportunities for improvement of Linux performance and Linux performance tools abound. If you find a performance problem that annoys you, fix it or report it to the developers and work with them to fix it. Either way, no one else will be hit by the problem, and the entire Linux community benefits.

Performance Tool Locations

The performance tools described in this book originated from many different locations on the Internet. Fortunately, most major distributions have pulled them together and included them in the current versions of their distributions. Table A-1 describes all the tools, provides pointers to their original source locations, and indicates whether they are included in the following distributions: Fedora Core 2 (FC2), Red Hat Enterprise Linux (EL3), and SUSE 9.1 (S9.1).

Table A-1   Locations of Performance Tools

Tool	Distro	Source Location
bash	FC2, EL3, S9.1	http://cnswww.cns.cwru.edu/~chet/bash/bashtop.html
etherape	None	http://etherape.sourceforge.net/
ethtool	FC2, EL3, S9.1	http://sourceforge.net/projects/gkernel/
free	FC2, EL3, S9.1	Part of the procps package: http://procps.sourceforge.net/
gcc	FC2, EL3, S9.1	http://gcc.gnu.org/
gdb	FC2, EL3, S9.1	http://sources.redhat.com/gdb/
gkrellm	FC2, S9.1	http://web.wt.net/~billw/gkrellm/gkrellm.html

continues

Table A-1   Locations of Performance Tools (Continued)

Tool	Distro	Source Location
gnome-system-monitor	FC2, EL3, S9.1	Part of the GNOME project, and available from: `ftp://ftp.gnome.org/pub/gnome/sources/gnome-system-monitor/`
gnumeric	FC2, EL3, S9.1	`http://www.gnome.org/projects/gnumeric/`
gprof	FC2, EL3, S9.1	Part of the `binutils` package: `http://sources.redhat.com/binutils`
ifconfig	FC2, EL3, S9.1	Part of the `net-tools`: `http://www.tazenda.demon.co.uk/phil/net-tools/`
iostat	FC2, S9.1	Part of the `sysstat` package: `http://perso.wanadoo.fr/sebastien.godard/`
ip	FC2, EL3, S9.1	Part of the `iproute` package: `ftp://ftp.inr.ac.ru/ip-routing`
ipcs	FC2, EL3, S9.1	Part of the `util-linux` package: `ftp.win.tue.nl:/pub/linux-local/utils/util-linux`
iptraf	FC2, S9.1	`http://cebu.mozcom.com/riker/iptraf`
kcachegrind	FC2, S9.1	Part of the (v3.2 or higher) `kdesdk` package: `http://kcachegrind.sourceforge.net/cgi-bin/show.cgi`
ldd	FC2, EL3, S9.1	Part of GNU `libc`: `http://www.gnu.org/software/libc/libc.html`
ld (The Linux loader)	FC2, EL3, S9.1	Part of `binutils`: `http://sources.redhat.com/binutils`

Tool	Distro	Source Location
lsof	FC2, EL3, S9.1	ftp://lsof.itap.purdue.edu/pub/tools/unix/lsof
ltrace	FC2, EL3, S9.1	http://packages.debian.org/unstable/utils/ltrace.html
memprof	FC2, EL3, S9.1	http://www.gnome.org/projects/memprof
mii-tool	FC2, EL3, S9.1	Part of the net-tools: http://www.tazenda.demon.co.uk/phil/net-tools/
mpstat	FC2, S9.1	Part of the sysstat package: http://perso.wanadoo.fr/sebastien.godard/
netstat	FC2, EL3, S9.1	Part of the net-tools: http://www.tazenda.demon.co.uk/phil/net-tools/
objdump	FC2, EL3, S9.1	Part of binutils: http://sources.redhat.com/binutils
oprofile	FC2, EL3, S9.1	http://oprofile.sourceforge.net/
proc filesystem	FC2, EL3, S9.1	The proc file system is part of the Linux kernel and is enabled in almost every distribution.
procinfo	FC2, S9.1	ftp://ftp.cistron.nl/pub/people/svm
ps	FC2, EL3, S9.1	Part of the procps package: http://procps.sourceforge.net/
sar	FC2, EL3, S9.1	Part of the sysstat package: http://perso.wanadoo.fr/sebastien.godard/
script	FC2, EL3, S9.1	Part of the util-linux package: http://www.kernel.org/pub/linux/utils/util-linux/

continues

Table A-1 Locations of Performance Tools (Continued)

Tool	Distro	Source Location
slabtop	FC2, EL3, S9.1	Part of the procps package: http://procps.sourceforge.net/
strace	FC2, EL3, S9.1	http://sourceforge.net/projects/strace/
tee	FC2, EL3, S9.1	Part of the coreutils package: ftp://alpha.gnu.org/gnu/coreutils/
time	FC2, EL3	http://www.gnu.org/directory/GNU/time.html
top	FC2, EL3, S9.1	Part of the procps package: http://procps.sourceforge.net/
valgrind	S9.1	http://valgrind.kde.org/
vmstat	FC2, EL3, S9.1	Part of the procps package: http://procps.sourceforge.net/

Although not denoted in the table, Debian (testing) contains all the tools listed except procinfo.

Installing oprofile

lthough the system profiler oprofile is a powerful performance tool, its installa-
tion/use can be tricky. This appendix describes some of the issues when installing
oprofile on Fedora Core 2 (FC2), Red Hat Enterprise Linux (EL3), and SUSE 9.1
(S9.1).

B.1 Fedora Core 2 (FC2)

For FC2, Red Hat provides packages for oprofile that should be used rather than those
downloaded from the oprofile Web site. The uniprocessor kernel does not provide the
necessary oprofile drivers. Red Hat packages the necessary oprofile kernel modules
with the smp version of the kernel. If you want to run oprofile, you must use the smp
kernel, even if you are running it on a single-processor machine.

B.2 Enterprise Linux 3 (EL3)

For EL3, once again, Red Hat provides packages for oprofile that should be used rather
than those downloaded from the oprofile Web site. The uniprocessor kernel does not
provide the necessary oprofile drivers. Red Hat packages the necessary oprofile kernel
modules with the smp or hugemem versions of the kernel. If you want to run oprofile,
you must use the smp or hugemem kernel, even if you are running it on a single-processor
machine.

More details on using `oprofile` in EL3 are provided at `http://www.redhat.com/docs/manuals/enterprise/RHEL-3-Manual/sysadmin-guide/ch-oprofile.html`.

B.3 SUSE 9.1

For SUSE 9.1, SUSE provides packages for `oprofile` that should be used rather than those downloaded from the `oprofile` Web site. All versions of the SUSE kernels (`default`, `smp`, and `bigsmp`) provide support for `oprofile`, so any of the supplied kernels will work.

Index

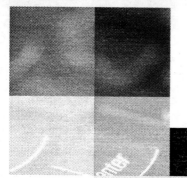

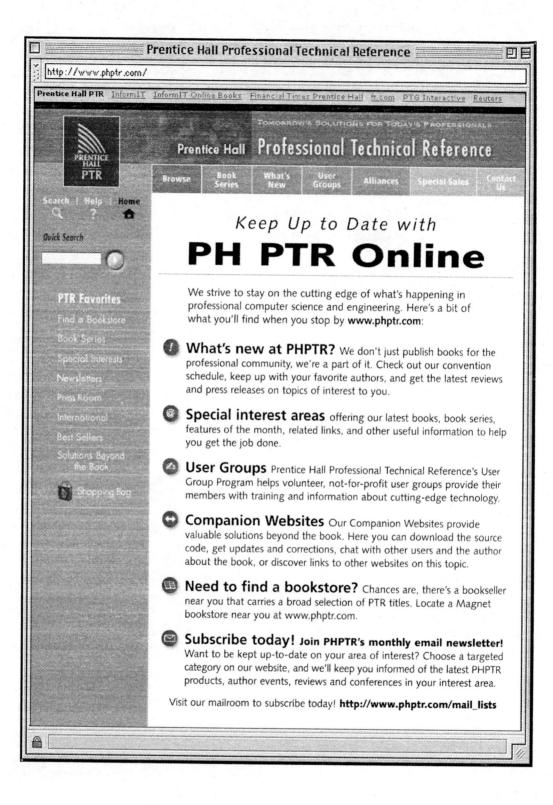